WORLD EDUCATION SERIES

Education in Modern Egypt

World education series

GENERAL EDITOR: DR BRIAN HOLMES
Professor of Education, Head,
Department of Comparative Education
Institute of Education
University of London

Education and Development in Latin America

Laurence Gale

Education in Communist China

R. F. Price

Reforms and Restraints in Modern French Education

W. R. Fraser

Education in a Small Democracy: New Zealand

Ian A. McLaren

Education in Modern Egypt:
Ideals and Realities

GEORGIE D. M. HYDE

Professor Emeritus, American University,
Cairo

ROUTLEDGE & KEGAN PAUL

London, Henley and Boston

First published in 1978
by Routledge & Kegan Paul Ltd
39 Store Street,
London WC1E 7DD,
Broadway House,
Newtown Road,
Henley-on-Thames,
Oxon RG9 1EN and
9 Park Street,
Boston, Mass. 02108, USA

Typesetting by HBM Typesetting Ltd,
Chorley, Lancashire
and printed in Great Britain by
Lowe & Brydone Ltd

British Library Cataloguing in Publication Data

Hyde, Georgie D M

Education in modern Egypt. – (World education series).
1. Education – Egypt – History – 20th century
I. Title II. Series
370'.962   LA1646   78-40141

ISBN 0 7100 8879 5

*To all my students in Egypt, England and
all parts of the world*

Contents

Contents

Acknowledgments

A book of this nature can only be written with the co-operation of many people most of whom, like the teachers and their pupils, who allowed a foreign educationist to listen to lessons, examine exercise books and engage in discussions will inevitably be nameless. Such co-operation, from whatever source is gratefully acknowledged.

Three groups of people made a significant contribution, beginning with those concerned with educational visits, during a period when 'open doors' were still such a novelty that one headmaster, having failed to get in touch with his immediate superior to confirm that the visitor's permit was valid, played for safety by offering her refreshments and allowing her to peer at the girls in their classroom from the bottom of a staircase! I am very grateful to the Minister of Education and the Minister of Higher Education whose permits made it possible to see for myself the normal daily programmes in all types of educational institutions. There were no problems after I had approached Mr Abu Shady, Under Secretary for Education (now Governor of Kafr el-Sheikh), who, assisted by Mrs Mona Kamel arranged visits in the Cairo and Giza governorates to schools of all kinds and literacy and adult centres. A very interesting and fruitful period was also spent in Alexandria, thanks to the courtesy of Mr Fahmy Gabr, Under Secretary for Education, and his staff who arranged for visits to Special Schools, literacy centres, including those used for factory workers and adult educational centres. During all my visits arranged by the Ministry there was ample opportunity for meeting officials at all levels to discuss projects, problems and plans. I am also indebted to Dr Bekri, then Director of Sers el-Layyan Centre for inviting me to attend an international conference giving insight into the problems of illiteracy and demonstrating some of the latest methods of dealing with them. The kind provision of transport, not only by the Ministry but also by the Arab Socialist Union is much appreciated.

The material for this book was collected mainly from 1969–75 in

Cairo. During much of this period not only was it difficult to approach busy officials whose resources were stretched on account of the war situation, but, for security reasons, access to government buildings and official documents was, understandably, denied to foreigners. My debt to the local Press during this period is acknowledged throughout this book: the excellent coverage in the field of education is a tribute to the importance attached to it by the Egyptian Government and the Editor of the *Egyptian Gazette*. Permission to use and quote liberally from this excellent source of information and, to a lesser extent from the Arabic newspapers, *al-Ahram* and *al-Gomhoureya*, has added flesh to the bones of official literature. The latter, however, provide the core of information, supported by interviews with busy officials at the ministries and other government offices notably Professor Dr Shafik Balba'a, Secretary General, Supreme Council of the Universities; Dr M. Saber Selim, Director, Science Department ALECSO; and, at the Ministry of Education: Mr Mansour Hussain, Under Secretary; Dr Mohamed Mahmoud Radwan, First Under Secretary and President of the Teachers' Association; and Dr Fouad el-Bahey el-Sayed, Director, National Council for Educational Research, all of whom spared the time to answer innumerable questions.

Finally, my thanks go to all who have contributed to the publication of this book, notably to Professor Brian Holmes, General Editor of the series, who read the manuscript and made suggestions about the organization of the chapters, which transformed them from a miscellaneous collection to a cohesive unit; to Dr Abd el-Aziz El-Koussy, Professor of Ain Shams University, Egypt, a distinguished educationist, who not only encouraged me to write the book but kindly agreed to write a Preface; and to Dr Munir, Minister-Counsellor (Information) of the Egyptian Embassy, London, who has kindly co-operated with me in his official capacity.

GEORGIE D. M. HYDE
Reigate, Surrey and Cairo, Egypt

The author and publishers are grateful to the following for permission to quote from the works cited.

Amir Boktor, *The Development of Expansion of Education in the United Arab Republic* (1963), by permission of the American University in Cairo Press; Georgie D. M. Hyde and Josette G. Abdalla, 'Psychological

Services to School-Aged Population in Egypt' in *Psychology in the Schools in International Perspective* (1977), published by International School Psychology by arrangement with the Editor, Calvin D. Caterall, PhD, prior to publication; Yusef Saleh el-Din Kotb (ed.), *Education and Modernization in Egypt* (1974), Ain Shams University Press; Robert Mabro, *The Egyptian Economy 1952–1972* (1974), by permission of the Oxford University Press; Saneya Abdul Wahab Saleh, *Attitudinal and Social Structural Aspects of the Brain Drain: The Egyptian Case* (1975), unpublished MA thesis, American University in Cairo; Joseph S. Szyliowicz, *Education and Modernization in the Middle East*, copyright © 1973 by Cornell University Press, used by permission of Cornell University Press; *Assessment of Children's Needs in Egypt: Final Report* (1974) and Herman D. Stein, *Planning for the Needs of Children in Developing Countries: Report of Round-Table Conference* (1963), by permission of UNICEF; Samuel Makarius Tawadros (ed.), *Assessment of Children's Needs in Egypt: Report of the Psychological Committee, the National Centre for Social and Criminological Research, Cairo* (1973), and *Mental Health and School Work* (1974), el-Nahda el-Masriya, Cairo; Magdi Wahba, *Cultural Policy in Egypt* © UNESCO 1972, reprinted by permission of UNESCO.

The Ministry of Information, Cairo were extremely helpful in supplying documents and information including documents obtained from the Ministries of Education and the Supreme Council for the Universities, including reports, plans, tables, etc. Reports include those of the Ministry of Education and al-Azhar, the National Centre for Educational Research, the Unedbas Mission to the Arab Republic of Egypt concerning the reorganization of secondary education (1975) and the World Bank survey of Egyptian education (1975), ministerial decrees and issues; republican laws, issues and decrees, government and ministerial plans, university calendars for Cairo and Ain Shams; *The National Charter* (1962), *The October Working Paper* (1974).

The newspapers the *Egyptian Gazette* (1969–75 and 1913), *al-Ahram* and *al-Gomhoureya*.

World education series

The volumes in the World Education Series will treat national systems of education and, where appropriate, features of different systems within a particular region. These studies are intended to meet the needs of students of comparative education in university departments and schools of education and colleges of education and will supplement the growing volume of literature in the field. They may also appeal to a wider lay audience interested in education abroad.

As an area study of a national system each volume presents an accurate, reasonably up-to-date account of the most important features of the educational system described. Among these are the ways in which the school system is controlled, financed and administered. Some account is given of the various kinds of school within the system and the characteristics of each of them. The principles of curriculum organization and some aspects of teacher education are outlined. Of more interest, however, is the analysis which is made in each volume of the unique national characteristics of an educational system, seen in the context of its history and the sociological, economic and political factors which have in the past and continue now to influence educational policy.

The assumption behind the series is, however, that common socio-economic and educational problems find unique expression in a particular country or region, and that a brief analysis of some major national issues will reveal similarities and differences. Thus, while in each case the interpretation of policies and practices is based on the politics of education, the interpretative emphasis will vary from one country to another.

The framework of analysis for each volume is consequently the same, attention being drawn in the first section to the legal basis of educational provision, followed in the second section by an analysis of the political considerations which have and do influence the formulation, adoption and implementation of policy. The role of political parties is described where appropriate and the influence of the church or churches on policy examined. Attention too is given to the activities of pressure groups at national, regional and local levels. Changing industrial, urban and familial patterns are used to show how educational needs are in process of change and what difficulties arise when innovations are attempted. Again, each author touches on the extent to which economic resources affect the implementation of policy. The analysis relates principally to the thirty-year period between 1945 and 1975 but relevant aspects of the pre-Second World War period are described and the chains of events are seen in historical perspective.

Finally, in the third section some account is given of problems which arise within the educational system itself. Those which appear to the author of particular interest and importance have been treated in some depth. Others have been referred to so that readers may consult other sources of information if they wish. Broad problem areas in education have, however, been identified. The points of transition within a system between the first and second and between the second and third stages of education give rise to problems of selection and allocation. Under conditions of expansion, created by explosions of population and aspirations, traditional solutions are often thought to be no longer adequate. The attempts made to meet these new situations are described. So too are the relationships and debates about them, between the various types of school at different levels of education. For example what are the possibilities of transfer between academic, general and technical/vocation schools at the second stage of education? And where these different types have been replaced by some form of common or comprehensive school what kinds of differentiation exist within the single school? At the third level of higher education what relationships exist between institutions providing general education, professional training and research opportunities? In some systems a form of dual control is growing up with the universities retaining much of their traditional autonomy and the technological institutes and teacher education institutions increasingly feeling the influence of government agencies. Again, after a process of differentiation in course content in the first stage of higher education there is now a tendency for the first year (or two) of college or university work to be regarded as a preparatory year (or years) with common or somewhat similar courses of studies for all students.

Particular attention has been paid to the problems which arise in the area of teacher education. Movements in most countries are in the direction of bringing together the previously separate systems of training for elementary and secondary school teachers. Common entrance prerequisites to different training institutions may now be required. Where this is not yet the case training colleges usually make it possible for students to obtain, during the course of their studies, a certificate which grants entry to the university and highest (in prestige and status) forms of teacher education. The place of teacher education in the structure of higher education is, in short, discussed in each of the volumes. So are debates about curricular content and methods of certification.

Finally, some attention is given to the interaction of the schools and other social agencies. Among these the health services, youth organizations, the family, the Church, industry and commerce have been regarded as important. Where special note is not taken of such institutions the impact they have in the schools is dealt with throughout the volume as a whole.

The framework in short is intended to facilitate cross cultural studies through the series as a whole. Basic educational legislation is referred to in the belief that it gives the most reliable and valid source of national goals or aims in education. The problems of putting these into effective action are socio-economic-political and educational. Comparisons can be made, therefore, between the aims of education as expressed in national legislation and between the main factors which inhibit or facilitate practical provisions in accordance with these aims.

BRIAN HOLMES
General Editor

General editor's introduction

In twenty-five years the leaders and people of Egypt have achieved a great deal. After the 1952 Revolution the new government embarked upon a whole series of measures designed to modernize the country. Government initiatives had to be taken against a background of centuries of tradition and the influence of colonial powers. The educational system, in particular, had been profoundly influenced by French and British missionaries and by educational practices in these two countries. The political revolution and complete independence did not of themselves solve everything. Successful modernization depends in the long run on the skill with which new ideas and patterns of behaviour are incorporated into traditional frameworks without alienating the majority of citizens. In Egypt, as elsewhere, the key to modernization has been the application of science and technology in the interests of industrialization and scientific socialism. In response to this need, changes in educational policy and practice have been inevitable. The analysis made by Professor Hyde of the constraints surrounding the rapid and successful transformation of the educational system has relevance for most countries pursuing policies of 'modernization'.

The relationship between higher education and economic development is fairly obvious. In Egypt universities have been expanded, new departments and institutes have been set up and attempts have been made to plan research and development. A National Planning Committee and the Academy of Scientific Research have been involved in policy formulation and the organization of research. Under a Supreme Council for the Universities, existing and new universities are free to conduct their affairs within budgets allocated by the government. There has, of course, been a shift of emphasis from the humanities to the applied sciences – engineering, agriculture and medicine. Development has been planned to meet the need for more and more technologists. A striking feature of university expansion has been the way in which al-Azhar University, which in 1952 had faculties of Islamic law,

Q'ranic studies and Arabic language and literature, has been brought into the mainstream of development. It flourishes under a Ministry of al-Azhar Affairs as a testimony to the fact that Islam, the declared state religion, thrives in modern secular Egypt.

It is, therefore, less to Islam that we should turn than to the economic and political problems post-1952 leaders faced as we seek to assess the success of plans to improve the educational system. Foreign political influences had encouraged the growth of English medium secondary schools. Success in the preparatory departments of these language schools ensured admission to government secondary schools and subsequently to the universities. Life chances in the civil service were greatly enhanced. Thus while some progress had been made by 1952 towards the creation of a system of free primary schooling, illiteracy rates were very high and the proportion of children who failed to complete the course (wastage) was also very high. Traditional opposition to the education of girls and women had to be overcome. Differences of provision between rural and city areas had to be ironed out. Attitudes to skilled and semi-skilled work in industry had to be transformed. The status and prestige enjoyed by white collar jobs had somehow to be modified. The domination of examinations had to be reduced in spite of the fact that they provide clear incentives to students and measures of success for teachers. Consumer preference for 'general' rather than 'technical' courses has not been easily changed in spite of the needs of industrialization. The more adequate education and training of teachers have been issues of concern to government planners. There has also been some attempt to reduce the power of the central authorities in the interests of local participation. As in many countries the constraints have been considerable and planners have had to face difficulties created by the need to pursue simultaneously rather conflicting aims in education, namely the provision of education to all as a human right and the need to allocate resources to education in a way which will best serve the aims of economic development.

Success itself has created problems. Many well-trained graduates have chosen to seek employment abroad, thus depriving the country of the trained manpower it needs. Such a 'brain drain' is a common feature. On the other hand the government's policy of seconding trained personnel to other countries has been most generous and, in the long run, imaginative. In the short term it has placed additional strains on the educational system. These circumstances have given Egypt a key role to play in the Arab world. The succession of wars has made further demands on an economy in which vast differences exist between rural and city life and between illiterate peasants and the educated professional class. Some, but not all, of these difficulties are common to most developing countries.

It is, of course, because many of the problems faced by educationists in Egypt are found elsewhere that this case study has wider relevance. If the problems faced and the conditions under which they are found can be replicated in many parts of the world, this case study illustrates very clearly the particular responses made by Egyptians to the challenge to modernize. Their aims have not been significantly different from those expressed elsewhere since 1945. They have been to raise standards of living for the mass of people, to create new and just political systems and to provide education as a human right. A comparison of the policies adopted to achieve these aims and the success and failure of them is of considerable interest to Comparative Educationists. Many of the problems known to us in the early 1950s have not yet been solved. After twenty-five years of serious and sincere endeavour in Egypt it is not unreasonable to make some assessment of the success and failure of policies adopted and put into practice in that country.

Professor Hyde has made such an assessment. Sympathetic yet critical, the analysis is based on careful research, long experience of the Arab world, a period of teaching recently in the American University in Cairo and many discussions with friends and officials in Egypt. The judgment of Dr El-Koussy is worth repeating. 'This book, which reflects a high degree of objectivity, fairness and sincerity in the educational cause will be welcomed in Egypt for the analytic overview of the Egyptian educational system it provides.' I think it will do this and more. It should have considerable appeal to all those who are committed to the 'planned development of education' who yet wish to evaluate critically success and the conditions under which failures in planning are likely to occur. It illustrates the areas in which policies are likely to succeed and draws attention to the reasons for delays in the realization of the hopes of educationists and the expectations of parents and pupils. As a case study of a system of education which has been 'planned' after the overthrow of a political system, it adds a new dimension to the volumes published in this World Education Series. Hopefully it will provide a model which subsequent authors can follow.

BRIAN HOLMES

Preface

by Dr A. A. El-Koussy

Ain Shams University, Cairo

There is a feeling among educators nowadays that if you write about education in a newly developing country you must hasten to publish it before it gets out-of-date. This actually happens even with accounts in the international, regional and national statistical handbooks. Professor Hyde's book succeeds in delineating the educational picture of modern Egypt within the last twenty-five years by showing its dynamics, its historical background and its future possibilities. By making this approach she has brought into relief the main trends and characteristics, thus overcoming the above difficulty.

The author took as a landmark the 1952 Revolution which radically changed the whole life and politics of the Egyptian people. She assumes that great political movements are usually accompanied by radical educational changes to help solidify and support the new régime. Indeed education in Egypt in 1952 has been given, as she records, a top priority among the various activities of the country, accelerating by leaps and bounds the progress already made following the establishment of the first Egyptian Constitution in 1923.

Progress does not mean that we are not aware of the handicaps and obstacles. There are still children of school age who are not registered in schools, while schools and universities are congested with students in numbers outweighing the facilities and resources, both human and material. These are scarce in a country that has faced five big wars in twenty-five years. To this problem must be added that of the large proportion of children under fifteen years of age (45 per cent as compared with 20 to 30 per cent in developed countries) which makes necessary a competitive examination system, with all its drawbacks. These problems are clarified in this book.

Professor Hyde has worked in education for about twenty years in the Middle East, culminating in her experience at the American University in Cairo, where she has both contributed and extended her knowledge of Arab culture and the Arab way of life, which she has learned to understand and appreciate. Her wide travel and varied experiences in other parts of the world provide a frame of reference for her studies of Egyptian education made after many personal visits to schools and educational institutions to collect data. She is well qualified to produce this present study, which, had it been written by an Egyptian educator, would probably have reflected either sympathy or involvement with the system, thereby satisfying some Egyptian educators while making others over-critical. (This characteristic is not confined to Egypt, but appears to be universal.) It is better for such a book to be written by a candid observer from outside, whose scientific standpoint is less influenced by personal involvements and sympathies.

This book, which reflects a high degree of objectivity, fairness and sincerity in the educational cause will be welcomed in Egypt for the analytic overview of the Egyptian educational system it provides. It will also be welcomed in other Arab and other developing countries since it presents a comprehensive case study with both diagnosis and prognosis of a sister country. The work will also be a good source for educators in other parts of the world, particularly those interested in comparative research. It will help them to appreciate the contribution of Egypt to the enrichment of mankind in general.

I

The context of education in modern Egypt

Introduction

Prelude to the Revolution

After nine years of British rule, in 1923, Egypt became nominally independent and achieved her first written Egyptian constitution. In theory she was to be ruled by a constitutional monarchy, with power residing in the people, but in practice the king had not only executive authority but legislative power. Most of his subjects were illiterate peasants living a feudal-type existence in the thousands of small hamlets throughout Egypt. Their political awareness was minimal. Qubain (1969), Ammar (1966), Taha Husayn (1948), and other writers of the period have described how their lives were governed by an unwritten common law developed through customs, practices and traditions of their families, villages and religious bodies, 'sources of law which they could recognize and obey loyally because they emanated from their own environment' (Qubain). The most powerful influence, the Moslem religion, pervaded every aspect of their lives although already Islam was becoming increasingly subservient to the state, its law, through foreign influence, being superseded by civil law.

Other agents of change were at work. Internal migration (estimated at about ten million during the first half of the century) increased after the Second World War, owing to the depressed conditions of agriculture following disruptions of trade. The tendency of industry and new services to concentrate in the larger towns made them attractive to job-hunters, creating all the socio-economic problems attendant to the rapid expansion of an urban population, unskilled and disorganized, lacking the leadership, protection and neighbourhood sanctions of their previous mode of life. It was the disillusionment, resentment and misery of these masses, whose slum dwellings in crowded quarters contrasted painfully with the spacious homes and the amenities enjoyed not only by city Egyptians but by foreigners, that sparked off the riots of Black Sunday in Cairo during January 1952.

Meanwhile, at the other end of the social scale, the politically orientated intelligentsia suffered disillusionment with what claimed to be a liberal, democratic régime. Although three-fifths of the Senate were elected by a form of universal suffrage, the king could exercise a veto, adjourn parliament and rule by decrees or prevent the leaders of the elected party from forming a government or maintaining it. This treatment was experienced by the popular Wafd party, which, says Qubain (1969), 'was suspended in 1930 and nullified by imposition of martial law eleven out of the fifteen years between 1937 and 1952'.

Gamal Abdul Nasser, who organized the 'Free Officers' movement from among his fellow students at the Military Academy in 1942, had ten years in which to study and learn from Egypt's two previous attempts at revolution. He concluded that they had failed because they surrendered to a 'pseudo-democracy' of alien origin which failed to break the tyranny of feudalism and was dominated by a ruling class which was insensitive to the sufferings and misery of the masses. For Nasser political freedom was meaningless unless combined with economic and social freedom.

After the military junta had declared the 1923 Constitution abolished in favour of rule by decree, the monarchy itself (which at first had been preserved by Farouk's abdication in favour of his infant son) was abolished and a republic declared. All political parties were dissolved and their properties sequestrated. A committee of lawyers was given three years to draw up a new constitution under a new one-party government consisting mainly of members of the Revolutionary Command Council.

The state of education in 1952

The 'wind of change' had also reached the educational world by 1952, the main advance since independence in 1923 being in the field of primary education, which had been so badly neglected during the British occupation. The new Egyptian government had inherited a system of education virtually unchanged since 1836, when Mohammed ʿAli created a modern European-type system to exist side by side with the traditional religious system dominated by al-Azhar. Certain characteristics of this system persisted not just till Egypt received her independence, but until, under Nasser's influence, al-Azhar came to terms with modernization.

2

Mohammed 'Ali's plans for Egypt, embracing a strong modern army, scientifically equipped modern factories for spinning and weaving to replace small home industries and a strong fleet to protect the Eastern Mediterranean, could not be carried out by Egyptians lacking scientific training, so he not only provided modern colleges to fill the educational gap but also sent students on educational missions abroad and invited European teachers to Egypt. His educational ladder in terms of priorities thus began at the top, with secondary schools created to supply college students and, in time, primary schools to feed the secondary schools. It is not surprising that enlightened educators ever since have had a tough time trying to create an image of the primary school as an institution in its own right, serving the developmental needs of its pupils rather than what El-Koussy referred to as 'a miniature version of a secondary school'.

During the British occupation the number of secondary schools was increased by benevolent organizations, the medium of instruction being English, which facilitated the employment of their students in the Civil Service. These private schools, which were mainly run by foreign communities, were known as language schools or mission schools. Their modern curricula gave them great prestige, so their primary sections fed the government secondary schools as well as the private schools while their secondary sections led to the higher professions and many well-paid government posts. During this period they were completely independent.

There was no expansion of government non-fee-paying elementary education until the Egyptian Constitution made it compulsory from six to twelve years, a declaration of intent not likely to be fully realized until half a century later. However, in spite of the setbacks resulting from the king's interference with government, solid progress was made to give the intelligent poor at least a chance to step on the modern educational ladder. There was a marked increase in the percentage of the Budget used for elementary education, 15 per cent in 1920, 39 per cent in 1945 (El-Koussy, 1953). The gradual removal of the second-language teaching from the primary school made transfer from elementary to primary school possible and by 1945 elementary pupils were able to compete in the primary school examination for secondary places. The abolition of primary-school fees, including payment for school books, materials and school meals in 1949, created a single status school at this stage, resulting in a rush not only for primary school places but for places in the government's kindergartens. It is significant that Egypt, prior to 1952, had started on the road to free education, which, in view of her rapidly increasing population and limited finances, inevitably led to at least the temporary lowering of standards. One immediate effect was the law in 1951 confirming that formal education was compulsory and free from six to twelve years. This meant the closure of some excellent kindergartens which had been staffed by Egyptians trained in England and the inclusion of six-year-olds in the primary schools, whose class numbers expanded rapidly with increasing demand. This was an inevitable retrogressive step.

Other trends which would be developed by the future revolutionary government were the increasing attention paid to technical education, which in 1951 became part of the secondary system, and the increased provision for the education of girls, whose numbers had doubled since 1945. A variety of education schools for the training of teachers had been established, including a special institution for training rural teachers in what were considered appropriate skills for the sons of fellahin (peasants), but the point of entry was completion of a primary school education.

In 1952 Cairo University had four faculties, Alexandria University was established and a new university, Ibrahim Pasha (shortly to be re-named Ain Shams), had been opened in 1950. Subjects involving sciences, such as medicine and engineering, were taught but 'modernization' had not yet become the key word in higher education. The Science Faculty at Cairo University had already been strengthened by the incorporation of three notable institutes, the Helwan Observatory, the Institute of Oceanography and the Desert Institute of Egypt. The modern universities, however, served an élite aristocracy and, to a lesser extent, the upper middle classes, who could afford to pay the fees. They alone of educational institutions were allowed to operate under their own laws. The Ministry of Education, which had passed entirely into Egyptian hands had made some attempt at decentralization by creating educational zones, each with its bureaucratic hierarchy. However, the Directors' power was limited, the Ministry having complete control not only of manpower and finance but of detailed curricula, textbooks, examinations and discipline.

To summarize, far-reaching reforms had been made in education since Egypt had attained independence, but long-term planning had been minimal: the many inadequacies included money, well-trained and specialized teachers and administrative staff, buildings and equipment. Writing just before the Revolution, El-Koussy (1953), stated,

> one of the greatest hindrances to all progress lies in our inability to reconcile the two main educational theories, the one demanding that plans for reform should start with quantitative development, in the belief that quality will follow; the other advocating initial concentration on quality and the setting of a high standard, with quantitative development to follow. Future leaders will have to serve both ends simultaneously and will have to attack the self-defeating factors in an effective way.

The Constitution of 1956

By 1956 the Revolutionary government under the leadership of President Abdul Nasser was ready to incorporate in a new constitution the basic principles to guide the new republic. Egypt was formally declared to be a sovereign Arab state, a democratic republic and an integral part of the 'Arab nation'. Sovereignty belonged to the people, Islam was the religion of the state and Arabic became the official language. To preserve its sovereignty and independence, imperialism and its agents would need to be eradicated and a strong national army established. The democratic ideal would be pursued by breaking the bonds of feudalism, ending monopolies and controlling the influence of capitalism over the system of government. Social justice would be the right of every citizen.

Some post-revolutionary issues and their implication for education

National integration

It is self-evident that national integration becomes a priority in the political programme of a revolutionary leader or party to ensure that the new régime lives long enough to carry out the policies designed to change the conditions that led to revolution. This is particularly so in the case of a country like Egypt whose 'Free Officers' achieved their initial success without the civil war and mass executions of opponents typical of so many other revolutions.

The post-revolutionary issues are all concerned with the problem of finding a common ground between sections of the population that, historically speaking, had little in common but their faith in God. As the Revolution was the enemy of social and economic as well as political evils, appropriate legislation would inevitably benefit one section of the population at the expense of another. Integration could only take place if national pride could reconcile the interests of those who would materially lose on the deal, with the masses who for centuries had been so fully occupied with economic survival that a change of government was less important than a change of master. President Nasser had much to say about the failure of the 1919 popular revolutionary movement which, he said, resulted in a 'sham democracy' of reactionaries. The Constitution of 1956 demanded that disparate elements be integrated and authority shifted in the direction of social justice.

Secularization

Until the Revolution, the integrating factor not only in Egypt but the whole Arab world had been Islam, which had been a whole way of life covering not just personal conduct and relationships but legal, political, social, economic and educational aspects. There were still those who thought that an Egyptian 'renascence' implies a return to a strict adherence to the Islamic faith and practice. This belief had been reinforced by the temporary successes of the Moslem Brotherhood, but Islam was regarded by Nasser, himself a devout Moslem, as inadequate to deal with problems of Western origin. Sharabi (1966), points out that it was the political disintegration of the Ottoman Empire that made possible the separation of the functions of church and state, which, in turn, made compatible the existence of socialism and Islam. In his view disintegration of the Islamic hold resulted not only from the decline of Islamic Law but also from the secularization of education which began with the introduction of technical schools and Christian missionary schools. The exact role and function of Islam in the modern Egyptian educational system was an issue to be resolved in the next few years, but in 1956 it was clearly given the status of state religion.

Education of the masses

The 1956 Constitution declared that sovereignty belongs to the 'people', that is, to every Egyptian subject, male or female, including the 75 per cent who at that time constituted the illiterate masses. The preparation of these citizens (on whom, ultimately, the success of the Revolution would depend), for carrying out their democratic responsibilities was a crucial issue. The failure of previous governments to provide a good public educational system was regarded by educationists, economists and politicians alike as the main cause for Egypt's backwardness. Radwan (1951), describes an education system in which the only provision for the majority of Egypt's fast-increasing population was 'on the job' training in the field or workshop, which enabled the trainee to earn enough to cover his daily needs of food, shelter and clothing. This he calls 'education for serfdom'.

The status quo was fortified by religion, politics, extremes of poverty and riches and the social class system which kept the masses of people 'in that state of life to which it had pleased God to call them'. The land system was one of private ownership, and, says Mabro, even after legislation to improve the fellah's lot there was 'no extension service, no attempts to expand education in the villages'. After Egyptian independence some attempt was made to improve the quantity and quality of rural education but it was inadequate in both directions. The economy played its part in resisting change. According to Mabro,

In 1952, before the land reform, 2,000 owners held 19·7 per cent of the total area, some 1,177,000 feddans [acres]. At the other end of the spectrum more than 2 million persons owned between themselves 778,000 feddans or 13 per cent of the total area. These owners were virtually landless; some lived in the towns or worked in the villages having leased their plots to neighbours or relatives; others rented land to supplement their holdings. Finally, landless peasants formed a sizeable group estimated at 1·3 million families.

For the Revolutionary Government a crucial issue was therefore the raising of the standard of living of the mass of the people, freeing them from the bonds of feudalism and providing them with enough education to acquire both practical skills that would benefit themselves and the state and political skills that would enable them to carry out their democratic function.

Land reform, involving a re-distribution of wealth was inevitable if this were to be achieved, but it had to be done without disrupting production and marketing. For a full account, Mabro (1974), gives excellent coverage. For the present purpose, a few points (summarized from Mabro) will suffice. The Land Reform Law of 1952 fixed a 200-feddan [acre] ceiling on personal ownership, (extended to 300 if there were wives and children), amended to 100 in 1961 and 50 in 1969. Until 1953, landlords could sell excess land. Terms of compensation under 1961 law were generous (4 per cent interest and fifteen years' redemption) but in 1964 all interest payments were discontinued, the bonds becoming irredeemable and completely worthless. The Agrarian Reform Authority concentrated on the requisition and re-distribution of land together with the organization of co-operatives. The land was to be distributed in small lots of 2 to 5 feddans, depending on the quality and needs of the beneficiaries, priority being given to permanent workers of the estate, then farmers with large families and then the poorest members of the village, all of whom had to pay the compensation (later reduced to a half, then a quarter), over thirty years (later lengthened to forty), and pay the annual interest of 3 per cent and 15 per cent charges (both abolished in 1964). The agrarian reform laws since the 1960s have been used to compensate families of officers or soldiers who fought in Yemen or the wars against Israel as well as graduates from agricultural schools and faculties. Distributions are currently being made following the reclamation of land in the Delta and desert areas. No beneficiary can sell, sublet or subdivide the land and 'all are required by law to join a co-operative society which assumed, under the direction of an official, some of the functions of the displaced landlord – provision of inputs and credit, marketing of the crop and maintenance of fixed equipment, mainly irrigation pumps. . . . Minimum daily wages were stipulated' (Mabro, Chapter 4).

The co-operatives (which, in time, were extended to embrace new industries as well as agriculture) were designed to take care of basic skills necessary for subsistence living, but society would never become integrated at this level. The urgent need was for universal literacy and a basic education that would enable the highly intelligent among the workers to qualify for the various grades of management. The literacy drives and legislation to give every Egyptian child a free and compulsory education are described in the following chapters. The development of their political skills would result from their new and important status in the community under the guidance and patronage (in its best sense) of the Arab Socialist Union (ASU).

The role of the Arab Socialist Union

Apart from his own charismatic personality, the Arab Socialist Union was Nasser's special contribution to integration. After winning the power struggle he had abolished not only political parties but any other organization that might become a political liability. There were still potential opponents, such as the Moslem Brotherhood; power had to be centralized while the new régime developed policies and strategies. The Suez Canal crisis in 1956 added a new dimension to his struggle, strengthening his belief that Egypt's internal problems stemmed from the evils of imperialism and its agents. His success enhanced his image not only in Egypt but in the whole Arab world: the time was ripe to mobilize not only the economic social assets of the country but its manpower resources. In 1961 the former was achieved by the nationalization of leading industrial and economic enterprises and the latter by the organization of the Arab Socialist Union. (It is significant that it was not named the 'Egyptian Socialist Union' underlining the 1956 Constitution declaration that Egypt was 'an integral part of the "Arab nation"'.) It was re-organized again in 1968, a new National Assembly being elected from its members.

The Arab Socialist Union, often referred to as the 'working alliance' represents the interests of the entire labour force of Egypt: farmers, workers, intellectuals, national capitalists, members of organized professions, the armed forces and even students. It is therefore a vast structure at times duplicating the normal functions of trade, professional and political organizations.* No other political body is tolerated but trade and professional groups such as co-operative societies and the Teachers' Syndicate which exist side by side with the ASU are represented on its committees. For example, the Teachers' Syndicate is affiliated with the ASU Committee for Education and some members hold office in both organizations. Parliament is not an ASU body, nor are its members elected to represent the ASU as such, but, as Egypt is a one-party state, in practice no one becomes a member of parliament who has not previously been selected for office at some level by the ASU. The two organizations are co-ordinated by a parliamentary com-

* The party system was re-introduced in 1976 (see pp. 208–9). The special role of the ASU is in process of being defined.

9

mittee. There appears to be some overlap of functions, but whereas parliament legislates, the ASU is largely an executive body. The President works with a consultative committee consisting of four leaders: the Deputy President, the Prime Minister (selected by the President), the Head of Parliament (elected by the members of parliament) and the ASU leader. In matters affecting the interest or welfare of the masses, it is the ASU leader who is charged with carrying out the policy. For example, in the literacy campaign, the ASU were made responsible for the population at large, that is, those who are not workers in the public sector of industry or a government department. In 1960, under a law for the re-organization of the Press, the ASU had the responsibility of forming a Higher Council of the Press which would guarantee support for ideological and political sentiments in line with socialism. (This interpretation of 'complete freedom of the Press' has since been amended.) Another important function of the ASU is to develop popular organizations and syndicates which can be used as sounding-boards for the feelings of the members. As observed by Abd-el-Rahman (1974), 'The development of such movements is an endless source to the conscious leadership that directly receives the reactions and responses of the masses.' More directly the working population can make its voice heard through the hierarchical structure of the ASU. Any group of persons in a village, public organization, factory, occupation, geographical area, etc. can be set up as a 'basic unit' or 'conference' which elects a committee of one-third of its members every other year. The committee, with the help of the secretary and his assistant and, if desired, sub-committees, is responsible both for receiving and carrying out directives of the Higher Committee of the ASU and for sending it monthly reports of activities. At the next level is the conference and committee of the ASU for the city, district or organization which comprises more than one basic unit. The 'conference' is made up of all the 'committees' in the basic unit and, in turn it elects its own committee. This pattern is repeated, forming larger and more responsible circles until the level is reached of the General National Congress and the Committee of the ASU for the Republic, which is the highest authority. From its General Committee is elected the Higher Executive Committee which is a decision-making body with a Secretary-General and a Secretariat with thirteen departments. This complicated structure is described by Abd-el-Rahman as 'The authority which represents the people striving to accomplish the Revolution's potentialities and safeguarding its true democratic values'. It is a structure, in fact, that can be accommodated to extreme centralization or an extremely democratic process. Its potential for indoctrination and informal education of Egypt's liberated serfs cannot be over-estimated.

The revival of Arabic

Language has always been a unifying and integrating factor in national movements, notably in the unification of Italy and of Germany in the nineteenth century. Gaining the support of the masses has involved educating them in the vernacular, which wins in the linguistic battle of survival by sheer force of the numbers for whom it is the only means of communication. For hundreds of years the Egyptian people were governed by foreigners who did not attempt to study Arabic, a difficult, oriental language with a classical structure, using its unique alphabet from right to left. It was kept alive in its pure form as the sacred language of Islam, the vehicle for worship in the mosque, for the Holy Q'ran and Hadeeth, the Islamic Law and doctrines and a vast literature of poetry and prose to delight and tease Arab scholars. After the opening of modern Language Schools, the middle classes, like the aristocracy, showed their superiority by conversing in the European language in which they had been educated, while their illiterate servants communicated in a local Arabic dialect having what Bernstein describes as a 'restricted' vocabulary adulterated (or enriched, depending on the point of view), by words acquired during successive foreign occupations. All were familiar with the Q'ran, which is daily broadcast from the mosques.

Szyliowicz (1973), points out that Mohammed 'Ali's school system which used Arabic as the medium of instruction was an early factor in integrating a new Egyptian administrative élite, which in time achieved equality of status with the ruling Turco-Circassian group. He states that

the decision to use Arabic in the schools was, in fact, based upon the simple consideration that the majority of students knew only that language, but the consequences were far-reaching, for the existing dichotomy of language and culture was destroyed. Until now, communications between the ruling class, which spoke Ottoman Turkish, and the Egyptians, who spoke Arabic, had been severely limited, thus maintaining societal cleavages and restricting the opportunities for mobility. Now the foundations were laid for the emergence of Arabic as the national language and, in time, for the cultural integration of society. . . . in 1858 it was decreed that all official correspondence be conducted in Arabic. . . .Within a few decades Arabic completely replaced Turkish, thus signifying that a circulation of élites had taken place within the Egyptian bureaucracy.

Before the end of the century, intellectuals like al-Afghani, Abdu and Lutfi al-Sayyid not only expressed the new nationalist spirit in their writings, but came to grips with the problem of adapting an ancient language to mass media such as the Press and school. Newspapers had only been intelligible to a small literate section of the population, but reforms in the Arabic language, mainly associated with the work of Rifa'ah Rafi al-Tahtawi, drew the attention of orientalists and Arabs themselves to the scope and flexibility of the language. Hourani (in Ahmed, 1960) claims that Rifa'ah was the first Egyptian who saw Egypt as a nation distinct from the general body of the Islamic Community: 'Every land has a planet from whose horizon the sun rises. Our Egypt is the planet of Africa, the highest minaret and the warm sun of its horizon.' More than a century later, President Nasser was to develop this theme.

While Abdu concentrated on the importance of knowledge of Arabic for a revival of Islam and its literature, others, through the Press, which now reached an expanded audience from the new literate class educated in private primary and elementary schools, hoped to influence the public in appreciating the importance of education in the national language as a nationalistic weapon. Somehow the revival of Arabic and traditional ways of learning had to be reconciled with the modern scientific approach of Western cultures. The concept of a modern scientific education using Arabic as the medium of instruction was expressed by Lutfi al-Sayyid in the national newspaper, *al-Jaridah* (12 December 1913, translated by Ahmed, 1960): 'To my mind the preservation of the language and the enthusiasm for serving it by re-invigorating its life through new styles and idioms are proof that a nation has personality and self-respect.' Nearly two decades later the founding of the Academy of the Arabic Language shifted the concept of Divine Revelation to that of scientific analysis of the language, leading to its adaptation to the requirements of modern science and technology. The Academy, which flourished under the guidance of Egypt's most distinguished scholar, Taha Husayn, now has to its credit not only a standard dictionary of classical literary Arabic based on historical principles, according to the latest lexicographical practice, but a journal of linguistic studies and a library of over ten thousand books. Perhaps its greatest achievement has been to help the establishment of Arabic as, perhaps, the greatest unifying factor not only in Egypt but in the Arab world. Since four years before the Revolution all Egyptian children, whether in state or private schools had to study Arabic, and, since it was made officially the state language in the Constitution of 1956, it has increasingly become a medium of instruction at all levels of education. Although this is politically satisfying and accords with the national pride of the Egyptian people it has created some educational problems which are still being debated.

Modernization

'Modernization' is a complicated concept that can be discussed at all levels ranging from philosophical and psychological attitudes towards living, to the arrangement of desks to form groups rather than rows in the modern classroom. Badeau (1966), describes it as a sociological term implying change: 'a widespread shift in the centre of attention away from the familiar past to the modern, if nebulous, future'. In Egypt it is a key word to describe the application of science and technology, as practised with varying success in the West, and socialism, which draws its inspiration from both East and West, to every aspect of government. The term is used in connection with the administration, the legal system, the economy, industry and agriculture, manpower control, education, insurance, welfare and family planning. The ingredients are familiar: universal compulsory and free education, worker participation, welfare from the cradle to the grave, improved communication, up-to-date laboratories, workshops, equipment of all kinds to facilitate research, scientific and technological education and the training of personnel at home and abroad to provide scientific leadership in all fields and political education at home to ensure that no citizen loses the opportunity of democratic participation.

Such a comprehensive change in the pattern of living must have negative aspects: the old order must be overthrown in order to make way for the new. In Egypt the traditional liberal ideal had been tried

13

and found inadequate: it has moved to what Badeau calls 'a more radical programme of modernization . . . based on the conviction that there must be a total change in the social structure before a truly progressive modern state can emerge.' The enemies of modernization were seen in Egypt as foreign political domination and the feudalism of church and state, expressed in private ownership of most of the land and the means of production and wealth in general, leaving power in the hands of religious, economic, social and political élites.

The former, constructive aspect has, in Egypt, been given more prominence than the latter, destructive aspect: Islam, written into the Constitution as the state religion, was to be reformed but not destroyed in the process; landowners were to be allowed to keep enough of their feddans to ensure a good life, but they would be expected to use modern methods of increasing production; the private sector whether in industry or commerce or education would be subordinate to the public sector, but its importance in the modernization programmes would ensure not only recognition but survival, where necessary through government aid.

The other characteristic of 'modernization' as interpreted by Egypt arises from her situation geographically and historically in the Middle East. She looks beyond her national boundaries, identifying with whole of the Arab world. Therefore, with the establishment of the Arab League and all its subsidiary organizations, she throws her weight on the side of any modernization programme involving her partners, regardless of differences in political ideology.

Expressed policies

The National Charter, 1962

Looking back on the first ten years of the Egyptian Revolution, President Gamal Abdul Nasser claimed that 'the sole basis of work was the famous six principles carved out of the demands and needs of the people's struggle.' (These were embodied in the Constitution of 1956.) He was confident of ultimate success because 'On that day [23 July 1952] the Egyptian people re-discovered themselves and opened their eyes to their enormous latent potentialities.'

The President then reviewed the circumstances faced by the struggle of the people of Egypt and the steps they took to ensure control of the production machinery, to dissolve differences among classes as a means to real democracy and to establish new social relations, based on new values to be given expression by a new national culture. In this they were guided by 'a deep consciousness of history and its effect on contemporary man on the one hand, and of the ability of man in turn to influence history, on the other,' and an 'unshakeable faith in God, His Prophets and His sacred messages which He passed on to man as a guide to justice and righteousness'.

The Egyptian Revolution not only turned into a strong driving force providing the whole Arab world with energy and renewed vigour, confirming its unity, but had far-reaching effects on the liberation movement in Africa, Asia and Latin America, while the Battle of Suez helped all oppressed peoples discover infinite latent powers in themselves.

Continuing his review of past events, Nasser defends the necessity of the Revolution resulting from outstanding changes after the Second World War, including other nationalist movements in Asia, Africa and Latin America, the emergence of a communist camp of enormous force, the great scientific and technological advance suddenly achieved in methods of production and the increasing weight of moral forces in the world, such as those provided by the United Nations Organization, the Non-Aligned States and world opinion. Reverting again to the past struggles of the Egyptian people from the Islamic conquest till modern times, Nasser asserts that, in spite of dreadful experiences, the spirit of the people was never broken; 'the great disasters . . . prompted them to store up energy which they discharged at the appropriate moment.' He then records previous revolutionary efforts and analyses their failures, until the sudden and complete collapse of the system.

The President follows this with an essay on 'true democracy', which must be popular and progressive: 'in the life of a nation, as in the life of an individual, the way to maturity and clarity of vision is through trial and error. . . . Political democracy or freedom in its political aspects are of no value without economic democracy of freedom in its social aspect.' He details the many factors that made a mockery of the 1923 Constitution: the pressures on voters, the open forgery and the buying of votes. Inefficiency and corruption forced thousands of agricultural labourers to live in conditions akin to forced labour in return for starvation wages and no hope for the future. 'Work became a commodity in the production process to be bought by the exploiting capital at the terms best serving its interests.' Education was subject to the same abuse:

> Successive generations of Egyptian youth were taught that their country was neither fit for nor capable of industrialization. In their textbooks, they read their national history in distorted versions. Their national heroes were described as lost in a mist of doubt and uncertainty while those who betrayed the national cause were glorified and venerated.

Thereafter follows an elaboration of the six basic principles of the new Egyptian democracy.

The next section is on the inevitability of the socialist solution, 'imposed by reality, the broad aspirations of the masses and the changing nature of the world in the second part of the twentieth century. . . . Scientific socialism is the suitable style for finding the right method leading to progress.' The people's control over all the tools of production would be achieved by creating a capable public sector to bear the main responsibility for the development plan and a private sector that would, without exploitation, participate in the development within the framework of the overall plan. Planning must be a 'scientifically organized creative process that would meet the challenges facing our society.' Nasser regarded the July 1961 laws as the biggest triumph of the revolutionary drive in the economic field. These covered the principles of nationalization in the fields of production, industry, trade, finance and land and the opportunities for the private sector. Mistakes might be made through inexperience but 'at any rate it was inevitable that the major national interests should be handed over to the people even at the cost of facing temporary difficulties.'

In the section on 'Production and Society', Nasser stresses the importance of family planning supported by modern scientific methods. Standards of living should be raised 'through economic and social planning without sacrificing the living generations of citizens for the sake of those still unborn.' This could be achieved by doubling the national income every ten years. In agriculture this would not be done by nationalization but by increased individual ownership, supported by means of agricultural co-operation which would enable the farmer to use the most modern machines and scientific means to raise production. (He then gives details of the land reform laws of 1952 and 1961.) It is industry, however that 'is capable of realising the greatest hopes in the

field of social and economic evolution. . . . Only industrial scientific
work can explore the wealth of the Egyptian land and exploit its
natural and mineral riches to serve progress.' Agricultural and mineral
raw materials need local industrialization, providing local work and
markets, while consumer industries would lessen the need for imports.
Industrial planning would also ensure sources of foreign currency for
development. Nasser then discusses the importance of balancing the
needs for heavy industry and consumer industry and the position of
labour and labour unions in the new system. The importance of an
efficient system of transport receives attention. In industry 'the maintenance of the role of the private sector beside that of the public sector,
renders control over public ownership more effective . . . by encouraging competition within the framework of the general economic planning'. Foreign capital has also a part to play: foreign aid with no strings
attached, unconditional loans with easy repayment are accepted with
gratitude and limited foreign investment in unavoidable circumstances.
The aim is to use the national wealth to ensure the happiness and well-
being of every individual. This involves 'Equality of opportunity'
expressed in the right for medical care, including health insurance, the
right of an education to suit abilities and talents, the right to a suitable
job, insurance against old age and sickness, opportunities that will later
enable them to become responsible leaders; in all these women must be
regarded as equal to men and free to 'take a constructive and profound
part in shaping life', while the family, 'the first cell in society' must be
afforded all means of protection. The welfare society is able to formulate new moral values reflected in a free national culture which includes
freedom of religious belief, from which is derived the eternal spiritual
values, a message of progress and man's right to life and freedom. God
in His great wisdom has made equality of opportunity the basis of His
judgment of all people. (Then follows an essay on freedom.)

> The freedom of an individual to shape his destiny, to define his
> position in society, to express his opinion, and by means of his
> thought and experience and hopes to take an active part in leading
> and directing the evolution of his society is an inalienable human
> right which must be protected by law.

The role of the Armed Forces is to protect the progress of social construction against external dangers, so they must be scientifically
equipped, but 'We must always bear in mind that the needs of defence

should never have the upperhand of the needs of development.' The aim is 'peace based on justice' but 'our society has to be always ready to support peace by power, for the sake of the freedom of the homeland and the citizen.'

The last three sections of the Charter deal with three subjects very dear to Nasser's heart: the socialist application and its problems, Arab unity and foreign policy. Problems in education arising from the application of socialism are discussed in a later chapter. In general, Nasser's emphasis is on peaceful achievement of his aims: 'The creative energies of peoples can shape the morrow without being driven towards it through mass bloodshed.' This is made possible by scientific progress: 'Organized national action which is based on scientific planning is the path leading to the desired future.' Planning with reference to social and economic objectives 'should be translated into detailed programmes to put within reach of the machinery of production.' These must take count of time limits, allotted investments, quantity and quality as related to time and cost. 'Every citizen should be aware of his defined responsibility in the whole plan, and should be fully conscious of the definite rights he will enjoy in the event of the success of the plan.' He emphasizes that clarity of experience and of thought are essential; the citizen must be able to make sense of the socialist doctrine. Success involves organization to meet the dangers inherent in great periods of social change: 'The greatest means of insurance against these dangers, however, lies in the exercise of freedom, particularly through elected popular councils.' Nasser then discusses at length the importance of freedom of constructive criticism and the mean by which the freedom of the individual can be reconciled to freedom of the leadership. Much attention is also given to the place of science, described as 'the weapon with which revolutionary triumph can be achieved.' Atomic energy for war is not an objective, but for prosperity it is able to perform miracles in the struggle of national development.

Nasser speaks of Arab unity as though, by 1962, it could be almost taken for granted: 'The concept of Arab unity no longer requires a meeting of the rulers of the Arab nation to portray solidarity among the governments. . . . Unity has passed this stage and is identified with Arab existence itself.' The existence of differences is a proof of unity. With great skill he makes virtue of all the obstacles that have previously stood in the path of a complete Arab unity and outlines the great and conscious efforts that must be made to ensure its final achievement.

Finally he lays down the principles of foreign policy that 'runs in three channels, dug deep and straight by means of the struggle of a brave people that stood against, and triumphed over, all kinds of pressure.' These are: war on imperialism and domination, labouring to consolidate peace and international co-operation for the sake of prosperity. There is no contradiction between these ideals: Arab unity, a Pan-African movement and an Afro-Asian solidarity, a close spiritual bond that ties Egypt to this Islamic world and loyalty to the UN Charter, which is the outcome of suffering of peoples in two world wars, separated only by a period of an armed truce.

The Permanent Constitution of the Arab Republic of Egypt, 1971

After the traumatic defeat of Egypt in the 1967 war with Israel, Nasser saw the need to re-unite as quickly as possible the various disillusioned and frustrated groups who had reacted by blaming each other for the national setback. With typical flexibility, he announced the preparation for a new constitution based on ten guidelines. Besides reiterating the nature of Arab nationalism and socialism, it would institute democratic reforms. The President only lived to get his proposals accepted by a referendum of the people in May, 1968: the Constitution itself was issued by his successor, President Anwar El-Sadat, in 1971.

In the interim period, the new President began what he called 'the rectification of the revolution', a description calculated to make clear that he was not criticizing what had taken place during the leadership of his predecessor, but was marking a new stage in the revolutionary process. Its purpose was a liberalization of the régime, which, in time, compensated foreigners who had lost property as a result of the Revolution, returned sequestrated property of Egyptians, or, if that was not possible, gave compensation and set free people detained without trial, with the option of returning to their former posts or receiving a pension if they were too old. At the time this could be regarded as a popular move designed to ease the path of one who was taking over from the most charismatic and successful leader in the Middle East. However, his subsequent record has shown a president consistently peaceful in his intentions and moderate in action but able to strike when the security of the state itself is endangered.

Naturally much of the Permanent Constitution is based on the principles of the 1962 Charter but it is more specific, laying down safeguards in those areas of living which are of special concern in a one-party state. Rights and freedoms are very much emphasized, their protection being guaranteed by the independence of justice. Citizens are guaranteed their freedom and privacy: nobody may be arrested or searched either in person or in his home or be imprisoned or restricted in his personal freedom unless there is a judicial order. To attack these freedoms is a crime for which the state must provide compensation. The safety of society and its political régime, however, are in the hands of a socialist General Prosecutor, whose duty it is to safeguard them 'to protect the socialist gains and to maintain adherence to socialist conduct'.

The October Working Paper, 1974

This, the most important political document in Egypt's history since the National Charter, was produced by President Sadat after the October War of 1973 as a re-appraisal of Egypt's aims and objectives in the light of twenty years of 'Revolutionary' government culminating in military success against Israel. Although achievement was limited, for Egypt and her neighbours, the world could never again be the same as prior to the October War. The Egyptian nationality 'that does not know fanaticism, but practises sacrifice in defence of its land and rights and to safeguard construction and progress' had 'transcended the confines of being a mere slogan to become a palpable, well-defined action.' Internally, the rectification movement 'withdrawing all forms of exceptional measures, and ensuring stability of laws, rules, institutions and relations within a clear-cut framework, known beforehand to the citizens, through which they can exercise their political, economic and social activities', was made possible because the Revolution had attained the stage of order and stability. Political and social freedom were interdependent, so it had been decided to remove Press censorship. Arab nationalism had reached a new stage: 'The Arabs succeeded for the first time in joining ranks effectively, and agreeing jointly on definite actions, notwithstanding any political or social differences.' Political unity is a lengthy process, but, said Sadat, 'We also have to benefit from other nations to the effect that interrelated economic interests constitute the material bases for every successful political unity . . . economic co-operation can bear fruit and can be furthered despite different political and social systems.' As a final comment on what he calls 'milestones along the road', President Sadat faces his critics:

Fear befell those who alleged that we wanted to annul the
Charter or go back on our socialism. . . . Basic principles do not
change with the change of circumstances, otherwise they would not
have risen to the level of principles. It is only the application
which should be changed and this is what we are doing.

Perhaps the most controversial change has been the 'open door'
policy with its welcome of foreign investment and advanced technological knowledge accompanying it from the whole world, both east
and west, because, says Sadat, 'We are fully aware that versatile and
varied economic relations constitute the material basis for the freedom
of our political movement.' The open door economic policy would
supply the most modern technological means towards the rapid and
intensive industrialization needed to promote exports by raising their
standards.

In the section on 'Social Development', President Sadat records what
he calls 'a few basic observations' concerning education, for

the time has come to begin seriously this difficult task of
revolutionising the systems and concepts of general education and
culture of all sorts and standards from the eradication of illiteracy
to general technical and university education, to scientific and
technological research.

He regards the most important development in world education and
research to be 'the elimination of the distance between thought and
action', so that it is no longer limited to rigid study curricula, but 'has
become organically linked to the actions and requirements of society.'
To achieve the twin targets of understanding and harmonizing with
his society as well as acquiring the basic skills for serving it, an enlightened, educated individual needs a system that 'should be diversified
as much as possible, to respond to the need for various expertise,
specialisations and skills required in development.' Certain types and
stages of education should be linked to the environment, rural or
urban, field or factory, to maintain the bonds between the educated
individual to his environment for their mutual benefit. Likewise there
should be closer bonds between educational institutions and industrial
establishments. He hopes that in this process the theory of the social
differences between one form of education and another will be eliminated, so that the need of the country for skills and expertise can be met

'to raise the value of work or labour as the primary social value.' Thus it will be possible 'to get rid of this overwhelming disease whereby many consider education as the instrument for acquiring a special social privilege, while the principal target for some educated people has become office-jobs irrespective of their value in the movement of society.'

The second of the education targets is supported by the modern theory of continuous education, a necessity in an age in which scientific, technological and technical knowledge progresses with such speed that machines become obsolete as soon as they are manufactured. To keep abreast with knowledge, the educated person must have access to up-to-date libraries, institutes, research and reading centres, as well as modern books, magazines and periodicals. Seminars and constant training programmes are required at all levels of industry, while utilization should be made of 'all the means of modern science to collect, store and distribute information, and to raise the standard of knowledge given to the students in the schools, universities and institutes.'

Finally, expenditure on technological research, which should be co-ordinated and directed to the requirements of Egypt, is regarded as 'investment in heavy industry' because 'not only does it help development in the near future, it also guarantees its continuation and rising rates in the long run.' The aim is to enter this field as partners, especially in the Arab world. All this is possible because 'Arab man [has proved himself] capable of genuine production, once he is supplied with the suitable circumstances.' The Egyptian man is distinguished by his faith, which, as understood today,

> is pure faith, free from fanaticism . . . remote from irresponsibility and belief in superstitions, and does not deny man's will and the will of society to face the ever-changing circumstances of life, supported in this by the brain which God has given him and which distinguishes him from the rest of God's creatures.

In short, education and research are to be the ultimate means of achieving the main national tasks following the October war. President Sadat makes his own summary of these in the October Working Paper:

> Economic development at rates that exceed all we have achieved up till now.

Preparation of Egypt for the year 2000 so that means of continued progress may be secured for the coming generations.

Open door economic policy at home and abroad to provide all guarantees for funds invested in development.

Effective and comprehensive planning which guarantees the realization of the great goals of society through science and knowledge.

Consolidation and re-orientation of the public sector thus enabling it to take the lead in development.

Social development and the building up of man.

Entering the age of science and technology.

Civilizational progress based upon science and faith.

An open society which enjoys freedom.

A secure society in which the citizen enjoys peace of mind as to his present day and his future.

2

Problems related to education

The 'problem approach' in comparative education

This book is concerned with the problems faced by the government of
Egypt and specifically the Ministry of Education in the process of
implementing the policies inspired by the guiding principles of the
Revolution, as they affect the political, social and economic life of the
country. Although ministerial problems affecting specific legislation,
organization and practice are the main concern of this survey, to be fully
appreciated they need to be seen in the context of problems of a global
nature having their source in the events and situations already described,
since their solutions will also need to be found within that context. An
attempt will be made to show the inevitability of the problems, within
the conceptual framework of critical dualism, and to indicate the steps
being taken at all levels to find solutions or make the right choice
between opposed decisions, when compromise would be ineffective.
Inevitably an analysis by an outsider, especially of such a complex
situation will be guilty of over-simplification, but, by using as a basis
the declared Egyptian policies, and, in subsequent chapters, the problems
as perceived by the Ministry of Education, it is hoped to minimize the
margin of error.

Holmes (1965), suggests that Popper's (1946), distinction between
two types of law in any society, the normative and the sociological,
provides a useful framework for the 'problem approach' in comparative
educational studies. He describes normative laws as those resulting from
governmental legislation, which can be accepted, rejected or changed
by man, (with or without penalty) at any time, besides codes of
behaviour, value systems, taboos and beliefs which have become
formalized by long use, but are open to challenge in an 'open society'.
Changes in legal and social norms can themselves be the source of
problems. However, the concept of critical dualism assumes that there
are also sociological laws which man is less able to control, but which
enable him not only to understand the operation of social institutions,

but predict social transformation. According to the theory, sociological laws stem largely from functional relationships within institutions, the clearest example being found by the author in studies of social mobility, which trace the evolution of a 'gentleman' in three generations of more selective education. In this study it is not proposed to get involved in the ramifications of Popper's somewhat obscure theory in all its aspects but to bear in mind that a study of society needs to take account of both its normative and institutional patterns, and to recognize that incompatibility between them gives rise to problems, which, unresolved can induce conflict.

In Egypt, changes in both normative and industrial patterns are necessary if she is to achieve her revolutionary aims of evolving a society that is both socialist and modern. The problems involved demand both short-term and long-term solutions, with constant re-appraisal, and, where necessary, 'corrective movements', so that compromise between the ideal and the reality can be achieved, thus reducing the necessity to demand balance before the slow process of full integration of its disparate elements has been fulfilled. A few basic groups of problems will be discussed below.

Modernization

In his most recent and extensive study of education and modernization in the Middle East, Szyliowicz (1973), states that difficulties in defining modernization include 'the great problems involved in conceptualizing how education is related to its achievement'. He continues:

> Only in recent years have social scientists begun to investigate this relationship empirically and analytically, and, although there is wide-spread agreement that education contributes directly to modernization, no adequate body of theory is yet available that would permit the testing of specific hypotheses with data from the Middle East.

He finds that conceptually the most precise relationship and also the most universally sought strand of modernization is in economic development.

> Practically every country in the world is seeking to achieve a rapid rate of economic growth, and underlying the huge investments being made in education is the belief that formal

25

schooling is a major variable determining the rate and level of economic development.

Neil J. Smelser and Seymour Martin Lipset (1966), who discuss this belief at length, find that 'the various ad hoc generalizations that have been made in this area remain largely in the category of "unproven" and, not surprisingly, some of them contradict each other', for example, one drawing attention to the increase in economic growth due to increasing amount of skill and another the undermining of conditions of growth due to the frustrations suffered through 'overexpansion' of educational resources. They cite evidence from a number of sources that increased education made for economic growth in the United States, Japan and the Soviet Union 'long before anyone could argue that the demand for the educated equalled their increased supply', quoting Clark Kerr that the United States 'got started very early using education largely, or at least philosophically, for political reasons and then this turned out to be a great economic asset.' There appears to be little conflict in Egypt's basic policy to expand her educational provision to the limits as a prerequisite to modernization.

The problem lies in the distribution of education at the various levels, a balancing feat which often appears to create further problems in its attempts at solution. The discussion by Smelser and Lipset above suggests that evidence has been produced in various parts of the world staking the claims of literacy, primary education, secondary education and higher education respectively to be of supreme importance. The choice for Egypt is difficult because she has limited financial resources, a large uneducated population, a costly programme for rapid industrialization and her political ideology demands that education in a welfare state shall be the birthright of every Egyptian, boy or girl. All stages of education have periodically received special attention. The concerted action to combat illiteracy and steps taken to draw into the primary school system all children of primary school age, as well as the development of intermediate education in the preparatory schools will be discussed. However, financial support has long been weighted in favour of higher education, particularly in the expansion of the universities. Boktor (1963) claimed that the number of students then enrolled in the universities, higher institutions and other organizations offering courses beyond the secondary level exceeded the number in England, Wales and Scotland combined, although the population of the United Kingdom was then double that of Egypt. He also pointed out that, in fact, the colleges which form the nucleus of university provision were all opened during the period when illiteracy was near 100 per cent and university education the privilege of a moneyed élite. With the revolution there has been a phenomenal expansion of higher education to meet both socialist aspirations and manpower demands in the wake of industrialization and modernization programmes. According to Smelser and Lipset (1966), data from investigations appears to suggest that technological growth may depend most on high levels of university enrolment as it is in these institutions that attitudes and skills needed in modernization programmes are fostered. The type of educational growth therefore becomes more important than the amount: how far are the university courses relevant to those much-needed attitudes and skills? Smelser and Lipset point out that it can be argued that the American, Japanese and Communist university systems are the most appropriate for developing countries because their inclusion of technical and vocational courses makes them less élitist and more likely to be viewed as agencies training for a wide variety of occupations. Japan is cited as being highly successful in developing an educational system that enhanced those occupations that were needed for modernization. Egypt has begun working on these lines, but, as President Sadat has himself pointed out, one technical secondary school costs the government as much as about twelve general secondary schools. Every year the problem is aggravated by the addition of about a million babies to the dependent population.

Population explosion: family planning education

The latest sample census which took place in Egypt in 1966 showed an average annual rate of growth of 2·54, which is one of the highest in the world, being almost double that of the USSR and USA and more than double that of the United Kingdom and France. According to Hanna (1974), it doubled in the forty-three years between 1917 and 1960, and at the present rate could double again before the end of the century. Population fertility seminars organized by the head of the Central Mobilization and Statistics Agency in 1971 produced some interesting facts relevant to all the problems facing the country. That year the population reached 34 million, almost equally divided between male and female, including 6 million in Greater Cairo, representing an

TABLE 1 *Population projections – selected age groups in thousands as at 1 July*

Age group	1972	1973	1975	1976	1980	1985	1990
6 through 9	3,624		3,856		4,338	4,897	5,513
10 through 14	3,902		4,153		4,672	5,274	5,938
15 through 19	3,449		3,670		4,129	4,660	5,247
20 through 23	2,369		2,521		2,836	3,201	3,604
6 through 23	13,344		14,200		15,975	18,032	20,302

(*Source:* Bureau of Mobilization and Statistics – The Bureau figures are considerably higher after 1975 for the age groups 5 through 14 than those recently prepared by the Cairo Demographic Center.)

Age group	1972	1973	1975	1976	1980	1985	1990
6 through 11	5,180	5,300	5,515 (5,725)	5,660	6,210 (5,846)	7,010 (6,119)	7,890 (7,020)
12 through 14	2,340	2,390	2,490 (2,730)	2,550	2,800 (2,832)	3,160 (2,920)	3,560 (3,028)
15 through 17	2,070	2,190	2,420 (2,449)	2,440	2,480 (2,784)	2,800 (2,827)	3,150 (2,927)
18 through 22	3,160	3,260	3,460	3,530	3,780	4,260	4,800
12 through 17	4,410	4,580	4,910	4,990	5,280	5,960	6,710
6 through 14	7,520	7,690	8,005	8,210	9,010	10,170	11,450
6 through 22	12,750	13,140	13,885	14,180	15,270	17,230	19,400
6 through 13	6,700	7,140	7,250	7,400	8,150	9,050	10,300

(*Source:* Mission estimates of school-age projections based on the projections provided by the Bureau of Mobilization and Statistics given above. The Cairo Demographic Center projections are shown in brackets. For purposes of the planning exercise carried out by the mission ANNEXES, the Bureau of Mobilization and Statistics projections have been used as being the official views, although the Demographic Center appear more realistic on the basis of recent indications of a considerable drop in the birth rate.)

For purposes of intake into primary of 6-year-old children, the mission uses MOE figures for 1975 to 1980 and Cairo Demographic Center figures for 1981–1990 as given below:

1975 – 961	1979 – 970	1983 – 1,034	1987 – 1,166
1976 – 949	1980 – 985	1984 – 1,049	1988 – 1,204
1977 – 959	1981 – 1,013	1985 – 1,074	1989 – 1,243
1978 – 964	1982 – 1,020	1986 – 1,110	1990 – 1,288

(*Source:* by courtesy of the Ministry of Education, Cairo.)

increase of one person in every 1·5 minutes. In the entire country the population was rising at the rate of 66,700 a month, a daily average of 2,223 or three persons every 2 minutes. Hanna (1974), attributes the explosion to a combination of improvement of health conditions, mainly due to better control of epidemic diseases, a rapid decline in the death rate and infant mortality with corresponding increase in life expectancy plus a very high fertility rate.

Such rapid population growth has profound effects on social structure, for example, the re-distribution of population. Hurewitz (1966), notes that the density in Egypt is roughly 70 per square mile, but that the density for the cultivated area along the banks of the Nile surpasses 1,800 per square mile, making it one of the most thickly settled agrarian districts in the world. The problem is complicated by the paradox that while the swollen agricultural population spills into the cities hoping to be absorbed by new government and private industries, agriculture itself has not kept up with the increased demand for food to support the increased population. Hanna sees such shortages as responsible for the rise in food prices which make government subsidies necessary, thus further disrupting the economy.

Mabro (1974), Hanna (1974), and Hurewitz (1966), all contribute to an analysis of the effects of the transformation of Egypt from a labour-short to a labour-surplus economy: 'the lag of economic and social advancement behind the numerical growth of the people' (Hurewitz) with accompanying strains on the administrative machinery which must handle the mounting public services, the consequent rapid expansion of the service sector which Mabro considers often to disguise the serious problems of unemployment in urban centres, and the migration of workers, mostly skilled, to jobs abroad (according to Mabro, an estimated 200,000 in 1972). To these problems can be added those felt in the Ministry of Education: the inadequacy of school buildings, equipment, personnel to cope with ancillary social services as well as teaching, and all the problems associated with a shift system and transport. To quote Hurewitz:

> It is baffling enough to mobilize resources, skills and leadership for the general uplift of a slowly expanding society, but the difficulties of planned development are compounded by the multiplying mouths to feed, children to educate and people to employ. Economists estimate that for every one per cent of

growth of population at least three per cent of the national income must be invested in development merely to maintain existing standards.

This applies to education as with other aspects of life in Egypt. Hence the stress laid by Mabro on the necessity of an understanding of the demographic processes through studies of the determinants of mortality and fertility, so that the quality of population forecasts, which he considers to be 'an important ingredient in economic planning' may make possible the design of effective population policies.

Since the Revolution such policies have had a place in national planning, beginning with the formation in 1953 of a National Committee for Population Problems to outline the policy for the country. Hanna (1974), mentions three important developments: the opening of a very limited number of family planning clinics in 1955, followed seven years later by the launching of the official birth control propaganda and the establishment in both urban and rural areas of a large number of clinics providing free oral contraceptives and IUD's, and the beginning of a national family planning project in 1966. This was a ten-year programme for reducing the birth rate to 30 per thousand by 1978. The plan concentrates, says Hanna, on the most fertile group of women, aged between twenty-five and thirty-four, in the hope of getting the quickest results.

Other educational programmes have followed. Changing a pattern of living which defies legislation is a very slow process which can only be measured by accurate statistics. This will be made possible by a technical aid agreement made in 1971 between Egypt and the United Nations Demographic Fund. The fund promised to contribute about £E 1·5 million towards making a general census in 1974. It would also strengthen national efforts in the fields of information, education and training, relating to family planning, besides helping in the execution of an experimental project to be undertaken jointly by mother and child welfare centres, vital medical research administrations and family planning centres, apart from scholarships to be granted by the Fund to students for studies abroad as well as additional consultative services.

The grant was a tribute to the fact that Egypt is at the top of the list of African, Near and Middle East countries which undertakes positive efforts to find solutions to demographic and family planning problems. In the family planning area typical activities are illustrated by the programmes arranged for the observation of a 'family planning week' in 1971. These included a contest to choose the best private centre of family planning in each governorate that has ten centres, a series of seminars arranged by the Ministry of Social Affairs in co-operation with the General Society of Birth Control, a Ministry of Health programme of meetings and seminars in the health units throughout the Republic, a special edition of the *Public Health Magazine* on family planning, a number of booklets on family planning published by the Ministry of Culture, and a series of seminars organized by the Cultural Palaces and Information Offices in the governorates with the theme of modern methods of birth control and its economic effects. During that week all information media, including the cinema and theatre, participated in the campaign for informing people of social and economic aspects of family planning. Also the ASU took part. (*Egyptian Gazette* 29 March 1971).

It is uphill work trying to convince the peasants that a large family is a liability rather than an asset. As an Egyptian interviewed in a recent television programme on Egypt pointed out, there are still peasants whose annual income is about £50. Where are they to get the money to pay for labour on their land, if it is not supplied by their children? An advance towards the solution of such a complex problem raises many other important issues. Nevertheless, some progress is being made: the birthrate of 45 per thousand in 1952 decreased to 39 per thousand in 1968 and to 36 per thousand in 1970.

Meanwhile movements of the population, such as the drift to the cities and towns are not spontaneous only in character. In order to ease population problems the government has initiated schemes that involve organized internal migration. Reference has already been made to the distribution of reclaimed agricultural land. Other schemes involve the resettlement of displaced persons due either to the war with Israel or projects such as the High Dam and the new settlements in the Western Desert now irrigated by artesian wells. With more than 50 per cent of her population under the age of fifteen years, it is vital for Egypt to use her manpower to the best advantage.

Manpower problems

It is patent that Egypt, unlike many Western countries, does not need foreign labour to man her factories or provide semi-skilled labour. Nor have her leaders ever doubted the quality of her citizens, demonstrated during the Suez crisis and the October War by the armed forces. 'God's most important gift to Egypt', says Sadat in the October Working Paper (1974), 'is its people and our chief national wealth is our manpower.' With quantity and quality assured, the problem is a temporary one which can be solved by education and training. Sadat continues:

> Like all resources, it [manpower] has to be developed. The development of manpower means first and foremost increasing its capacity to give and to work by providing food, clothing, health services and housing and improving its human potential through culture, education and training.

The time for inferiority feelings is past:

> The Egyptian worker has proved no less capable of assimilating modern technology than the Egyptian soldier. Egyptian experts have demonstrated both at home and abroad that they are of the highest calibre, by any standard. Our country is neither lacking in educated young people nor in technical and administrative expertise. Still, the tasks lying ahead call for more.

The key problem is planning, a concept quite alien to the traditional Arab way of life. (One could digress here: although planning is accepted as a necessity of modern living, even educated westernized Arabs often find it difficult to make decisions ahead of time.) At the national level, the first planning commission, headed by the Prime Minister, met three years after the Revolution. However, the study of manpower had to be deferred until the results of the 1960 census came out in 1962. It thus missed the first educational plan 1965–70, but was in time for the second educational plan 1965–70, a detailed plan, worked out by the Ministries of Higher Education and Training and the Higher Council of the Universities to cover the various aspects of education. The standing Commission to study the manpower situation started to work about 1963.

Since then, but notably in the Seventies, attempts have been made to work out long-term policies to solve shortages of teaching staff at the various levels of education, linking training schemes to shortages in precise areas of industry, with special attention to vocational training centres and technical education and the closing of bottlenecks in the bureaucratic framework. One very important task of the Ministry of Manpower has been to recommend dates for the first appointments of university and higher institute graduates for the approval of the Ministerial Committee for Graduate Employment. Unfortunately there has been a time-lag between graduation and appointment that is very difficult to overcome, though it has been bridged partly by national service in the forces or the community. For example, the Egyptian holders of the 1968 and 1969 technical and vocational secondary certificates, who had applied to the Ministry of Labour for appointment, did not receive their letters of appointment until April 1971, but at least they were in the queue. Close co-operation exists between the Ministerial Committee on Manpower and the Ministry of Education. In 1972, for instance, when the Ministry of Education reported a shortage of 8,570 teachers of languages, mathematics and sciences, the Ministerial Committee on Manpower agreed that all university graduates at a certain level finishing their studies at the end of the second session should become teachers in those specializations where shortages existed. On the other hand the Minister of Education decided to postpone conscription for certain specializations. (*Egyptian Gazette*, 1972). Other means of meeting shortages included the re-employment of retired teachers and authorizing school science inspectors to work as teachers for part of the school year.

By 1974 the Ministry of Manpower had prepared the first scientifically planned guide to vocational classification to be used for planning and developing manpower on the national level. It not only gave 1,512 classifications of professions but would facilitate the keeping of records of job applications. It was recommended that a suitable committee be appointed to keep it up to date. Meanwhile about 1,376 engineers and architects of 1973 vintage were called up for compulsory service in the government and public sector during 1974 and the Higher Council for Training presided over by the Minister of Manpower decided to set up twenty specific committees to operate within the different sectors of the state and to recommend a unified training policy within each sector, and link the policy of wages and incentives to higher skills and productivity standards.

In spite of intensive studies of manpower since 1963, the Ministry of Education was faced with a shortage of 20,000 teachers for the year 1975. Drastic measures were taken, such as raising the pension age for teachers and calling on employees in the public and government sectors who were qualified for teaching to submit applications for transfer to the Ministry of Education or the Directorates of Education in the governorates where they worked. Paid overtime would also be compulsory for serving teachers. Intensive studies during 1975 suggested that the problem was not so much a matter of shortage but of a disequilibrium between supply (the number and quality of graduates) and the demand. The report of the Unedbas Mission (1975) suggested this is 'due to the fact that secondary education tends, in its quantitative growth, to meet the pressure of "social demand" rather than to meet manpower needs and the demand of higher education.' It also noted the reluctance of institutions, companies and banks to offer field training for secondary school students and lack of co-ordination between those institutions when such training does take place. Finally, steps need to be taken to remove the bias against technical secondary education.

This situation is well understood by Egyptian educationists and the planners. A re-distribution of manpower has been planned for 1976. This would include a reduction of manpower in government bodies, local administrative units and the public sector, that is, an onslaught against bureaucracy and a re-organization of policies on salaries, incentives, promotion, training, social insurance, pensions and other personal services. The problem facing educational planners is to reconcile the drastic measures mentioned above to alleviate the shortage of teachers while at the same time the Ministry of Manpower and Training is planning equally drastic projects to absorb redundant manpower, such as long-leave exportation of Egyptian manpower. The solution appears to lie with the educational planners. Meanwhile, the Egyptian, like the British, government tries to alleviate the problem by creating jobs for the young unemployed. Towards the end of 1976, out of an appropriation of £E 14 million provided in the State General Budget for the purpose, the Minister of Finance allotted an extra £E 2 million to provide jobs for 1974 university graduates and 1973 graduates of the intermediate technical institutes.

Women in modern Egypt: family and community education

The term 'manpower' can no longer be limited to the male sex: the concept of women's liberation is no longer confined to political enfranchisement but is now associated with every aspect of living.

Historically the treatment of women by men has been hallowed by custom and sanctified by religion, so that attempts to change women's roles generate both confusion and emotion. This has happened in Islamic societies where fundamentalists interpret their sacred writings to defend a social pattern which Western men sometimes envy, but which allows no justification in a modern society. There have, of course, always been individuals in Islamic society who have respected as well as loved one wife and shared their affection towards their children without regard to sex, but in conservative, traditional societies and peasant communities change comes through a slow process of education. Legislation can abolish the veil overnight, penalize wife-beaters and forbid the murder of unmarried pregnant girls, but these customs continue until the female, through education, becomes financially independent and aware of the means of protection.

In Egypt, according to Sumaya Fahmy (1974), the average per-centage of two-wife marriages for the years 1950–4 was 8·96 per cent and for the years 1965–9, it was 8·08 per cent, which she attributes to a flagrant misinterpretation of the Q'ran motivated by 'domination, need to prove virility, craving for excitement and so forth'. In 1971 it was the well-known Egyptian writer, Soheir el-Kalamawy, who was re-elected Secretary-General of the General Union of Arab Women at the seventh congress in Tunis, who appealed for an end to polyga-mous marriages 'so that Arab women can retain their dignity and personality'.

The Charter of 1962 is clearly in favour of women's liberation: 'Woman must be regarded as equal to man and must therefore shed the remaining shackles that impede her free movement so that she might take a constructive and profound part in shaping life.' Freedom, how-ever, does not imply disintegration of family life:

> The family is the first cell in a society and it must therefore be afforded all means of protection so that it might be better able to preserve the national tradition to rejuvenate its texture, and to carry along the whole of society in the direction of the goals set by the national struggle.

Since then the Arab Socialist Union has defined woman's status and her role in post-revolutionary Egypt. In 1971, the ASU Secretary for Youth opened the first training course for girls of the Nasser Socialist Youth Organization, which drew two hundred and fifty girls of the organization from all the governorates. The participants studied social services in the field of family and child welfare, carried out campaigns for family planning projects, besides working out plans for the welfare of servicemen and evacuees. They took part in discussions on the ideological and political aspects of the Revolution and the role of girls in the war effort. Emphasis was on the establishment of leadership recruiting centres in all districts and provincial towns for young women at all levels who had leadership qualities and were prepared to give full-time public service. Co-ordination of all feminist organizations was urged, and the development of activities such as first aid and nursing to contribute to the work of the Citizens' War Committees.

The beginning of a new stage in the history of the feminist movement in Egypt came a year later with the establishment of a women's secretariat at the Arab Socialist Union. The First Secretary of the ASU Central Committee, who opened an educational course for about three hundred and fifty women leaders in the political, social, cultural and labour fields, said that the current role and participation of the Egyptian woman was 'boundless, beginning in the home and ending in taking up the burden with the Egyptian man of the war'. Participants took part in a top level debate on the war effort and the Programme for National Action as well as discussing their status in the various fields of the political organization. The women's affairs committee of the ASU hoped that they would be prominent in activities related to family planning, literacy and in combating high prices and other social problems. Under this impetus, only a month later the Minister of Social Affairs addressed a conference in the Fayum governorate of a thousand feminist leaders who had completed a special training course to serve the villages. The theme was the catching up of the villages with modern civilization, but stress was laid on women's role in the war. By the time that the war started a year later, in 1973, the practical role of women had been defined: to work to minimize the number of casualties by protecting the lives of families and looking after the wounded. The details included combating rumours by getting correct information from the ASU governorate secretariats so that the public might be informed of the facts, by using abundant popular foods, making contact between wounded and families, giving blood donations, guiding people to air raid shelters. Experience led to re-organization bolstered by £E 200,000 provided by ASU funds for feminist activities and to ensure that feminist organization rapporteurs should be able to work on a full-time basis. By 1974, under the leadership of Egypt's first lady, Jihan el-Sadat the women leaders were clamouring for the initiation of a women's organization independent of the political organization, for a bigger representation at all levels of constitutional and political institutions, for not giving one person two posts at the same time, and for staging new elections for all the trade unions without interference by any authority. The campaign was well-timed: the Arab Socialist Union Women's Secretariat worked out a plan for 1975, the International Women's Year, including consolidation with other women's movements in the Third World, Arab countries, Africa and Asia. Mrs Sadat also called for an 'Arab Women Week' to be celebrated in all Arab countries as a symbol of solidarity and co-operation among Arab women. Their enthusiasm and dynamism were rewarded when President Sadat, in his capacity of Chairman of the ASU, issued a decree, forming the ASU Feminist Organization, specifying its structure and condition of membership. (If you can't defeat them, enlist them!) The structure follows the ASU pattern already described, the aim being to raise the standard and capability of the Egyptian woman, socially, politically and economically, with an emphasis on the family bonds and the means of their consolidation, while the immediate tasks included solving the career women's problems, taking part in family planning, child and mother care and illiteracy campaigns, rationalization of consumption and improving the status of women in work. A formidable package!

It is hoped by feminists that these measures will encourage Egyptian women to exercise the rights that they have acquired by legislation since the Revolution. These include the right to vote and be eligible for election to all publicly elected bodies on equal terms with men, embodied in the 1956 Constitution and all subsequent constitutions. As Sumaya Fahmy (1974), points out, very few women avail themselves of their opportunities, nor do they insist on their own and daughters' rights to education at all levels according to their capacities, including receiving vocational guidance and training according to ability and interest. In the majority of families the role of the wife is complete submission to her husband, who demands that her energies be concentrated on producing babies and attending the daily needs of the family. If she lives in a rural area, she will also have to labour in the fields and tend the animals that enable life to be carried on at a subsistence level. Ramzia el-Gharib's (1974), description of Egyptian family

37

life in a rural community (which is where 62 per cent of the whole population lives) appears to indicate a suitable area for studying the sociological laws referred to by Holmes (1965). The family pattern is governed by traditions which are very resistent to change, although, as el-Gharib points out, in the past twenty years there have been social changes which affect those patterns. Briefly, in rural areas family life is based on consanguine, not conjugal, relationships and it is an extended family system. Family ties are strengthened by obligations in times of crisis and difficulties which even extend to the children of divorced members. In other words, the family has an inbuilt social services structure which, regardless of poverty, makes it independent of outside help. The class gap is still wide: the middle and upper class male in many cases still supports the womenfolk, while they confine their activities to family and domestic affairs and good works, whereas the peasant needs the help of both his wife and daughters in the daily struggle for existence. The father has supreme power over the family, which can lead to much misery, but not invariably, as Egyptians are an affectionate people, very fond of children. Divorce is easy for the man, which makes it possible for him to cast off the wife and keep the children after she has served him faithfully for many years, a position which is being remedied by current legislation. In fact, the woman is covered legally both for the choice of a husband and the right of refusal, as well as financial protection. She cannot, however, according to Islamic law, divorce her husband, unless it was specifically agreed in the contract. As Sumaya Fahmy (1974), points out, it is very difficult for a girl to exercise her rights, even if she knows them:

> To demand the stipulation of divorce on her wedding day, a bride would risk offending her bridegroom. This is frowned upon by both families. So the bride in the majority of cases gives up her right to divorce. This is a good example of how ineffective laws can be when men and women have been brought up to believe in and to practise psychological attitudes which are contradictory to the values embodied in the laws.

There are, says el-Gharib (1974), three family problems of socialization: child discipline, with its sudden transition from the mother's permissiveness up to the age of six years, to severe discipline thereafter; the ignorance of parents who lack education; and the preference for sons. The solution to all such problems, discussed more fully below, is seen by women and a growing number of men to lie in girls' education at all stages and women's education in a community setting.

In 1973, on the occasion of the centenary of the first state Egyptian girls' school, President Sadat was reported as paying a glowing tribute to Egypt's women for their important contributions to the success of the Revolution:

> Women are now found in all spheres: scientific research, industry, agriculture, trade, art, education, social service, the press, medicine, the law profession, sports, planning and others. In the countryside there are women who are putting up a different kind of struggle. They stand by their husbands and children to promote the welfare of the society by providing its needs of food and cloth. In factories women help push the wheel of production vigorously forwards. (*Egyptian Gazette* 4 April 1971)

Girls' education has certainly come a long way since, as Boktor reports, Teheshmeafet, third wife of Khedive Ismail, founded a European-type school for girls, that is, privileged girls. Previous to that, Amin Samy Pasha, a former educationist, wrote in his book on education in Egypt (cited by Boktor, 1963),

> When the Council of Public Instruction in 1836 recommended the foundation of girls' schools, the suggestion was considered immoral. The efforts of the promoters of female education at that time ended in the establishment of a maternity school in which not one single Egyptian girl agreed to be a student. Ten Abyssinian slaves were therefore recruited and housed in that school to pursue their studies and justify its existence.

It has been a long hard struggle to justify spending money on girls' education, and, in spite of the progress expressed in policy and provision, many formidable problems remain.

One problem, which is still a matter for debate, is the kind of education that should be offered: for forty years, education for girls, limited but in great demand, still concentrated on domestic arts and moral education. Men were patently nervous that the freedom of women and girls to leave the home even when chaperoned, would lead to a deterioration of morals. One wrote in 1913,

> We would ask what has become of our morality when every day we see our husbands taking their wives and children to

cinematograph shows where the loosest love romances are exhibited and they are allowed to be present at scenes where love intrigues are given full scope. Such scenes often teach them the thousand and one tricks and strategems that lovers make use of in order to attain their ends and escape detection. We again ask where are Egypt's morals when we see our Egyptian women showing such keenness to visit cinematographs, where amorous spectacles are reproduced that bring a blush to the cheek of humanity in general. We ask again, where are our morals when we behold our women appearing in public in, so to say, erotic fashions, which make the least jealous man ashamed to behold! (*Egyptian Gazette* 10 April 1913)

One answer was to confine education to the requirements of their roles as wives and mothers. Lord Kitchener wrote in his report:

The demand for girls' schools shows no tendency to decrease. Reference was made in last year's report to the want of suitable accommodation and properly qualified teachers, which makes it difficult to keep pace with this growing movement, but some progress has been made in the past year. In the elementary schools specially set apart for girls, the education authorities are endeavouring to develop instruction on practical lines and to give early training in household management. Mistresses have been specially appointed with this object, their duties including the supervision of the cleanliness and physical condition of the children. In order to provide a course of training in these domestic subjects, a new section has also been added to the elementary training college for women teachers at Boulac. Similarly, in the girls' primary schools, kitchens and laundries have been attached to the buildings and the personal staff strengthened by the appointment of trained domestic science teachers. Following on the same lines, the special necessities of girls' education are being kept clearly in view in the preparation of the plans for new girls' schools to be erected in Cairo and Alexandria. (*Egyptian Gazette* 28 May 1913)

The accent on feminine roles persisted in the preparatory schools where boys studied music, singing, physical education and agriculture, while the girls learned needlework and domestic science, and when the first girls' secondary school was opened in 1920, the object was to prepare them for domestic life. However, the Revolution brought new attitudes to girls' education after 1952. Laws were passed stating that boys and girls must be provided with equal opportunities at all stages of education, and, where it could be done without giving offence, co-educational schools were introduced. Nevertheless the domestic bias for girls persisted, in spite of the fact that twelve 'needlework' schools for girls which had been provided at great cost had attracted very little demand. Girls who failed to get a place in a general secondary school, could join a 'Female Culture School' and, after hobbies and practical studies were introduced into the general secondary syllabuses, needlework and domestic science were provided for the girls, while the boys had four choices. In technical education, however, the girls managed to break away from the domestic orientation. With industrialization there has been an increasing demand for young girls to work as clerks in industry and commerce, so the commercial secondary schools are more popular for girls than boys. Other specialized training for them can be found in music, ballet, language schools, industrial courses and nursing. Theoretically they can train at university level in all professions open to men.

As equal pay for equal work has been long established in Egypt, the prospect for educated girls seems attractive, but the great problem remains: what kind of life are they being educated for? Of course there is room at the top for girls of high calibre, but even university graduates are absorbed by overmanning the civil service. At the secondary level, the time-lag between getting a certificate and getting a job becomes longer and longer, which is very puzzling to, for example, a domestic servant who has allowed his daughter to complete her education at a commercial secondary school in the belief that she will reward his sacrifice by earning 'good' money as well as raising the family status. At present, roughly half of Egypt's swollen and increasing population is female, but, according to el-Gharib (1974), in spite of the efforts to educate them, 'there are still about 80 per cent illiterates and only 0·3 per cent university educated women.' What will happen to the girls seeking work when 100 per cent attend school to the age of fifteen years, and a corresponding proportion complete secondary school and seek higher education? It appears that, especially in rural areas this is a problem which will become an increasing concern to the Ministry of Manpower, and, indeed, a number of other ministries as well as the

TABLE 2 *Quantitative development: comparative statistics of classes and pupils in the general, technical education and teacher training schools, the percentage of increasing or decreasing and the percentage of girls (for the school year 73/74 to 74/75)*

Stage	Classes				Pupils						Increasing and percentage of boys and girls in 1974/5						Percentage of girls	
			Difference		1973/4			1974/5										
	1973/4	1974/5	No.	%	Male	Female	Total	Male	Female	Total	Male	%	Female	%	Total	%	73/4	74/5
Primary	94,347	97,619	3,272	3·5	2,422,052	1,497,809	3,919,861	2,518,121	1,556,772	4,074,893	96,069	4·0	58,963	3·9	155,032	4·0	38·2	38·2
General preparatory	27,160	29,870	2,710	10·0	726,720	372,571	1,099,291	789,509	413,529	1,202,038	62,789	8·6	40,958	11·0	103,747	9·4	34·0	34·4
General secondary	8,437	8,803	366	4·3	217,515	106,088	323,603	226,784	113,542	340,326	9,269	4·3	7,454	7·0	16,723	5·2	32·8	33·4
Technical secondary	9,400	10,263	863	9·2	216,416	104,911	321,327	231,585	116,721	348,306	15,169	7·0	11,810	11·3	26,979	8·4	32·6	33·5
Teacher training schools	903	976	73	8·1	17,787	13,441	31,228	18,865	14,410	33,275	1,078	6·1	969	7·2	2,047	6·6	43·0	43·3

(*Source*: by courtesy of the Ministry of Education, Cairo.)

feminist section of the ASU. Among the findings of a study conducted by the family research unit at the National Research Centre (1971) on a random sample of 634 pupils in preparatory and secondary schools in the governorates of Cairo and Caliubia, boys and girls in rural communities have many more problems than those in urban districts, but for girls they are much greater. Village girls, in particular, experience boredom in class and suffer from inadequacy of extra-curricular activities; they are subjected to traditional pressures and are afforded little opportunity for independent thought. Currently special attention is being given to bridge the city–village gap. Farmers are being asked to boost their crops so that the village can be developed by re-building, boosting health services and other utilities, such as electrification, while decentralization in the departments of education and the universities is designed to match curricula with regional needs. It appears that problems arising out of girls' education need special attention before the compulsory education target is reached, not on the basis of sex discrimination but to anticipate their occupational needs. A modern state cannot afford to waste its womanpower resources.

Wastage

The concept of 'wastage', even in ordinary usage is complicated by the increasing use of 'recycling' processes which make one man's waste another man's resource. What appears to be basically an economic term becomes a moral issue when community interests are at stake, as in time of war or drought. In terms of individual development there is a tendency to think that, almost automatically, more and longer education cannot fail to be beneficial, education, that is, within an institution. When the public demand for education at the expense of the state far exceeds the financial resources available to provide it, the question of wastage is directed by educational personnel at all levels as well as the public at large to whatever aspect of the service appears to be economically unprofitable. Boktor (1963), commented:

> Fifty years ago compulsory education was declared impossible because it would have cost the State 1·5 million pounds. In 1959–60 the State spent 48 per cent of the ministry's total budget, or over 20 million pounds, on this type of education. Is it not time to question the expenditure of so much money, time and energy on a primary school system which is producing such meagre results?

43

Essentially this was the same question asked in England with reference to the results of raising the school leaving age to sixteen years. It crops up in discussions on 'formal' versus 'free' methods of teaching, 'general' versus 'vocational' education, 'selective' versus 'non-selective' education to which, in Egypt one might add 'male' versus 'female' and 'urban' versus 'rural'. As, in both countries, the expressed aim is equality of opportunity, the discussion is usually in terms of priorities.

School drop-outs, repeaters

The Ministry of Education in Egypt periodically investigates and reports on various aspects of wastage of its resources, examining not only social and cultural factors but possible inefficiencies in its administration. One of its main problems in primary education is the drop-out rate in the first five years, estimated in 1971 as about 18 per cent. (Drop-outs are defined as those pupils who started the education at a certain stage but left the school before completing the stage.) Financially this represented an estimated annual cost of £E 10 million as well as a loss of human resources, and an aggravation of the literacy problem. In the rural areas, where it is most common, especially among girls, many classes are under-used, which is not only considered a wastage of buildings and teachers but a discouragement to those who man this unpopular corner of the profession. Fahmy (1973), summarized the factors in the drop-out problem as:

1. Inefficiency of school administration, teaching methods, unsuitable curricula, lack of social and educational services to pupils, especially health services and school meals.
2. Inability of parents to pay the extra expenses for education.
3. The low income of parents especially in rural areas which makes them need the labour of their children in work at an early age.
4. The traditional pattern of Egyptian agriculture which requires the labour of children at an early age in certain agricultural operations.
5. The lack of interest on the part of the parents.
6. Old traditions and habits concerning the education of girls, which prevents them from going to school after a certain age.

The ways by which the Ministry of Education, in hand with the Ministry of Social Affairs and the relevant sections of the Arab Socialist

Union are trying to find solutions to these problems have already been indicated. This co-operation is in line with the report of a UNICEF round-table conference in 1964 (Ed. Stein 1965), which considered the problem of drop-outs or wastage in schools to be not merely an educational concern:

> This appears to be a problem that is not entirely within the scope of the educational system alone to manage. Health, vocational training, industry and other sectors would be involved in the development of the policy and plans affecting children of school age to help cope with both the prevention and with the consequences of wastage.

Wastage is also associated with the inadequacy of preparatory (intermediate) school provision. According to the Ministry of Education, in 1969/70 only 32 per cent of children completing primary education were admitted to free government and private preparatory schools, while 11 per cent found places in private fee-paying schools. Many of these children, lacking work-skills, become agricultural workers in the villages or end up by drifting to the cities where they pick up odd jobs: in either case they tend to return to illiteracy. Again, the lack of provision for slow learners at the compulsory stage has produced bottlenecks as children repeat one or more classes in an attempt to reach the entry standard for the next class. The problems of over-crowded classrooms are exacerbated by the wide age range using a specific desk and chair size, but many feel they are fortunate even to share the small number of desks available.

With the aid of UNICEF, the Egyptian government is now carrying out a programme for pre-vocational training to deal with such problems. Special centres have been established to provide primary school leavers and drop-outs with the knowledge and skills necessary for entering vocational training. By 1967 twenty pre-vocational centres giving training to 2,000 primary school leavers a year had been established.

Emigration: the brain drain

Wastage at the earlier stages of education is more than matched with losses sustained by what is termed the 'brain drain' at the postgraduate level. Because of the serious problem of finding qualified staff for the universities, it has been the policy of the Egyptian government to send about 10,000 to 18,000 graduates abroad every year, mainly to get higher qualifications in science and engineering, with an estimated return of about 500 a year to staff a new university faculty, which means having a doctoral degree, which is a prerequisition to appointment. These students, who represent the highest level of manpower in Egypt, have already received their education throughout school and university at the expense of the state. The loss of their services inevitably represents serious damage to the quality of teaching and research in Egypt in addition to the financial waste to the country of tens of millions of pounds.

Exact facts and figures of the brain drain are difficult to evaluate, as criteria vary with the different sources, but the following indicate the size of the problem. Adisheshiah cited by Szyliowicz (1973), reports that between 1962 and 1967, 2,400 professionals, 249 engineers, 138 scientists and 191 physicians left Egypt, of whom 70 per cent had PhDs. The situation for engineers is particularly critical, as five-year plans can absorb about twice the number available. Saleh (1975), has adapted a table taken from *al-Ahram*, 21 May 1969, which indicates the rapid increase of physician and engineer emigrants. She quotes official records as saying that the number of Egyptians who emigrated from 1962 to 1970 was 23,740, but that this includes more than one category. Saleh cites the break-down of emigrants in 1972, reported by the Centre of Industrial Development in the Arab League of Nations: 70 per cent were from the teaching profession and research workers who have a doctoral degree; 58·3 per cent of these were engineers and scientists and 17·5 per cent had a master's degree.

Reasons for the 'brain drain' are not entirely related to high salaries overseas and other economic advantages, although in an over-populated country with limited financial resources they are an inducement, especially to those who have experienced a high standard of living while studying abroad. Szyliowicz (1973), details the critical deficiencies in physical facilities for scientists and others in the home country: 'Confronted with inadequate facilities, a lack of recognition and support, heavy teaching loads, misemployment of skills, mediocre colleagues, uninterested superiors, and intellectual isolation, the able young scientist finds it extremely difficult to engage in productive research.' In her study in depth of the problem, Saneya Saleh has tried to find out how it is viewed by the Egyptian scientists themselves. Her sample is relatively small but she is confident that her data is generally representative of the views of Egyptian scientists of doctorate level who have spent at least five years abroad for postgraduate study and practical training. Her qualitative findings suggest many potentially useful lines for future research. All of her respondents appear to support Szyliowicz's view above, adding to it the necessity to work extra hours in order to make a decent living. However, it is the positive advantages rather than the negative factors in Egypt that 'pull potential migrants to the USA more than to any other country'. Countering these are strong emotional ties with the homeland and an appreciation of value systems which had previously been taken for granted. A typical respondent writes:

> What I miss here is the people. I think I am basically an Arab
> Egyptian Moslem. We have certain humanitarian characteristics
> which I don't think are found anywhere else. We put a great value
> on human relationships. We value a man because of his goodness
> to his fellow-men or his intellectual capability, rather than his
> wealth and power. We respect the porter because of his goodness
> and call him uncle out of respect for his age.

They keep their family ties and come for short visits, usually to work on projects and, at a later stage think in terms of helping what is still to them 'their' country, but . . . from the outside.

Concern for the situation is shown in President Sadat's speech to the Arab Socialist Union, 1974, reported in the *Egyptian Gazette*.

> The problem of the brain drain, for instance, is one that has to be
> solved. We must take measures for restoring our scientists. We
> must also find a solution to the problem of members of academic
> missions who do not return home after finishing their studies
> abroad; studies which are financed by the people. Yet, we know
> well enough that this is an international problem from which all
> the developing countries are suffering.

International conferences were held to solve this problem which even some advanced countries have suffered from at times of economic crises. 'All categories in the investigation above gave as "pull" work, high salaries, good libraries, facilities and grants for research, appreciation of good work, a challenging scientific atmosphere, organization and respect for time, and the pleasure of being in the middle of current scientific events' but the ten Egyptian experts questioned about policy agreed that restriction to leave at will could not be defended in a country which is so over-populated that 'there are four or five persons doing a task which could have been done more efficiently by one person,' but that 'in the case of those scientists whose higher education abroad was financed by the state, some kind of compensation to the country for the money spent on them is necessary if they wish to emigrate.' Twenty recommendations were made for study by the policy-makers, covering moral and material incentives to keep scientists from wanting to emigrate, while to curtail excess professional manpower it is suggested that there should be stricter educational screening, a limitation to the promotion of 'brain drain', re-allocation of excess labour in certain fields or departments and a creation and chanelling of capital into investments which would create new jobs for people in overstaffed occupational areas. Two trump cards remain: the close family and religious ties felt by the Egyptian emigrants, which remain a constant factor even when they adjust to the new life overseas.

Quality of education

Raising standards

The freedom of the Press having been restored, there has been considerable public criticism about the quality of education in Egypt, especially in the leading newspaper, *al-Ahram* whose well-known educational journalist ran a series of provocative articles in 1971, followed by recommendations and warnings. He compares in detail the standards reached by Egyptian and French schoolchildren, finding that at each stage the level is lower in Egypt: Egyptian preparatory equals French primary, Egyptian secondary, French preparatory, etc. He also finds that the French child knows more about the history of ancient Egypt than the Egyptian child.

Curricular reform

The curricula are attacked:

What should we teach these rising generations in elementary science, literature and art? A study of our teaching programmes showed that they are burdened, especially in the first stages, with two things: first, a heap of fragments and crusts of knowledge not at all proportionate to the capacity of the students to grasp or understand; second, heaps of national idiosyncracies and ideologies filling the programme under the name of 'national education'.

There is much more in this vein, capped by a plea for comparative educational studies:

We certainly need to compare our educational programmes with those of advanced countries, once every five years, to ascertain that the Egyptian student is not less scientifically educated, in any stage, than the English or French or Russian. (Louis Awad, *al-Ahram*, 26 January – 30 July 1971, in Arabic)

The theme was continued by President Sadat in a discussion on educational matters: 'If certain skills are lacking, the committee should seek them elsewhere, and study systems of education adopted in other countries, and apply what it considers suitable to us.' (*Egyptian Gazette* 1 April 1972) If the committee approached England it would find that the Egyptian complaints are sufficiently paralleled here in 1976 to provoke an exceptional speech by the Prime Minister. The problem in carrying out these injunctions is the lack of trained comparative educationists to make scientific comparative studies. According to one official, a certain amount of confusion results when educationists are sent on comparatively short missions to countries in various parts of the world, return and try to apply, piecemeal, what they have observed, without reference to the different philosophies underlying the educational fragment that is transferred. This problem has also not escaped the Press; in a long article discussing the problems of primary education the writer refers to 'the methods of teaching we import without understanding, the people who lay the plans for these programmes, without having any real contact with teaching, or practice'. (Samy Daoud, *al-Gomhoureya*, in Arabic)

New methods

Among the methods of teaching imported has been the increasing use of audio-visual aids, notably in the use of radio for language education. An experiment in the teaching of Arabic, French and English is currently being conducted and evaluated by the Ministry of Education. At all levels there is a trend to introduce more practical elements into curricula. In the fields of agricultural and technical education the need is obvious and the rate of progress dependent on the availability of plant and equipment as well as technicians. In primary education such changes can only be experimental in the short term, since whole generations of teachers need to be trained if the changes are to be meaningful.

However, where concentration has been based on a limited educational area, notably in the teaching of modern mathematics, success has been considerable. The main experiment was preceded, with the help of UNESCO, by a pilot study. Teachers were specially trained and the changes carefully organized, avoiding disruption of current programmes. With the establishment of the National Council for Education, Scientific Research and Technology, innovations in curricula and method are always subject to pilot experimentation, scientific planning and evaluation. All changes in the direction of education take place against a chronic shortage of buildings, equipment, books and, most important, teachers. The absence of large numbers of teachers serving with the armed forces during 1973 may have prompted the People's Broadcasting Service to begin new educational programmes for students sitting for examinations in all stages of education, a development which may meet some of the problems indicated above.

Examination reform

Traditionally examinations have always been a prominent feature of the educational system, success at each stage determining the possibility of entering the following stage. With the rapid increase in population and the growing demand for higher education, which always exceeds the supply, the pressure on children to achieve selection has created problems with no easy solution. Efforts to alleviate the system sometimes aggravate the cause of the problem. For example, allowing children who failed examinations for promotion in the early stages to repeat classes caused bottlenecks in primary schools already overcrowded; the system of external students, created in 1953, with the excellent intention of satisfying the aspirations of thousands of Egyptians to achieve a university degree, has, in fact, led to frustration for the students and serious problems for planners and administrators. Briefly, what Szyliowicz (1973), terms 'an extreme form of "do-it-yourself" approach to higher education' has, he says, produced thousands of students barred from attending classes, studying for examinations without any guidance whatsoever, depending on memorizing text-books, who add considerably to the burden of overworked examiners. Szyliowicz comments:

> A further consequence of this programme is that the aspirations of thousands of poorly trained individuals are further heightened. Possessing all the privileges of regular university students, they come to share the latter's expectations concerning future employment opportunities but they are, in effect, being poorly prepared for fields which are already saturated and in which there is no demand for their services.

During the last five years the Ministry of Education has taken many steps to lighten the examination burden in schools and institutes of education. Public examinations at the lower levels are being replaced by classroom examinations corrected at the school under supervision, while secondary school certificate examinations can, owing to the expansion of universities, be held at the governorate level. A report in 1975 from the National Centre for Educational Research suggests continuous assessment, with brief examinations at short intervals, a bigger examination after reaching the end of each chapter of the textbook and a comprehensive 'objective' examination at the end of the year. This appears to defeat the purpose of lifting the strain of examinations, which would become continuous and to encourage the learning of the textbook off by heart, a weakness in the system which has long been under attack, while not allowing time for modern creative methods to be used in the classroom. The 'objective' examination in particular, can lead to the indiscriminate cramming of facts which have not been understood or assimilated. The question of creativity has already been raised, so no doubt some compromise will be reached before the report is fully adopted.

Coaching

Any reform of examinations that would lessen the burden of homework would be welcomed by pupils and parents alike. The present system throws a great responsibility on the parents to see that the school day does not end when the child leaves for home but continues, in some cases far into the night. For small children the parents become teacher-substitutes, adding to the pressures endured in the classroom. There is no time for play, especially if the child is a slow learner. When the point is reached where specialized knowledge is required, anxious parents make incredible sacrifices to pay for coaching. This results in a paradoxical situation: education within the system is free from the primary stage to the university level, in order that every child in the socialist state should have equal chance to profit from it, but the teachers are employed by the parents in the evenings to give their children extra lessons to ensure that they pass their examinations, that is, by the parents who could obviously afford to pay fees. These, in the case of a university student, can amount to more than £700 a year for each child taught extra lessons. Coaching becomes big business when teachers are in short supply. The government would like to stamp it out, but that is impossible while teachers' salaries are so low and many join the brain drain to improve their standard of living. The Ministry of Education is trying to contain it by making it legal for teachers to offer a limited number of hours extra teaching for extra salary on the school premises. This is recognized as a part-solution; the basic problems remain to be solved. Meanwhile, according to *al-Ahram* and other local newspapers, the phenomenon of private lessons has become a characteristic of almost every household containing a student in any of the stages from kindergarten to the university.

Problems of children and youth

What of the school children and youth themselves, how do they view their problems? Two main sources are available: a national survey supported by UNICEF and carried out by the personnel of the National Centre for Social and Criminological Research in Cairo and the expressed concerns of students who can communicate through both their Arab Socialist Union organization and their independent students' unions.

The needs of children

The study of the problems of children, which covers the period 1966 to 1969, was Egypt's response to the call by a UNICEF conference for national policies for children based on their actual needs. Its main importance lies in the recognition of

an acute lack of accurate information about the nature and extent of the major needs and problems of Egyptian children, and, in addition, the corresponding lack of relevant data underlining whatever inconsistencies may be found between societal goals and systems' modes of satisfying children's needs in Egypt.

Henceforward, planning to solve children's problems would be an integrated part of national development plans. It is regarded as a pilot study on a nationwide scale, subject to all the difficulties of an ambitious pioneer effort, covering development stages from conception to the age of eighteen years. The steering committee argued that

if you could identify the problems, concerns and centres of pain of children and youth, you would at the same time be basically indicating some of their psycho-bio-social needs . . . the present investigation was more concerned with needs which have their roots in the 'circumstantial' climate into which the child is born and continues to grow and develop. The [main] line [was] therefore to try to assess the problems of children at different stages of their development in different social strata. (Assessment of children's needs in Egypt. Final report UNICEF, 1974)

It would be inappropriate here to attempt to cover, even in summary, this very detailed study of the problems of Egyptian children encompassing social, economic and educational features of the Egyptian background, the needs and problems of the pre-school child in the fields of health, nutrition, rearing methods, legal needs and problems arising when the mother works; the legal rights, needs and problems of the school-age child as they relate to family, custody, alimony and legal protection in general, health and nutritional needs, employment, educational opportunities and personal-social needs and problems. A few aspects have been selected for their relevance to the development of Egypt's educational policy.

It is noted that the sample used includes both fathers and mothers and those children attending school and non-attenders (ie. drop-outs, etc.). This is a recognition of the increasing importance of the roles of parents in their children's education (hitherto confined to the middle and upper classes) and of the need to meet the problems not only of children within the school system but of the unfortunates who still roam the streets and haunt the bazaars. No uniformity was found among the children's problems, which depended on sex, urban or rural domicile, the socio-economic level of the family, family size and the level of education, as well as working status of the father and mother. The services available in home and institution were described, but the survey of the conditions under which children live, of family expenditure and food consumption patterns showed that in

> the great majority of Egyptian families children are deprived of many essentials, a fact which is reflected not only in their health and nutritional status, but also in the pursuit of their personal interests, continuation of education and the fulfilment of other life aims.

The deprivations are responsible for high infant mortality rates, malnutrition and other diseases, incorrect family life and socialization methods, high rate of child labour, high rate of drop-outs, as well as non-attendance at primary schools (though free and compulsory) by almost 30 per cent in the six-to-twelve-years age group. Of special significance is that girls are more deprived than boys of many essentials, especially education and freedom of choice. The report indicates that in spite of Egypt's great efforts to provide services, they are 'in most cases deficient in many ways and very poor in quality'. The parents themselves aggravate the situation by failing to make use of technical education provision which would ensure a good living for their children in non-saturated areas of employment.

The report also points out the many inconsistencies between family practices and values and the goals and aims considered to be of national importance. These include the ignorance of wives and mothers, especially in rural areas, a strong tendency to think of manual work and skilled labour as inferior occupations with a corresponding reluctance to have their children educated along industrial and technical lines, discrimination against daughters, harsh discipline within the family, which frustrates the development of independence, and the pressure on students to gain admission to the universities and chase white-collar jobs, when, in fact the need of the country is for trained technicians, skilled mechanics and other manual experts.

The Egyptian government can claim that it is working to carry out the recommendations which follow this report: to pay more attention to rural areas, by providing community services, to ensure that girls are given the same attention concerning their needs and problems as boys, the increase of family planning units, especially in rural areas and the establishment of a 'National Planning Council for Children', which would co-ordinate the efforts of different ministries and public and social services and institutions. Finally, the investigation concludes that

Policies concerning children and families should be revised with a new outlook on actual social problems, and enforced with a courageous scientific attitude towards adopting a modern system suited to the needs of Egyptian children and the Egyptian family. (UNICEF, 1974)

The thousands of Egyptian children who reach the top of the educational ladder and spend three or more years studying at college or university are, like students in other countries, ready to discuss their problems with anyone who will listen. These appear to fall into two main categories: the socially acceptable, and political doubts and fears which are regarded as dangerous to the unity of the state. They are encouraged to express their problems (which might more accurately be described as 'grievances') through the student unions, the student branch of the Arab Socialist Union and counselling facilities described under 'student welfare'.

Student problems

Egyptian universities hold seminars periodically to give students the opportunity to discuss their problems relating to their studies and to have general discussions on the political situation. Union membership is not compulsory, so it is possible that half of those attending may be non-members. Apart from welfare (already discussed) the main problems seem to be related to shortages of scientific equipment and books, which are annual causes of frustration. To ease this situation the Higher Council of the Universities approved in 1972 the establishment of a university book fund with a starting capital of £E 100,000 and to make arrangements for providing university textbooks at the lowest possible cost. However, the decision to apply the principle of one textbook for every subject even if it was taught by more than one professor, to insist on every professor teaching one class for a minimum period of two years and in no circumstances to change a textbook before two years, so that a student who failed and had to repeat the year would not be compelled to obtain a new textbook, must, in view of very inadequate library facilities, be a source of intellectual frustration. In spite of this 'solution' the problem continues and in 1974 the cabinet took steps to facilitate the import of university textbooks as well as foreign volumes and reference books at reasonable prices. The following year a central book agency was created to ensure that books reach students in time and at suitable prices, and to help members of the teaching staff to print their books and distribute them more easily. To keep the prices down a republican decree was issued exempting university teaching staff from taxes on their profits from textbooks. The textbook problem has been detailed here, as it assumes an importance in the Egyptian study programme not found in, for example, English universities, where no textbooks are prescribed and there is no direct relationship between the course, the textbook, the author-professor, the student and the examination.

More difficult are problems arising from demands by students for the right to discuss political affairs in a way that expresses or implies criticism of the existing régime. Freedom of speech, which is seen as a mark of maturity, is traditionally exercised by young people who have only recently escaped the fetters of childhood, discovering that they have an opinion on any topic you like to name. With increasing social awareness they are sensitive to environmental shortcomings which they see as the outcome of faulty policies. Having no real power to change their world, they exercise a power of protest expressed with varying degrees of violence. In normal times such behaviour from students is tolerated by democratic countries provided that the demonstration does not involve law-breaking such as destruction of property and endangering life and liberty. Egypt's situation is not yet normal, nor can it be until a solution to the Arab-Jewish conflict has been found. Student attacks on the government are seen as undermining the solidarity that is necessary to achieve Egyptian political aims. Naturally students are not a party to military secrets, and it seems possible that while they were staging their protests against lack of support for the Palestinian cause, plans to invade the occupied territory in 1973 were already in hand.

By European and American standards student unrest in Egypt is mild in its eruptions, but, in the context of normal public behaviour by adults as well as youth it is disturbing the university authorities as well as the government. In 1972, students who had taken part in the incidents were allowed to return when the universities re-opened, except for the leaders who were interrogated by the Public Prosecutor. Even they were allowed to visit the universities and talk to staff. Meanwhile discussions took place with the student unions, and a fact-finding sub-committee of the Arab Socialist Union prepared a report for the People's Assembly. In the subsequent debate the students' right to freedom differentiates between self-expression and sensational slogans, abuse and rumours, for 'insult is a crime both inside and outside the university halls'. (*Egyptian Gazette*) A deviationist faction, who cared little for the homeland or the students, had infiltrated into their ranks, formed demonstrations, published wall magazines full of abuse of state institutions but had made no definite demands. Recommendations from the People's Assembly urged that more attention should be paid to youth problems both by themselves and the government, a revision of university regulations, more employment opportunities should be given to university graduates, student unions should be elected and that religious and spiritual values should be cared for in all stages of education. It was suggested that tolerance should be shown towards the views of the country's youth who were 'expressing the conscience of society'.

The President's reply was to reveal the seizure of evidence of Marxist-inspired plans to establish 'Committees for the Defence of Democracy', their mission being to 'struggle against the repressive measures, police and administrative intervention and statutes which suppress freedoms as well as disallow the freedom of publication, expression and meeting.' They had intended to declare the withdrawal of confidence from the existing students' unions and to form what they called the 'National Democratic Union of Students' so that they could control student affairs. It was also revealed that the activities had been started by an employee of the General Construction Company, for personal and financial gains, who subsequently admitted trying to incite university students to hold anti-government demonstrations to exert pressure on the government for the release of students pending investigations. There was general relief and gratitude from youth organizations when, almost on the eve of the October War, the President decided to withdraw the cases against students from the courts. The state Minister for Youth, referring to it as a 'wise and revolutionary decision', regarded it as 'an invitation to young people to do their duty at the present crucial stage in an atmosphere of security and freedom, guided only by their sense of responsibility and commitment to the national goals.' The October War gave Egyptian students fresh outlets for their energy and patriotism and has been followed by a period of peace in the universities, giving time for the investigation of 'legitimate' grievances.

The student unions have suffered a setback in so far as they now co-exist with the student section of the Arab Socialist Union which has the power of the political organization behind it. However, as sympathizers with the African students' movement and members of the International Students' Union, they appeal to students who want to be a part of a world association as well as an Egyptian or Arab organization.

3

The educational system: problems of control

Centralization versus decentralization

In education the government proposes and, to a great extent, the civil service body (in Egypt including the teachers as well as the Ministries of Education) disposes, so the relationship between the decision-making political body and the educational executive hierarchy is crucial to the successful solution of educational problems. There are some interesting points of comparison and contrast between the situation in Egypt and in England during the period covered by this survey. The basic relationship, which to a large extent determines all the hierarchical relationships, depends on the relative dependence or independence of educational policy from political dogma.

Periodically in England, there is a call from educationalists to remove education from politics, that is, to make educational decisions on educational grounds rather than to use them to support a political policy which may be changed at the next general election. It is argued that the country's children are being used as pawns in a power struggle in which neither side has all the best educational answers. The reply assumes that the concept of education extends beyond the school walls, being an integral part of the fabric of living, so cannot be divorced from other aspects of government. From the latter point of view it is but a short step to think of education in terms of the economic and social needs of the state and the contribution that should be made by its young people. Thus, in 1976, we had the unprecedented experience of listening to a British Prime Minister making a major speech expressing concern about educational standards and raising questions about curricula, organization, methods of teaching and other educational matters, hitherto regarded as the prerogative of the teaching profession. In periods of social change issues become confused, but one fact became clear when a by-election in the north of England resulted in a change of a political party in local government: the decision to reverse a political policy to adopt an overall comprehensive system of state education was also political. Decision-making in education, however obscured by theories of education taught in the colleges and bolstered by social and psychological research is ultimately political.

In Egypt this aspect of educational control has been less complicated owing to the one-party political system. Continuity of government for nearly a quarter of a century has favoured a singleness of purpose, creating stability and releasing the energies of administrators and educationalists to concentrate on the details of implementing national policies and solving the problems involved as efficiently as possible. Until recently, efficiency has been equated with centralization.

Historical factors as well as more recent events have conspired to centralize educational administration in Egypt. As Galt (1936), commented, for centuries Islam had preached the virtue of acquisition of knowledge directed towards a faithful execution of religious duties which allowed no individual or social deviation, When a European system was introduced by Mohammed 'Ali (1830–40), it followed the centralized pattern characteristic of French education, a pattern which the British failed to change during their occupation of Egypt. Galt, complaining of the ill effects of centralization on education in modern Egypt, remarked that

> Egyptian education presents no compelling philosophy like
> Fascism or Communism to warrant perpetuation of such a
> centralized machine for indoctrination. In Egypt the educational
> wheels of indoctrination are all set up, but there is no natural
> ideology to be indoctrinated. The wheels grind on for their own
> sake.

The price of stability, he thought, was stagnation. Two years later decentralization began with the division of Egypt into educational zones, including two or more provinces. Manned by an army of director generals, local controllers, advisory committees, technical advisers, inspectors and numerous sub-committees, the wheels still ground on until Gamal Abdul Nasser in 1952 supplied the 'compelling philosophy' and 'natural ideology' to use the machine.

With the consolidation of the political régime, the widespread distribution of the Arab Socialist Union units, expansion of education and plans for re-mapping Egypt into socially homogeneous, natural, geographical and integrated units, decentralization of education has become an important aspect of a general policy to attract Egyptians of all classes and occupations away from the over-popular and over-populated cities. At first the pace was slow: Boktor (1963), reported the existence of twenty-seven decentralized independent zones all over the country each with its own administration. At present governorates are being encouraged to adapt syllabuses to the needs and interests of the local population, but financial decentralization has yet to be worked out: even in Alexandria, the government allowance from Cairo has been itemized and only a relatively small part has been used freely for public services. However, in 1974, educational zones were re-organized and upgraded. Every governorate now comprises a zone and in certain districts of the Cairo, Alexandria and Giza governorates there is an administration of the first level. Moreover, every city in the other governorates is permitted to establish an educational administration with a director whose occupational status will depend on the number of schools and classrooms in his competence. The Ministry of Education provides directors for the newly established administrations, while the educational zone provides staff either from its own ranks or other personnel in the governorate. (Ministerial Issue No. 49 for the year 1974)

Educational policies and practices tend to go round in circles, so that one who has taught, say, for forty-five years periodically encounters a 'new' method of approach to teaching or discipline, supported by enthusiastic literature from America which appears to be an 'old' method clothed in the latest fashionable psychological terms. (Behaviour therapy is a case in point.) Educational administration in terms of centralization and decentralization appears to be, in Egypt, approaching the point in the circle that England is leaving. During the period of Galt's protest against decentralization, in England the transition was made from a completely decentralized financial structure, resulting, for example, in widely different salary scales for teachers and the provision of secondary education, etc. (depending on local tax levels), to centralized responsibility for major building projects, a national salary scale and other measures aimed at giving rural communities the same level of educational opportunity as those found in the cities and the suburbs. Egypt is hoping to achieve the same objective by decentralization. At the same time the Egyptian administration, as shown in the details below, is trying to liberalize the administration by various methods: changing the image of the inspectorate by turning it into an 'advisory' body, giving head teachers more freedom in the running of their schools, encouraging flexibility in curricula and modern approaches to teaching, all in the name of efficiency and with the desire to raise standards, while in England there is a strong political move to cut down the freedom of head teachers to run their schools in their own way without interference, to increase the power of the inspectorate and to establish at least a core curriculum which every child must follow. These measures are also being discussed with the object of increasing efficiency and raising standards. Perhaps both countries are moving towards a balanced solution.

The structure and scope of the Ministries of Education

The ministries

As indicated, efforts by the Ministries of Education to solve educational problems are made within the political framework, which outlines their responsibilities and restraints. While the main responsibility for education and training lies with the Ministry of Education and the Ministry of Higher Education, other ministries train manpower for their own specialized needs, providing both formal and informal programmes. The Ministry of al-Azhar is responsible for a complete network of schools and colleges which operate outside the public sector and for religious education. The private sector and voluntary teaching, such as private coaching and organized literacy classes are subject to governmental restraints, but the universities are outside ministerial jurisdiction.

Until July 1961, the Ministry of Education carried the responsibility for all levels of education except the universities. Rapid expansion in the field of higher education made desirable a split in the administration, so, as far as institutions are concerned, its main responsibilities are for primary, preparatory (intermediate), secondary general, secondary technical (commercial, agricultural and industrial) education and primary teacher training. Such is the growing concern for switching from a concentration on quantity to quality of education in Egypt that the scope of ministerial activity is gradually increasing. For example, recently two new departments have been added to those discussed below. These are: a separate department for broadcasting educational programmes by radio and television, which co-operates with television staffs and personnel from the Department of Educational Aids; and a Department for Military/Training Affairs which had been affiliated to the preparatory and education sector. The responsibility of this department is to provide military training for both boys and girls in the secondary stage, and to train the boys in military exercises and the girls in medical care. (Law No. 46 for the year 1973 and Ministerial Issue No. 131 for the year 1974)

The Ministry is subject to Republican Issues which reflect national policies and affect other ministries, but formulates its own regulations relating to internal administration. During the period 1973/5, the government established the National Council for Education, Scientific Research and Technology for designing long-term policies in these areas and suggesting general policy for developing national facilities. It is also responsible for studying the possibilities of international co-operation and exchange of experience in those areas, and for co-ordinating the various efforts made, as well as following up and evaluating the designed plans with the purpose of developing future policies. The Council has been formed of leaders in the field of education and of experienced experts in its various branches and specializations, leaders who have gained public fame for their superior abilities and efficient contributions over a long period of time at home and abroad. (Republican Issue No. 615 for the year 1974)

After 1961 education above the secondary level became the responsibility of the new Ministry of Higher Education. Technically the universities retained their independence, but an attempt was made to integrate them into the government system by the creation of the Supreme Council of Universities, under the presidency of the Minister of Higher Education, which is responsible for planning and research both in the universities and in other institutes of higher education.

The main functions of the Ministry are as follows:

1. to plan for and retain control over the Higher Technical Institutes and Technical Training Institutes, although individual institutions are given a good deal of freedom in the management of their own administrative affairs;
2. to carry out advisory functions and planning functions in the universities as a major member of the Supreme Council of Universities;
3. responsibility for student missions abroad, award of scholarships and all other matters relating to foreign students;
4. admissions to higher institutes and universities on the basis of examinations.

These functions and those of the Supreme Council of Universities together with instructions for the organization of Higher Education Institutes and universities are detailed in Law No. 49 (1972), modified by amendments in subsequent years.

The Supreme Council of Universities

This Council meets the need to co-ordinate the heterogeneous collection of universities, colleges and institutes of diverse origins that together represent higher education in Egypt. It is a formidable task owing to the extreme decentralization of these institutions in contrast to other levels of education (Qubain said in 1966 that 'Each college and indeed sometimes each department within the small college is a world unto its own'), but necessary, as duplication is a luxury that Egypt cannot afford in terms of manpower or finance. Problems arising from the unprecedented expansion in this sector of education in recent years have already been discussed and some details of the institutions themselves will be found in the chapter on Higher Education.

The Supreme Council of Universities consists of the Minister of Higher Education (president), vice-president of each university, a member to be selected annually by each university council from among deans of the respective university faculties, five external members known for great interest and experience in university education and public affairs, nominated by the Council, and the Secretary General of the Council. Co-ordination in the field of higher university education covers university studies and academic degrees, teaching in corresponding faculties, institutes and departments of universities and university teaching posts. The Council is also responsible for planning the general policy of university education and scientific research in universities, which aims at orienting the academic work to serve the nation's needs in accordance with its national, social, economic, cultural and scientific objectives. It also determines the fields of specialization of the professorships, the creation of new fields and the equivalence of foreign degrees, as well as deciding the number of students to be admitted to the different faculties of each of the universities and formulating the regulations for admission. Within the framework of its responsibilities, it sets up by-laws of the universities and approves faculty regulations, but is limited to comments on the government grants given annually to each university.

The educational system: problems of control

The Council sets up committees of specialized university professors from Egypt and abroad or suitably qualified persons to increase its efficiency. For example, there are thirteen committees covering all disciplines forming sub-committees to deal with matters concerning university studies. Other committees evaluate the academic work of applicants for university posts, deal with the equivalence of degrees at various levels awarded by foreign institutions, and deal with cultural relations affairs with foreign universities and institutions in the field of higher education and scientific research. A general secretariat headed by a secretary general, ranking as a vice-president of a university, with five years' minimum experience as a professor takes care of the administrative and financial aspects of the specialized units. (Source: personal communication and notes and pamphlets from the Secretary General of the Supreme Council of Universities, Cairo, 1976)

Planning

As indicated above, the Ministries of Education and Higher Education have been charged by the government to produce a ministerial structure that will enable the country, through its educational system to solve its manpower problems at all levels. The natural bureaucratic response to such a grave and comprehensive responsibility is to organize innumerable committees and open countless files. However, law and order are to be preserved by scientific planning.

The National Council for Education, Scientific Research and Technology

Gamal Abdul Nasser recognized that national planning was essential to organize strategies and harness all Egyptian resources to carry out his political, social and economic policies. A National Planning Committee was founded in 1956 to collect information from the public and private authorities about their proposed policies and projects which they should follow up and evaluate. However, the scope of the Committee's tasks, which affected every aspect of the economy, led to its upgrading to become the Ministry of National Planning, which coordinates information from experts, research workers and specialized study groups. This information, general and statistical, is the basis of the five-year plans which became a feature of Egyptian politics after 1960.

Every ministry now has a planning sector with a director who co-ordinates plans of its various branches, with due attention being paid to the results of relevant researches. He also acts as a liaison officer to the Minister of National Planning. The whole task of planning has been taken over with enthusiasm: there are yearly plans, five-year plans, ten-year plans and even plans spanning the next twenty-five years. The problem lies in the provision of a framework which will ensure that each plan, however minor or subordinate, has its appointed place in an overall strategy. Egypt has the advantage of learning from the experience of expert planners who subject her projects to a detailed evaluation before granting financial help.

In education, planning is centralized at the Ministry of Education but the Educational Zones contribute by giving information about their needs and facilities. An expressed policy is that the governorates should be self-sufficient in education (Report 1973), but, as far as can be ascertained, implementation is not included in a ten-year plan which began in 1972/3 and will end in 1981/2. The principles and main objectives were outlined in the Annual Report (1973). They can be summarized as follows:

Principles:

the absorption of all children of compulsory school age;

compulsory school age to be raised to fifteen;

elimination of private and paid lessons;

raising standards, especially in science;

linking education and the needs of society;

eradication of illiteracy.

Main objectives:

equal opportunity for all citizens;

provision of skilled and well-equipped manpower;

introduction of modern science in curricula and method;

educational, medical, physical and psychological care of students at all
  stages;

programme of literacy education and education of the handicapped;

centre for educational research;

continuous assessment as main part of the examination system;

co-ordination between the different bodies concerned with education at different levels.

Most of these principles and objectives are in general terms, making progress assessment a co-ordinating exercise, but the Report on 'The

Development of Education in A.R.E. during the Period 1973/4–1974/5'
indicates that more detailed planning is in progress and that some items,
such as the Centre for Educational Research (described below) have
already been achieved. Problems related to the implementation of these
principles and objectives and the steps taken to find solutions will be
found in subsequent chapters. Examples are the introduction of
modern mathematics in some preparatory schools and attempts to
improve buildings and equipment. A noble attempt to give every child
a school place is, in some cases, being achieved by gross over-crowding
of classes and double or treble sessions daily. There are so many factors
over which the Minister of Education has no control that, however
careful the planning, it is at this stage impossible to assess the chances of
100 per cent primary school attendance in 1980, quite apart from the
raising of the compulsory age to fifteen years.

The Ministerial Committee on Education

Meanwhile, following the establishment by the government of the
National Council for Education, Scientific Research and Technology
for designing long-term policies, the Minister of Education in 1974
formed a Ministerial Committee on Education composed of officials
working in these areas. The members discuss their policies, plans and
responsibilities, project new laws and issues of their respective departments, discuss the National Plans for Research and the distribution of
manpower, and approve plans of co-operation and exchange of experiences on a scientific basis. (Ministerial Issue No. 185 for the year 1974)

There can be no doubt that during this period of rapid change the
new National Council has a useful role and that the Ministerial Committee has a function of supplying the groundwork for discussion at
the national level. There is equally no doubt that the experts involved
are capable of fulfilling their important duties. The snag is that the
Council is likely to be composed of 'the mixture as before' since the
qualifications for membership cover a quantity and quality of experience only acquired by those whose services cover not only a high
administrative position, often entailing much travel, but membership of
numerous committees. It is to be hoped that the government is seizing
this opportunity of waiving aside the normal procedure of hierarchical
stepping stones to include at least a proportion of young, able scientists
in its Council, who have the time and energy to give priority to this

work. There is evidence from both overworked officials at the top and frustrated graduates returning from overseas training that adjustments in the rigid promotion system might alleviate the manpower situation. Meanwhile the Minister of Education has delegated some of his authority to his Under-Secretaries of State, by appointing a Head Under-Secretary for Education. This will free him to co-operate and to participate to a greater degree in the management of education at the central level. (Ministerial Issue No. 130 for the year 1974)

Re-organization within the Ministry

The year 1974 witnessed a tremendous effort to meet the need for modernization within the Ministry. Ministerial Issues Nos 84 and 134 are responsible for the re-organization to encompass the following sections:

1. Office of the Minister and the Planning Sector, jointly charged to supervise the following departments: The General Department, the Council for Directors of Education, the Department of Development Plans, the Department of Organization, the Department of Statistics and the Department of Public Relations.
2. Supervision and follow-up for General Culture Education responsible for supervising the instruction of general culture education subjects, the General Department for In-Service Training, the General Department for Audio-Visual Aids, the General Department of Libraries and Museums, and the General Department of School Activities.
3. Administrative and Financial Affairs Sector responsible for the following General Departments: Finance, Administration, Personnel, Administration and Financial Supervision and Affairs of Law.
4. Central Educational Services and follow-up of Educational Zones, responsible for the following General Departments: Books and Textbooks, Laboratories, Examinations, follow-up of Educational Zones and Private Education.
5. Primary Education and Teachers Preparation Sector which supervises the General Departments of: Primary Education, Teachers' Preparation, Adult Education and Literacy.
6. Preparatory and Secondary Education Sector which is in charge of the following General Departments: Preparatory Education,

Secondary Education, Physical and Social Education and Cultural Relationships.

7. Technical Education Sector which is responsible for General Departments of: Industrial Education, Supervision of Technical Subjects, and Technical Equipment and Instruments.

Educational Consultants and Supervisors It is self-evident that plans to improve the quality of education need a follow-up service by competent supervisors who are able both to assess as well as act as liaison officers between the planners, teachers and officials engaged in executing the plans. This ministerial problem has partly been resolved by the establishment of a sector of supervision in the Ministry of Education itself, making it possible to transfer educational consultants from the National Centre for Educational Research to the Ministry, making a two-tier advisory service, which if co-ordinated should improve efficiency. With the move has come a re-definition of the responsibilities of consultants. They must

join in the committees for studying curriculum development, textbooks and educational books, take part in meetings which are held for studying the general policies for each educational stage and its problems, strengthen the relations among the staffs working in the field and get in touch with the organizations which are responsible for the specific subject matter and its method of teaching, suggest the research and experiments which can be applied in schools and participate in carrying out such research, visit schools and carry out field trips to Educational Zones.

There are specific consultants for technical education, whose responsibilities are defined as follows:

Carry out the studies and research which aims at developing the quality of education in the certain specialization, hold meetings with the concerned departments of planning, curriculum, textbooks, supervision, school administration, student affairs and examinations for studying the problems they face and try to solve them.

All educational consultants must, in their own fields of specialization, also supervise the work of general inspectors and co-ordinate their efforts in the development of educational supervision in all the stages and types of education. (Ministerial Issue No. 55 for the year 1974)

The supervisors, who are conceived as experienced people who can guide and help their colleagues to the advantage of the schools are divided into two categories: the administrative leaders in the offices of the Ministry of Education itself and in the Educational Zones, and the educational supervisors who supervise the instruction in the schools and institutions, and who guide the teachers and evaluate the pupils, the curricula, the textbooks, the school activities and the whole educational process. (Ministerial Issue No. 180 for the year 1973)

The objective of all these detailed instructions is to define the responsibilities of the supervisory staffs at all levels right from the senior teacher up to the supervisor, senior supervisor and the general supervisor. It would be difficult to conceive of a more watertight chain of inspection and advice to test curricula and textbooks to guide and evaluate teachers and pupils, hoping thereby to raise standards of education. The system, however, raises certain important questions. What is considered to be excellence in teachers and head teachers? Are they low-grade civil servants whose function is to carry out precisely the orders received from above? Is initiative inappropriate for teachers? Does the head teacher find any scope for creativity in his (her) job? An Egyptian American who broadcast his comments on Egyptian education while attending a conference on 'Egypt in the Year Two Thousand' found that educational institutions were lacking individual personalities. He felt that this was a sign of immaturity. In the lower levels of education where creativity should be a great feature of teaching and learning, the standardization of so many aspects of the educational experience leads probably to a less than just conclusion that, if you have seen one school, you may have seen the lot. To balance this impression, it must be recorded that in England, where for many years the head teacher has been 'king of his castle', some shocking results lead to a public enquiry from time to time, and that Egypt is in the process of changing the concept of an inspectorate to that of an advisory service, while England is debating the advisability of tightening its control.

In the final analysis of its problems, the Ministry of Education relies increasingly on investigations and research conducted by the National Centre for Educational Research which is now an integral part of its organization.

The National Centre for Educational Research

Before the Revolution one of the controllers under the Technical Adviser (later called an Under-Secretary) was a 'Controller of Projects and Research.' He was in charge of studies and research required by the Ministry of Education, involving examination of plans, policies and courses. This was not considered a full-time job, as, according to Matthews and Akrawi (1949), he was also expected to supervise the collection of information and to take charge of the Ministry library consisting of about 50,000 books in Arabic, English and French, which he lent to officials of the Ministry and teachers all over the country.

The Revolutionary Government, with its emphasis on planning a new order in Egypt, realized that if it were scientific, it could not be divorced from research, so in 1956 it established a Science Council, with the object of encouraging scientific research in all spheres of public life. To legalize these efforts, the state supplanted the Council by a Ministry of Scientific Research, with eight specialized councils, later creating an 'Academy of Scientific Research and Technology.' (Details can be found in the chapter on Higher Education.) Emphasis was on scientific research related to the fields of social and economic development and modern science. Inevitably the Academy's interests overlapped those of the Ministry of Education, since it participated in the development of scientific curricula, supported scientific societies and encouraged the holding of scientific conferences. Also it co-ordinated projects in the various industries, financing them and extending their scope.

By 1970 the Ministry of Education had decided to transform its Technical Research Department into a National Council for Educational Research which would be staffed by officers experienced in scientific methodology which could be applied to investigation and experimentation in the field of education. After comparative studies had been carried out and Egyptian needs and conditions considered, the Centre was established by Decree No. 881 of 1972, as a public agency under the chairmanship of the Minister of Education. (Source: its first Director, Dr Fuad el-Bahay el-Sayed).

According to Dr Fuad the objectives of the Centre are concentrated on improvement of education in all fields, providing sound scientific data to be available for policy-makers and planners, forming technical cadres in the area of educational research, conducting experiments and helping local organizations, while ensuring co-operation and co-ordination with specialized councils and centres in other states. The Board of Directors include representatives of the Ministries of Education, Higher Education, Manpower, Industry, Agriculture, the universities and their specialized faculties, the faculties of education, the Arab Organization for Science and Culture, the Science Academy, the National Planning Institute, the Arab Socialist Union Central Committee and the Education Committee of the People's Council.

By 1973 the Minister of Education, Chairman of the National Education Research Centre, was ready to set up the Centre's General Scientific and Permanent Committees. Care was taken that they should represent scientific and educational skills as well as services and production institutions. Members were drawn from the universities and higher institutes, teacher training institutes, experts on education with long teaching service, former ministers of the production and services sectors and the educational professions association. Each committee has a rapporteur and a technical secretary, its members being selected from advisers on study subjects and/or university professors who are in a position to devote their full time to the committees. (This would be an ideal situation which appears to be unrealistic at present.) The committees' work is planned to deal with field problems in all the educational zones.

The research workers themselves are organized into major sectors and units: Research and Experimental Sector, Documentation and Information Agency, Statistics and Computer Agency, Foreign Relation Office, Financial and Administrative Affairs Sector and offices attached to the Director of the Centre, each having its own responsibilities and functions.

In its short life the NCER has shown great activity including the appointment of nineteen standing committees. At present these are studying and researching in two main areas: school curricula at different stages of education and general aspects of education, such as school administration, educational planning and financing, pre- and in-service training of teachers, evaluation and testing, counselling and guidance, school buildings and equipment and technology of education. An example of research can be taken in the field of school curricula in 1974. As a result of the recommendations made by NCER experts and the Ministry of Education's Under-Secretaries, the Minister approved an experiment on introducing the teaching of English into the fifth and sixth forms of primary schools, to be carried out initially in all primary schools in Luxor, Aswan, Alexandria, Suez, Port Said and Ismailia the following year. In some of the larger schools in the governorates English would start in the third form. Another pilot experiment, on the development of education in rural areas, would be carried out in thirty-four village primary schools, involving special curricula aimed at linking the study programme to the environment and the local industries and crafts existing in each village. The Minister also decided to carry out a pilot study of his new plans for improving curricula, school books and teaching methods on the most up-to-date lines. Fifty schools representing the different stages were to be selected from the different governorates for this experiment. The procedure to be followed for this group of schools would be radically different from the one currently used throughout the Republic. There would be no ministry-imposed syllabus or set books. Workshops would be set up in each governorate to work independently on developing the school curriculum and training teachers in suitable methods of instruction. Non-traditional subjects would be taught in these schools as well as new branches of certain subjects which had been taught more or less in the same way for thirty years, especially in secondary schools. The new subjects would include astronomy and modern electronics. The experiments would take a whole year and the results would be assessed by the NCER and the Ministry's special departments before being applied universally.

In 1973, the Financial Administrative Affairs Sector approved a five-year plan to provide qualified personnel in different areas of science and education, by sending abroad four candidates annually on scholarships to obtain a doctorate degree in a specialized branch of either of these subjects.

The Documentation and Information Agency attached to the Centre issues the following publications: *Contemporary Trends in Education* (twice a year), *Educational Abstracts* (quarterly), *Educational Information* (monthly) *Guide to Educational Circulars* (annually) *Guide to Educational Laws and Regulations* (annually), and *Report on Educational Developments in the Arab Republic of Egypt* (annually).

It appears that, in the future, decision-making in the Ministry of Education will largely result from the work of the NCER. This is in line with the recommendations of the Marrakesh Conference (1970) that research bodies at regional and national level should be created to study problems of education along scientific lines and approve it accordingly. . . . In short, if education is to be really a powerful instrument for modernization, social reconstruction and economic development in the region, it must be based on educational research and its findings.

Finance

Unfortunately, the more scientific the research, the greater its demands on the annual budget. Even in the West, research is difficult to finance unless the subject is perceived to be of practical value, and this may be less obvious in education than in other fields, for example, in medicine. However, the decision on how much to spend studying education along scientific lines is made in the Ministry of Education, for, although the Plan and Budget Committee of the People's Assembly discusses general educational policy in the light of interim development plans, the Ministry of Finance has the final responsibility for allocation of funds; the state, having laid down general rules, leaves the ministries to make detailed decisions within the national guidelines.

After the Revolution, state expenditure on education increased rapidly, and is still increasing. According to Mabro (1974), the £E 23 million budgeted in 1952/3 was raised to about £E 126 million in 1969/70, at the same time as public investment in education increased from £E 2·5 million to about £E 33·3 million. After that, investment averaged about £E 25 million a year.

The Egyptian budget is complicated by the necessity to estimate the amount of foreign currency required in a fluctuating market. This applies particularly to scientific and technological equipment. The Ministry of Education adds to this problem that of importing textbooks and reference books which are essential for studies at the post-secondary level. Although a partial solution has been found in the increasing production of textbooks in Arabic and a law forbidding the re-export of textbooks paid for in hard currency, the problem is likely to increase rather than diminish with the increase in higher education.

Egypt receives considerable aid from outside sources, such as United Nations organizations, the World Bank and friendly countries in both East and West. The details are complicated, involving individual agreements in the form of gifts, loans, personnel, buildings and equip-

ment, and sometimes complete projects. An international body is likely
to ask to evaluate the project and recommend the form of aid. These
evaluations are extremely useful to Egypt at this stage of her development, when she is faced with the formidable task of covering in a few
years the developments that have taken place elsewhere over more than
a century.

The ministerial budget is a compromise between the requests from
all internal sources, including the governorates, and the provision made
by the Ministry of Finance. One official in a governorate outside Cairo
told me that if he needs fifteen million, he asks for twenty, knowing
that what he will get will be nearer to what he needs. This is probably a
world-wide practice. The amount received does not bear a one-to-one
relationship to the amount produced by the governorate, as the
principle behind the final allocation is that need is more important than
capacity to pay. Education also gains from local efforts and by cultural
agreements with friendly countries made at the national level.

The following report from government sources published by the
Egyptian Gazette (19 November 1974), covers not only some illuminat-
ing statistics, but gives insight into budgetry problems:

The Minister of Education, Dr Mustafa Kamal, said that the
budget of the Ministry this year amounted to £E 178·5 million,
an increase of £E 28 million last year. He pointed out that the
volume of wages and salaries hit the £E 137 million mark, an
increase of £E 11 million of which £E 4½ million are bonuses
for teachers who worked overtime. The Minister said that the
Ministry had worked out a long-term policy for the solution of
the shortage in teaching staff. A total of £E 100,000 has been
allocated for the Teacher Training Schools to enable teachers to
get 25 per cent more for their salaries with monthly subsidies for
learners equivalent to £E 2 for those getting 75 per cent of marks
and £E 3 for those getting more than 80 per cent. Other
allocations include £E 4 million for annual increments and the
employment of demobilized teaching staff members. The Minister
said that the Ministry's expenditures jumped to £E 22·5 million
in view of the high price of copy books and textbooks, the
implementation of the school meal programme at teacher training
schools, the operation of the new classrooms, incentives and
educational missions in the Sudan. The Minister explained that new

investment allocations increased by £E 7·7 million to cope with the expansion in all educational stages. The number of enrolled pupils of both sexes in primary schools this year was 738,000, while the set target was 722,000 only, a 78 per cent enrolment. He said that next year the admissions would cover 748,000 while 100 per cent would be made feasible by 1980. The Minister said that concentration in the secondary school stage centred on the technical education so as to represent in ten years' time 70 per cent, and the general education 30 per cent, instead of the present 52 per cent technical and 43 per cent general education. The Minister explained that this would entail new financial commitments, giving as an example that the costs of a general secondary school are in the region of £E 50,000, while a technical school costs fifteen times as much as this amount. The Minister declared that the new classrooms in the budget number 1,461. A total of £E 2·1 million of which £E 1 million is in foreign currency which has been appropriated for general projects and furniture. Debates then ensued about the educational operation and the Ministry's adoption of vocational training centres and technical education. Another aspect of the debate was the Grade 3 bottlenecks especially that there are 126,000 employees in the Ministry of Education alone.

4

The educational ladder

Problems as seen by the Administration

The responsibility of the administration only begins with the maintenance and improvement of the efficiency of the bureaucratic structure
and the development of scientific instruments of planning that will make
possible the implementation of national policies. At a second level its
duty is to implement the plans and maintain the processes of education
which provide their substance. Problems at the latter level arise mainly
because educational processes are slow to develop, as the recipients are
not accustomed to indulge in long-term planning, and expenses grow
rapidly, so there is never enough money available to implement the
ideal plan, making compromise solutions of immediate importance.

In the Report on the Development of Education (1973/4–1974/5), a
summary is made by the Ministry of Education of 'the most important
problems which face educational processes in Egypt'. They are listed as
follows:

the problem of combating illiteracy;
the problem of executing compulsory education for all children
as soon as possible;
the problem of drop-outs and repeating classes especially in the
compulsory stage;
the problem of counselling and guidance in the secondary stage in
relation to choice of branches of study;
the problem of providing educational services in villages and
remote areas;
the problem of developing the system of examination in the form
which can ensure sound education and at the same time limit its
weight on the pupils;
the problem of raising the standard of performance among
primary school teachers;
the problem of providing qualified and trained manpower in

77

different fields of production, which are necessary for economic and social development, besides allocating enough budget for equipment and facilities.

These problems can roughly be divided into two categories: those concerned with the quantity of education and those with quality. Education through literacy and compulsory education that avoids the wastage of drop-outs and repeaters must be achieved for all citizens, whether they live in the city or the village or remote settlement. At the same time, the quality of service must be improved by better teacher-training for the primary schools, reforming the examination system and guiding the secondary-school pupils, so that their choice of studies will meet the needs of qualified and trained manpower in different fields of production, making possible economic and social development. The solution to all the problems requires an adequate budget to cover equipment and facilities. As El-Koussy envisaged in 1953, the leaders of education are still needing 'to serve both ends simultaneously' and to attack 'the self-defeating factors'.

Some of the problems above were discussed in Chapter 2, in the context of their historical origins and national policies following the Revolution of 1952. In subsequent chapters they will be seen as part of the immediate concern of officials at all levels engaged in making the educational ladder available to as many of Egypt's children as possible, who are capable of climbing it. The search for solutions is also discussed.

In spite of her problems of population, finance, war economy and manpower, Egypt is trying to pursue her goal of continuous education. The educational ladder has progressively added new rungs over the years. The primary stage was, until 1943, reserved for an élite of fee-paying pupils. Most children at this level attended a four-year elementary school, which was free, legally compulsory and regarded as a complete education. An important stage in the development of Egyptian education was reached when, in 1943, fees were abolished in the primary schools, making possible a fusion between primary and elementary education. However, this plan was not implemented until 1953, when the revolutionary government passed Law No. 201, which not only unified the primary schools but extended this compulsory rung of the ladder for two years. The structure thus becomes:

Primary education: entry within the 6–8 age range: 6 years
Preparatory education: entry 9–14 years: 3 years

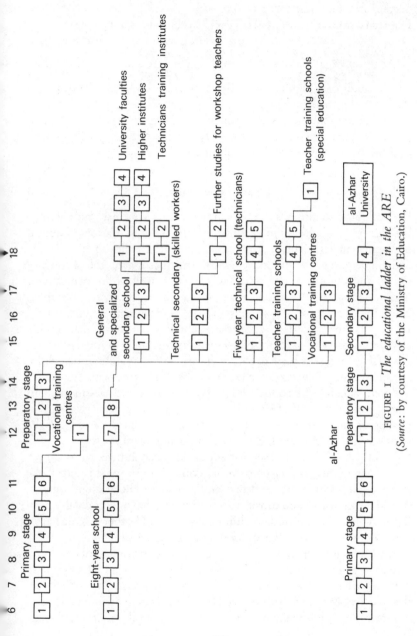

FIGURE I *The educational ladder in the ARE*
(*Source*: by courtesy of the Ministry of Education, Cairo.)

Secondary education: entry 12–17 years: 3 years
Higher education: entry 18–20 years: Technical training 2 years

Higher Technical Institutes: 4
or 5 years
Universities: 4, 5 or 6 years

The result of a highly competitive examination at the end of each stage determines the possibility of entry to the following stage and the courses open to the successful candidate. As the tendency is for Egyptian parents to regard university as the only worthwhile goal, the competition becomes very severe from the first year at school.

Primary schools

In developing countries there is a tendency for the primary school to be the cinderella of educational institutions: it lacks the missionary appeal of literacy and fundamental education, the informality of the nursery and kindergarten (where they exist), the prestige of the secondary school and the immediate practical appeal as well as the glamour of higher education. Whether or not he has been fortunate enough to enjoy the freedom of play in a pre-school environment or to run wild in his neighbourhood, the primary-school child finds that in the traditional school he is expected to spend many hours of the day sitting at a desk learning the basic tools of education. If he is an Egyptian child, he stands a good chance of having to share his desk with two other children, and his classroom with forty-four or more classmates. His school, too, will be shared with a similar group or even two similar groups of children who enter the building on the departure of the previous group. As one high official told me, some primary schools built for 500 children are used for educating 5,000 in three shifts, so the 1,500 leaving meet the 1,500 or more coming in, so what is left of the playground accommodates 3,000 at the end of the session: library, special rooms for art and music, field and garden have all gradually been taken over to accommodate children who would otherwise not get a chance to go to school. How can they be turned away?

However, as in all countries, the picture varies from school to school, city to city, governorate to governorate. For example, if the Egyptian child referred to above happens to live in the governorates of Aswan, the Red Sea, Mersa Matruh or the New Valley, he may be in a class of less than thirty children and be able to register at school before the age

TABLE 3 *Primary education teachers by qualification and sex*

Years	Qualified		Unqualified		Total			% qualified			Teacher-pupil ratio
	Males	Females	Males	Females	Males	Females	Total	Males	Females	Total	
1963–4	35,648	27,607	11,531	6,163	47,179	33,770	80,949	75·6	81·8	78·1	38·7
1964–5	37,871	29,167	10,901	6,214	48,772	35,381	84,153	77·6	82·4	79·7	39·2
1965–6	39,273	30,860	10,051	6,107	49,324	36,967	86,291	79·6	83·5	81·3	39·6
1966–7	39,146	31,555	9,396	6,004	48,542	37,559	86,101	80·6	84·0	82·1	39·7
1967–8	38,873	33,643	9,353	6,005	48,226	39,648	87,874	80·6	84·9	82·5	39·6
1968–9	35,856	36,096	8,515	5,985	44,371	42,081	86,452	80·8	85·8	83·2	41·1
1969–70											
1970–1	38,244	45,259	8,149	7,084	46,393	52,343	98,736	82·4	86·5	84·6	37·9
1971–2											
1972–3	37,613	44,956	8,077	6,729	45,690	51,685	97,375	82·3	87·0	84·8	40·9
1973–4					42,151	51,351	93,502				41·9

(*Source:* by courtesy of the Ministry of Education, Cairo.)

81

of six years. He may even have begun school at the age of six years but be still in the same class at seven or eight years, on account of having to repeat the class. In theory, the first two classes are infant or kindergarten classes, since this level was incorporated into the primary school, but, basically, the first class is what it claims to be, the first primary stage. There are none of those features of an infants' school: special furniture, equipment, space, informal organization, facilities for play, etc. Infant schools are not only very expensive to equip, but need skilled teachers who can help their pupils to bridge the gap between home and school. Small children are not interested in copying pages and pages of letters and figures. At present Egypt cannot afford good schools for infants. This raises the question of whether education is being advanced by enlarging classes to admit children under six years, before suitable provision can be made. Six years is already a very tender age for joining 'the rat race'. Perhaps there would be less repeating of classes if those under seven were to be admitted to a more informal programme. This would automatically solve the undesirable wide range of admittance at subsequent stages. Unfortunately one would still have to face the high cost of informal programmes.

The primary programme is subject-based, courses being given in religion, Arabic language, mathematics, general science and hygiene, social studies and citizenship, physical education, art education, music, home economics for girls and agricultural industries for boys. These are rather pretentious titles for what actually takes place in the classroom. The primary school administrators, head teachers and teachers are desperately anxious to introduce new methods and equipment. The curricula come under constant revision with appropriate modification of textbooks; teaching aids are produced, and during the last few years a start has been made to provide the schools with workshops and libraries. 'Music' is not always interpreted as screaming patriotic songs: some schools visited have small music groups where the children make music for themselves with percussion and other instruments. Physical education is too often what used to be called 'drill' given by an instructor in the style of a sergeant major on parade, but, with the encroachments made on field and playground, there is little scope for a more imaginative approach to this subject. The fact is that the 'modern' school is a complex organization inspired by attitudes towards learning and teaching and interpersonal relationships, not only between teacher and taught but the whole educational hierarchy, based on theories of child development and education demanding a methodology that allows for freedom of expression, individual and group work, much of which centres around the interests of the children themselves, taking place in an environment including accommodation and equipment that allows flexibility of use. In a country where maximum use of 'the plant' is essential and the 'shift' system is common, the criteria above are indeed formidable. Much frustration can be avoided if it is recognized that not all teachers feel happy and do their best work if striving to be 'with it' in education and some children find security and intellectual satisfaction in a more formal and 'structured' classroom. At primary school level the most important aspect is interpersonal relationships. If these are right, with teacher and child co-operating to produce a happy atmosphere, excellence can be achieved, and indeed is achieved in some Egyptian primary schools, in spite of difficulties.

In the overcrowded primary classroom associated with the 'class' method of teaching, it is not the children of high calibre who suffer: they will learn to read, for example, whatever the method used. Many of them come from a home background where books are available and parents are waiting to lighten the burden of homework. It is the less able and underprivileged children who need more interest and attention from the teacher, like, for instance, the boy from the back of a class who read to me fluently what was expected of him but from the wrong page! The traditional method of learning off by heart, which still has a useful function in the education of small children, is very hard to eradicate as the sole method of learning, unless there are facilities for hearing children read individually or in small groups. Experience has proved that any child can learn to read fluently, unless he is so mentally deficient that he needs to be in a special school, provided that someone is willing to listen to him regularly and help him to see for himself why he makes mistakes. The same applies to arithmetic. The Egyptian child has the advantage that Arabic is a phonetic language, so that given the sounds of a few letters and the key to the vowel sounds, he can quickly practise words for himself. In Arabic it is necessary for full advantage to be taken of the phonetic nature of the language so that the mechanics of reading are mastered quickly, leaving the teacher adequate time to concentrate on the difficult grammatical construction of the language. In large classes, in spite of up-to-date reading books and teachers' manuals, provided by the government, it is difficult to resist making a class write pages of 'alifs' with quiet concentration, rather than letting them practise out loud the combinations of various phonetic letters, each at his own pace, knowing the purpose of the exercise.

Meanwhile the Director of Primary Education attacks these problems on two fronts: the standard of teaching and the status of teachers. To improve standards of teaching, his strategy is to organize a group of about forty Chief Inspectors and experts to spend one week in a governorate visiting as many schools as possible. After a report has been prepared, he goes to the governorate himself to meet all the primary leaders, including head teachers and representatives of their staffs to discuss the report and their problems. In 1975 he concentrated on improving the quality of teaching reading and writing, linking the educational process with activities of the community and the inculcation of religious and social values. Teachers are likely to appreciate his guidance, for, as President of the Teachers' Syndicate, he is appalled by their low status, admires their enthusiasm and struggles for their rights.

The one-class school

In recent years Egypt has been adding to her agricultural land by various reclamation schemes and distributing it to worthy members of the population, such as families of war victims, displaced farmers and successful agricultural students. In the areas under discussion all the problems of rural areas are accentuated. It is very important that the children do not miss what is now their legal right – to reach at least the first rung of the educational ladder. It is also essential not to add to the literacy problem. In 1975 a new scheme was launched by the Ministry of Education to run one-class schools in those areas where the child population is scattered and relatively small. The plan is to open five thousand such schools over five years. The first thousand have already started, but the scheme is still in its experimental stage, so it is too soon to report progress. The first teachers are mainly drawn from the mosque and from teachers in retirement living within reach of the schools. They receive in-service training in the zone and a lesson-by-lesson guide. Children are accepted from six to fifteen years old, but in the Alexandria governorate, for instance, which has started with ten classes, accommodation for all six-year-olds is found in the normal schools, so the one-class school is only needed for late starters. The arrangement is flexible, to fit not only the agricultural cycle, but the

TABLE 4 *Preparatory education: teachers by qualification and sex*

Year	Qualified		Unqualified		Total			Percentage qualified	Percentage females
	Males	Females	Males	Females	Males	Females	Total		
1963–4	9,653	2,439	4,776	1,318	14,429	3,757	18,186	66	21
1964–5	10,102	2,838	5,539	1,237	15,641	4,075	19,716	66	21
1965–6	11,242	3,305	5,730	1,344	16,979	4,649	21,628	67	21
1966–7	12,883	3,826	5,950	1,344	18,833	5,170	24,003	70	22
1967–8	13,197	4,237	7,647	1,639	20,844	5,876	26,720	65	22
1968–9	13,136	4,552	7,199	1,755	20,335	6,307	26,642	66	24
1969–70									
1970–1	13,004	5,030	7,487	2,370	20,491	7,400	27,891	65	26
1971–2									
1972–3	12,730	6,161	6,764	3,100	19,494	9,261	28,755	66	32
1973–4	12,176	6,334	6,932	3,474	19,108	9,808	28,916	64	34

(*Source:* by courtesy of the Ministry of Education, Cairo.)

convenience of the teachers available. Among suggestions being discussed are the three-month summer session for the training of teachers, a 'mother' school in the nearest town or village, which will accept children whose intelligence obviously qualifies them for a more normal education, and the acceptance of rural candidates at a lower level in the teacher training schools, in order to encourage them to return as teachers.

Preparatory schools

If the amount of space taken in the public Press indicated the relative interest in the various educational institutions, the primary school, which educationalists rank as of vital importance in the educational ladder, appears to be lacking in 'news value'. The preparatory school receives even less publicity, perhaps because, in spite of its independence and re-defined functions, it is regarded as less than a school in its own right than as a bridge between the primary and secondary stages. Yet it has a distinct function in the present Egyptian system, since it marks the next stage in compulsory education.

The preparatory school can claim to be the product of the Revolution of 1952, having been created in 1953/4 by the Education Decree No. 2 of 1953, but it did not receive its independence until 1957. It is now a free intermediate school between the free compulsory primary school and the highly selective secondary school. In the intervening period, it has, itself, become less selective. Boktor (1963), reported that it received 20 per cent of the primary school population, although some of the successful candidates had to be accommodated in private schools owing to the shortage of rooms in the state schools. The 1975 estimate is 70 per cent, representing an expanding educational demand. Originally the school had a dual function: to prepare able children to continue their education in secondary or technical school, while the less able were prepared for practical work. Thus, like the primary school, it had the disadvantage of being a transitional stage for some pupils and a terminal school for others. The term 'practical', according to Boktor (1963), covered a variety of offerings later sorted out and distributed to other sections of the school system. He lists them as:

Preparatory Technical Schools (Agricultural, Commercial or Industrial) for males, and similar ones for females. Also under this heading there are co-educational schools, combining males and females.

Preparatory Practical Schools, for the pupils in the School of Light (Blind), Schools of Hope (Deaf and Dumb), Schools of Thought (Mentally Defective).

Schools and/or studies at a preparatory level, combined with apprenticeship. The pupils of these schools combine the usual academic course with practice in certain trades.

Schools of Caligraphy. The pupils of these schools specialize, more particularly in the various types of caligraphy (thuluth, riqa'a, kufi, etc.).

Experimental schools. These were opened in 1960–1 in ten localities: four in Cairo, two at Alexandria and the remainder at Giza, Zagazig, Tanta and Fayoum. . . . All of them have been intentionally concentrated in sections of the country where they will serve as laboratories for teacher training institutions.

Five years of experimentation showed that early specialization gave neither a good educational foundation nor skills that could be utilized in industry, so a ministerial decree of 1962 made the preparatory school an institution for general education only. Pupils study religion, Arabic language, a modern language, social studies and citizenship, mathematics (algebra, geometry and arithmetic) general science and hygiene, art education and music, physical education, home economics for girls and agricultural education for boys. It will be seen that the only distinctive feature is the addition of a foreign language to the subjects studied at the primary level.

Developments over the years have included modifications of the syllabuses, upgrading of teachers in this section by employing university graduates as far as possible, expansions of building and equipment, especially the provision of science laboratories and an increase in co-education. Modern mathematics was introduced in some schools in 1974/5. This is the result of a drive begun in 1971, the year that the Ministry of Education provided £E 100,000 to pay for modern laboratories in preparatory schools. An agreement was reached with the universities to develop the curricula of science faculties to include modern mathematics and to train the necessary teachers. An experiment was started in Alexandria and, while university professors were made responsible for following up the teaching of modern mathematics and science in the schools, the teachers themselves were offered £E 8 monthly as a bonus.

Competition for places in these schools has increased rapidly, especially since fees were abolished. The number of pupils has increased from 250,903 in 1959/70, to 1,203,038 in 1975. Owing to its general character, education in preparatory schools is mainly regarded as an opportunity for pupils to sort out their interests and abilities prior to the next stage in their education. To make this a reality, even more libraries and workshops, as well as vocational guidance facilities, are required, as only about 60 per cent will qualify for any kind of secondary education.

The eight-year school

With the help of an Eastern bloc country, Egypt is at present experimenting with an eight-year school which will give valuable experience in planning a framework for primary and preparatory education when she is in the position to raise compulsory education to fifteen years. At present the two schools cover nine years, and allowing for one repeat year following failure in the final preparatory examination, pupils in the top class may be eighteen years old. Of course demand for increased education may result in pupils wishing to continue their courses after reaching the compulsory limit, as happened in England in secondary schools when the same compulsory limit was reached, but 'compulsory' brings many problems related to the desire of older, non-academic children to throw off school restrictions and get a job. Scarcity of education creates a demand which may be a factor in the willingness of young men to take their lessons side by side with young boys who often outshine them.

The experimental school gives the Ministry of Education the chance to come to grips with such problems. The aim is to get children into school at six years old, so that this will eventually reduce the incidence of over-age children. The range of ability is likely to increase when selection no longer operates, and the Ministry, which is determined to switch from traditional to modern methods of teaching, will inevitably include group and individual methods which, together with remedial classes and groups, make possible automatic promotion at the early stages of education.

Studies at present include Arabic language, religion, English and

German, mathematics, biology, physics, chemistry, polytechnical subjects, home economics, history and geography, art education, music and physical education. This is a formidable list in view of the fact that pupils are admitted in the sixth grade, which is considered equal to the first grade in a preparatory school, so losing one year of primary education.

Currently the Ministry is thinking of expanding the experiment by establishing another eight-year school in Assiut, where the programmes would be linked to community development. This would be a step in carrying out the expressed policy of making education more meaningful in the governorates, where the social pattern differs in some respects from that found in urban Cairo.

Secondary schools

Egypt provides a very diversified programme of secondary education. This was not always so, since this stage of education was created originally to provide lower grade civil servants during the periods of foreign occupation. At that time it was élitist and fee-paying. Education was in such short supply that to accept any other than a white-collar job would have been unthinkable, especially as the guaranteed post offered security, prestige, and, for the very able, a chance of being sent to a foreign university.

The fortunate 60 per cent of preparatory pupils who continue their education at the state's expense are distributed in the following types of secondary school:

a. the General secondary school, which, after a common first year, divides into two branches: the humanities and the mathematics-science;
b. the Technical secondary school, which specializes in industrial, commercial or agricultural studies;
c. primary teacher-training schools; and
d. training institutions attached to other ministries.

General secondary schools

The majority of candidates opt for these schools, as the final goal of most parents, especially from the middle and upper classes, is a university education for their children, preferably by a direct route. The choice is limited to the cream of the candidates, very few of whom would reject such an opportunity. Within that group, which may exceed in number the capacity of the school, priority is given to pupils under eighteen years of age and those who live in the school district.

The course lasts three years, which, according to English standards, means that a minimum of four years' previous education is needed to be at the secondary level. This would cover the three-year preparatory period (which could be considered as lower secondary) and the sixth primary class, or the fifth primary class from the eight-year school. It is therefore not surprising that, in order to cover the various syllabuses and achieve high standards, pupils are sometimes burdened with so much homework that they complain bitterly of having to work far into the night. Frequent tests and the supervision of anxious parents, as well as coaching ensure that the required assignments are fulfilled.

The first year's courses, common to all pupils, are religion, Arabic language, history and geography, Arabic society, mathematics, biology, chemistry, physics, art education, physical education, military preparation and practical studies. Results of examinations and assessment in about twelve of these subjects is the deciding factor for choosing to spend the next two years studying the humanities or mathematics-science. Humanities students take all of the following subjects: Religion, Arabic language, first foreign language, second foreign language, history, geography, Arab society, sociology, economics, philosophy and psychology, art education, physical education, military preparation and practical studies, besides a choice of one or two subjects at a specialized level. Mathematics-Science students take all of the following subjects: Religion, Arabic language, first foreign language, second foreign language, Arab society, mathematics, biology, chemistry, physics, physical education, military preparation and practical subjects, besides one or two subjects at a specialized level.

These specialized subjects were introduced during the period of 1973–5 without reduction in the number of subjects taken or an extended course. This means that, allowing for physical education, military preparation and practical studies, the student who gets high enough marks enters the university after passing an examination of up to fourteen subjects, which may include two at the specialized level. It could be argued that such a broadly placed education is a better foundation for the university aspirants than the narrow specialization associated with 'A' and 'S' levels of school certificate which occupy the English

TABLE 5 *General secondary education: teachers by qualification and sex*

Year	Qualified		Unqualified		Total qualified	Total teachers	Percentage qualified	Percentage females
	Males	Females	Males	Females				
1963–4	5,689	1,408	2,036	494	7,097	9,627	74	20
1964–5	5,931	1,891	2,038	541	7,822	10,401	75	23
1965–6	6,416	2,137	1,910	529	8,553	10,992	79	24
1966–7	7,087	2,320	1,988	539	9,407	11,934	79	24
1967–8	7,847	2,553	2,096	542	10,400	13,038	80	24
1968–9	8,057	2,674	2,223	592	10,731	13,546	79	24
1969–70								
1970–1	7,972	2,730	2,428	811	10,702	13,941	80	25
1971–2								
1972–3	7,882	3,087	2,680	924	10,969	14,573	75	28
1973–4	7,596	3,099	2,782	1,143	10,695	14,620	73	29

(*Source:* by courtesy of the Ministry of Education, Cairo.)

91

student two or three years prior to his university entry. In practice it means that the university courses must take longer, especially in the sciences. The relative cost of school and university places may be a factor in a future extension of the secondary courses, as well as the man-power wastage involved when the weeding out of less academic students takes place at university level. Perhaps with this in mind, in 1971 the secondary education conference called for an extra secondary year to take the place of the lost year when the eight-year compulsory primary school becomes a reality. This would solve the problem if junior colleges or sixth-form colleges also become part of the system. The problem is how to distribute the academic load with the least expense and the least wastage of manpower.

Technical and vocational secondary schools

These schools, designed to serve industry and agriculture, are an inter-esting development in a country where manual labour has been cheap and plentiful, supplied by an ignorant populace trained to be content to live 'in that state of life in which it had pleased God to call them'. Mabro (1974), had analysed at length the problems of land reform and the development of industry from the Revolution of 1952 until 1972. A very brief summary of a few of his points will supply the background to the comprehensive provision for technical and vocational education which, apart from the literacy campaign, has been the most spectacular educational advance since the Revolution.

According to Mabro, after the rapid expansion of the nineteenth century, agricultural production, concentrated on the export of cotton, did not increase much owing to multiple cropping, the perennial irrigation which damaged the soil and inadequate drainage. He quotes E. R. J. Owen's comment covering the first quarter of the century that 'much of the investment in the agricultural sector was necessary to repair damage already done to soil fertility'. In the 1930s the second heightening of the Aswan barrage and a dam built by Egypt in the Sudan increased water supply and improved its regulation. Increase in crops was accompanied by the establishment of a modern textile industry leading to nearly a tenfold increase in local consumption. This was followed by advances in other industries: Portland cement, chemicals, paper, petroleum goods, industries supported not only by foreigners, according to Mabro, but by Egyptian capitalists. More money was released for education, but not yet for education directly related to industry and agriculture. There was no prestige or government security for the artisan. In the 1950s, according to Qubain (1966), vocational schools were mostly for orphans and destitute children.

Since 1952, the expressed policy has been not only to provide the necessary manpower to modernize existing and serve new industry, agriculture and the army, but also to reduce pressure on general secondary education resulting from the population explosion and the abolition of school fees. Such is the prejudice against manual labour that, given the choice, parents will pay large fees for having their children coached or educated privately rather than see them enter what they consider to be an inferior type of school. As recently as 1970 a research report (Fahmy M.S., 1973), showed that the overwhelming majority of fathers in both rural and urban areas sampled, regardless of income, preferred a general rather than any other type of secondary education for their sons, in spite of propaganda and inducements.

In 1971, the Central Council for Technical Education, established in the previous year, saw as its main task the preparation of long-term plans for developing all kinds of technical education, even including courses in the prestigious general secondary schools, particularly with a view of increasing the number of skilled workers. Part of the plan was the linking of this type of education with the production and services sections of industry so that courses would meet the requirements of specializations. These included chemical industries, electronics and architecture. The system of work in these schools, their status and administration were regulated by a group of ministerial decrees. To cover the cost, the Minister of Education allocated £E 1·5 million for 1973 and, for future projects, £E 2,767,000. Meanwhile, a number of schools in Alexandria, Aswan and other parts of the country were to be changed into technical schools.

There are two types of technical schools: a three-year school for training skilled workers and a five-year school for training technicians. However, if the three-year pupil shows the right aptitude, he may continue his studies and become a technician. Also the five-year pupil theoretically has the opportunity for training in a higher institute or university, although his chances of acceptance are not high at present. Technical education at both levels includes industrial education, agricultural education and commercial education. (Law No. 75: Technical Education for the year 1970)

There is no co-education in technical schools, but the schools are similar in aims, quality, entry requirements and examinations. They are usually chosen by children who fail to get into the general secondary school and without means to get a private education. With attention being drawn to the increasing importance of technical education, it is hoped that these schools will attract some children of higher calibre. This might happen if, for abler pupils, some higher science and mathematics courses were introduced, making possible the Ministry's intentions to open the way to higher education and the university. At this level such courses might be more useful than industrial psychology, for example, which is usually offered at the postgraduate level. At present, students study the following subjects: religion, Arabic language, a foreign language, science and mathematics, vocational fitness, first-aid, grouped under 'General Culture'; scientific principles for vocational and technical subjects and their application; practical vocation and technical subjects. In addition they have workshop drill and field experiences. Whatever the specialization, the course lasts five years.

Industrial secondary schools At present, according to the Ministry reports, the divisions and branches are:
Mechanical engineering division: machine-operating branch
motor car engineering branch
Electricity engineering division: electricity power and network
wire and wireless communications
The three-year courses for skilled labourers include the following branches:
For boys: tractors and agricultural machines
air-conditioning and freezing instruments
ships-motors
fishing: tools and equipment
general upkeep and maintenance of equipment
For girls: fur and leather industries
metal industries
electronic composition
mechanical instruments
beauty and hairdressing
laboratory specialists
clothes – mass production
decoration and arrangement

Agricultural secondary schools There are fifty-two agricultural secondary schools in Egypt, the largest, in Giza, educating 1,200 pupils, including five girls in the first year and more in the other years. Over 70 per cent of them hope to continue studies at an agricultural higher institute. The agricultural courses are general during the first three years, covering horticulture, livestock, milk-production, production of fruit juice (including mango and guava), making yogurt, other agricultural products, flowers, soil analysis, machinery and tropical plants. A mini-chemistry laboratory, equipped by an enterprising teacher, enables the science to be taught with the minimum of outlay. It seems quite clear, however, that, as in many Egyptian educational institutions, standards will not be able to be maintained or improved with the pressure of existing space and equipment. Some kind of compromise between the pursuit of educational democracy and educational excellence appears inevitable in the short term.

At the level of preparing technicians there are two divisions in agricultural education: general agricultural studies, with the purpose of preparing agricultural supervisory helpers, and specialized agricultural studies to prepare technicians for specialized fields. In the latter, students are given opportunities of practical experiences in schools and out-of-school farms and institutions. This is designed to enable the technician to relate school studies to community activities and to see the relevance of scientific theory to specific practical processes. The schedule of study gives a nice balance between general culture, scientific and technical studies with application and practical experience.

At the level of preparing skilled labourers, the branches include general agriculture, production of sugar cane, production of orchards, production of vegetables (each with up-keep of agricultural machines and tractors), animal production and plant production.

Commercial secondary schools These schools, which attract both boys and girls, have a single programme. Subjects studied are religion, Arabic language, first foreign language and translation, second foreign language, accounting, financial and commercial mathematics, applied secretarial work, English and Arabic typing, general knowledge, elected professional subject, economic geography and history, citizenship and physical education.

In general, there is a constant reassessment and modification in all branches of technical education, attention being taken to revision of curricula and textbooks, teacher-training and provision of equipment. The main concern is to link by every possible means, such as student work in community institutions during vacations, the relationship between school studies and factory, workshop and farm.

Diversity of courses at the secondary level is an important achievement in terms of modernization. Freedom of choice at this period of her development is a luxury that Egypt cannot afford, but flexibility is essential if manpower resources are to be fully exploited. In other modern systems of education, rigidity, as expressed in examination systems that determine a child's future at an early age, and training schemes that tie a man to one trade for life, are giving way to the concept of flexibility. Egypt is striving for continuous education but the insufficient overlap between different types of secondary school makes transfer from one type to another impossible, thereby practically excluding the technical child from the chance of getting to a university.

As found in England, parity of esteem between different types of secondary school is difficult to achieve when entry depends on examination success rather than choice, but, if the curricula have a common core, transfer at certain stages becomes possible. Egyptian educators, who have a special difficulty in attracting able students to technical education, are wondering whether the comprehensive secondary school would be an answer to their problem.

Teacher education and practice

The teachers' role in Egypt

Teachers, especially at the lower levels, are the natural target for complaints of the defects of an educational system. They are accused of ignorance, stupidity, lack of sensitivity and professional failure by parents, administrators and the public at large. They are expected to act as professionals in spite of an inadequate education, a too short training, having to teach large classes in the worst available buildings, lack of amenities, low status and low salary. Until these conditions are improved, the primary school teachers, having laid the foundation of learning, see their pupils pass on to other teachers with smaller classes, more amenities, better buildings, higher status and higher pay. Before the 1944 Education Act was passed in England, making necessary the employment of primary school staff to fill the gaps in the secondary schools, and the institution of a basic common salary scale, there was no social contact between the primary teachers who prepared pupils for the secondary schools and the secondary staff who received them.

From the literature, it appears that the Egyptian primary school teacher has not lacked the kind of criticism that should be more justly aimed at a system that regards the primary school as the least important rung of the educational ladder in terms of buildings, equipment, manpower and salaries. It may be years before Egypt is able to support a unified salary scale, post-secondary training and appropriate status for all her teachers, but, particularly during the last five years, there has been a growing awareness of the crucial role of teachers in every sphere of Egyptian development. Since 1972, the teacher's importance has been publicized by the observation of a Teachers' Day each year, beginning with a lesson in each class devoted to explaining to children the role of teachers in bringing up good, educated citizens. Activities include meetings of parents' councils, teachers' committees and the honouring of 'ideal teachers' (five from each governorate in each of four categories), by the Arab Socialist Union, and a final speech-giving ceremony organized by the Teachers' Association, with awards to leading educationalists, the main speech being read on behalf of President Sadat himself. In these speeches over the years, emphasis has been on the teachers' political role, their role in the war effort, in the building of a modern state ('the national edifice') and in 'moulding the Egyptian personality'. Certificates and investment bonds are distributed to successful teachers on these occasions and the profession is promised conditions of service commensurate with the responsibilities it shoulders. To quote a typical message from President Sadat (*Egyptian Gazette*, 2 October 1973),

> While we reap today the fruit of the effort exerted in the field of education since the Revolution, we have to double the struggle for establishing the best educational system . . . which should be capable of realizing our hopes and objectives and coping with local, Arab and international changes. Education must play its full role in the process of building up the contemporary state based on science and faith within the framework of an integrated educational plan which can help us occupy a worthy position in the world. . . . Congratulations on your magnificent national role. Our hearts do encompass you while full of hope and

optimism, for we know that you are fully aware of the greatness of the profession you are practising, a profession whose mention in the holy book of the Q'ran is proof of its greatness. May God guide your steps and peace be upon you.

Such a statement by the head of state is not surprisingly met by increasing opportunity for teachers to express their views with regard not only to professional but to political matters. This is done largely through the Teachers' Syndicate, which meets regularly to discuss professional problems or listen to invited speakers, but also through the Arab Socialist Union on whose educational committee it is represented and which keeps a watching brief on its needs and welfare. When a debate was launched on the desirability or otherwise of adopting a party system of government, it was the teachers who collectively voted for a party system. It is significant that the President thought that their views were sufficiently important to merit an address by himself during the final stages of the debate.

However, teachers, like other key workers, are subject to manpower considerations. They are guaranteed jobs, but the place of employment, transfer and promotion are determined, not by successful application in response to an advertisement, but by unified rules drafted by the Committee of Under-Secretaries and published as ministerial decrees. Thus it was stipulated in 1974 that the co-ordination department in each of the Ministry's sectors should fill the vacancies in any governorate by transference from other governorates to the same posts or corresponding ones. If there were vacancies left, the directorates of education would be entitled to appoint or promote their own employees, provided that, in Cairo and Alexandria, only 10 per cent of the total number of posts were locally filled and the rest through transfers. This policy seems to be aimed at ensuring a fair distribution of available manpower to provide equal educational opportunity, with special safeguards for governorates other than Cairo and Alexandria.

Teacher training

Teacher training has undergone many changes since Boktor (1963) gave details of the tremendous number and variety of institutions engaged in preparing teachers. Also the criticism levelled at the entire educational system by Egyptian experts, administrators and intellectuals in the sixties, reported by Szyliowicz (1973), have been met by vigorous action on the part of the Ministries of Education in the seventies. Teacher training is still piecemeal, as though the teacher of Primary VI class needed no overlap in content or method or knowledge of child development with the teacher of the first preparatory class, but the hierarchy has been reduced and the lowest level of entry raised.

The primary student teacher studies for five years after gaining a preparatory school certificate. In practice the decision to enter the Teachers' Institute implies a rejection for entry to a secondary school, either at the general or technical level, since high-level opportunities for teacher training would be available to successful candidates. Theoretically the first three years in the Institute provide an education equivalent to the general education given in secondary schools, but this seems unlikely at present, as the student is not obliged to sit for the competitive examination before continuing with two years of professional preparation. During this period, which is mainly occupied with methods of teaching the various school subjects and a day's practice every week, where there are the necessary facilities, the students may specialize in one of the following subjects or groups of subjects:

> Arabic language and social studies
> Science, mathematics, home economics (for girls) and
>   agricultural industries (for boys)
> physical education
> art education
> musical education
> nursery and kindergarten teaching

Within the limits imposed by inadequate buildings lacking modern equipment and the entry level, as well as the shortness of the courses, the maximum is being done to turn out teachers able to cope with the traditional-type curricula in an overcrowded classroom. A visit to male and female institutes showed them to be excellent of their kind, staffed by successful teachers or head teachers with invaluable experience and great enthusiasm for their task. Equally important, the students were lively and receptive as a group, giving the impression of growth possibilities in the course of in-service training. Each teaching institute has practising schools attached to it, which, if time allowed and the curricula were less rigid, would be suitable for experimentation as they are less crowded and have some facilities not found in every school.

Although the Ministry of Education is responsible for preparatory and secondary education, the training for teaching for these schools, which takes place at the post-secondary level, is the responsibility of the Minister of Higher Education. Yet teachers in all stages of the educational system in Egypt up to the completion of the secondary stage are engaged by the Ministry of Education, which pays their salaries, promotes and transfers them, as well as providing for their professional growth and in-service training.

In-service training

In-service training originated from the acute shortage of teachers as the various school levels became free of fees and the primary stage lengthened and became legally compulsory. The position was worsened by the decline in the number and output of teachers from 1967 to 1971 at the same time as the population explosion was beginning to contribute to the problem of school accommodation. Before the Revolution, Egyptian leaders had attributed the ills of their country to the failure of public education. Afterwards they pinned their hopes and faith to its rapid increase in quantity and quality: education would solve all their personal and national problems. In the words of Safran (1961), 'Ever since Egypt first became aware of the challenge of modern conditions to traditional ideology, education has been rightly viewed as the most important instrument for accomplishing the necessary re-adjustment.'

To meet the demand, various schemes were adopted for training at all levels, for primary schools, secondary schools and special subjects. Selection for suitability was not essential, since, in spite of all efforts, more than twenty thousand teachers were appointed without training (Sarhan 1974). After the Revolution the Ministry of Education adopted progressively higher standards for teachers at all levels by raising entry requirements and lengthening courses, but was still employing a vast army of untrained teachers who did not reach these standards. In-service training was the answer to this problem, which was accentuated by the lack of sufficient trained teacher-educators. Comprehensive plans were made to supplement training on the job with evening courses, vacation courses and careful inspection. Nevertheless, in 1963, Boktor could write:

> With the exception of occasional refresher courses of a more
> routine nature, there is nothing being done to enrich teachers

culturally and professionally. Books of real value are too expensive to buy, school libraries with a few books and periodicals are locked up most of the time and are beyond the reach of those who want to read. As a result, teachers, on the whole, do not grow. They teach the same thing in the same way and entertain the same ideas and methods to such extent that they become stagnant, plodding along in the same groove from the time that they start teaching until the time they retire.

To get Boktor's gloomy picture into perspective, it is necessary to keep in mind the size of the problem and the limitations imposed by financial and manpower inadequacies. The general training centre at the Ministry of Education was not established until 1955, only three years after the Revolution and only eight years before Boktor make his comment. This is not a very long time for covering the deficiencies of more than twenty thousand untrained teachers, as well as those who received insufficient training. In fact, the centre, as well as those established in the educational zones, catered for the needs of a wide variety of educationalists, including qualifying programmes, refresher courses, courses on new methods of teaching audio-visual aids, schools administration, guidance and special courses leading to promotion.

Although the Ministry is still concerned with 'modern' methods of teaching, an almost impossible achievement at the primary level where large classes prohibit group teaching and no provision is made for the slow and backward, attention is also being given to the quality and personality of the teacher. Obviously the thousands of inadequately educated teachers cannot be replaced, so why not give them the opportunity for self-improvement throughout their working life? In-service training is now viewed not just in terms of minimal qualifications, but as a continuous process linked with the concept of life-long education. Future candidates will, it is hoped, be in sufficient numbers for selective processes to be used. Says the Ministry,

> We have a well-organized teacher-training system which provides for a first accelerated training stage, followed by in-service training cycles. We have laws and regulations which regulate training cycles for teachers and other personnel in education. Professional growth and promotion depend mainly on the programmes of in-service training which teachers and educators attend.

The co-operative process whereby educational authorities, universities, teacher-training institutions and schools share in-service training of teachers is matched by the part played by industrial enterprises and socio-cultural institutions in programmes for technical school teachers. All personnel in education are covered: teachers, supervisors, administrators and non-professional staff. However, whereas all this activity is covered by a law of 1966, entitled 'Recommendation of the Status of Teachers', which provides that 'authorities should promote the establishment of a wide system of in-service education free to all teachers', further training for teacher-educators is regulated by the laws of colleges of education and universities, administered by the Ministry of Higher Education.

The changing role of the teacher, its influence on preparation for the profession and on in-service training

The Egyptian government was, with other member states, invited to participate in the 35th session of the International Conference on Education which was held in Geneva in September 1975. In answer to an enquiry from the UNESCO International Bureau of Education, a paper with the title above was prepared, the term 'teacher' covering 'all those persons in formal education who are responsible for and directly involved in the education of pupils in both public and private schools up to the completion of the secondary stage of education'. Owing to the shared responsibility for teacher training between the Ministries of Education and Higher Education two reports were prepared covering primary and post-primary teachers.

The primary section covers seventy-nine points which clarify the Ministry of Education's deep concern for teacher training at all stages. It can be regarded partly as a record of achievement and partly as a statement of intent, a blueprint for future development. The following is a summary of some of the points, which range from philosophical aims and objectives to declared policies already in practice or planned for the future. The headings are those used in the paper, and the brackets enclose comments by me.

The changing role of the teacher The teacher is formally concerned and intentionally prepared to educate the young with the purpose of bringing them up to live effectively in a society which is putting constant pressure on education to keep pace with all the recent changes and developments in Egyptian society. This involves a continual revision of aims and objectives requiring the teacher to perform new duties and assume new functions, to be a guide and leader rather than a transmitter of knowledge and bearer of information. His role will depend not only on the size of the school but the type of the community: he will need to adjust to new methods, new syllabuses and increasing facilities.

The relationship between changes in society and the role of teachers In Egypt social and economic changes have directly influenced the changing role of the teacher, especially the development of science and technology and the increased rate at which new knowledge is produced and circulated. It is necessary to prepare well-informed teachers capable of self-development and the pursuit of a life-long education.

Changes in Egyptian society which recently have affected the teacher's role
1. *Rapid increase in population* which raises the number of children who should be in school. Although only 75 per cent achieve compulsory education, the great pressure on school buildings and facilities leads to over-crowded classrooms and working in shifts. Accordingly teachers must cope with large groups needing individual attention, diverse activities and evaluation of growth and development.

2. *Economic and social development* which during the last two decades has been planned with specific aims to raise the standard of living and provide a decent life for every citizen. Accompanying social changes include urbanization and the drift from the villages to big towns and cities, creating demand for new educational opportunities. Thus schools and teachers must cater for pupils from widely different social and economic backgrounds and traditions. Teachers must study the environment in order to help parents understand their children and solve their problems. Their tasks cover parent education ranging from informal meetings and talks on social and religious occasions, such as preaching in the mosque and church, to formal teaching of adults in occupational and literacy classes.

3. *Changes in educational aims and objectives* relate to the quantitative expansion of education in Egypt, including universal education up to the age of twelve by 1980 and thence to fourteen or fifteen, demands to be accompanied by qualitative improvements in curricula, methods of teaching and the development of suitable aids and materials for learning. For this purpose a national budget has enabled the National

Council for Education, Technology and Research to make a plan for the school year 1975/6. (Here follows the one-room school project above.) Priority is being given to rural areas in order to remedy regional disparities and discrepancies. Pupils in deserts and remote areas will get school meals and transport, while their teachers will enjoy a 25 per cent pay increase and earlier promotion. Preparatory (intermediate) schools provide opportunities for the pupils to be guided towards the right kind of secondary education or transfer to a vocational centre in which they are prepared for employment. The whole educational system aims at preparing the young to participate effectively in re-shaping society and to contribute in the movement of reconstruction and development. The teacher is now considered to be the agent of innovation and change in his community.

4. *Changes in the structure of the education system* (Most points have already been discussed.) Large schools in big towns, cities and industrial areas need certain educational services such as counselling guidance and health care, including meal facilities and better sanitary conditions for pupils. Such schools can extend their services and offer their buildings to the community, the school staff providing personnel to help with, for example, family planning, agricultural affairs and difficulties in small industries. (This pre-supposes that the present over-use of buildings for the shift system is ameliorated.)

5. *Changes in content and method of education* (Most of this section is discussed elsewhere in the document.) The reviewing and up-dating of the contents of courses is required as well as the introduction of new courses, such as new mathematics, popular education and contemporary problems. 'Discovery' methods of teaching will help children leaving school at twelve years to develop their knowledge through self-learning. As leader of the community, the teacher, in his/her role as counsellor and guide, plans for all the activities of the children inside and outside the classroom.

6. *Diversification and integration of teaching personnel* Large classes add to the many functions of the teacher already mentioned, including playground supervision, clerical work, and grade records. The help is needed and sometimes provided of other personnel outside the teaching profession, such as doctors, nurses, social workers, secretaries, guidance personnel, specialists, vocational trainers and technicians, all working in close relationship as a team. These are augmented by part-time and temporary teachers.

7. *The need for improved status of teachers* whose roles and responsibilities should be matched with raising the level of their preparation and improving their social and economic status. Unfortunately primary teachers are still considered an inferior category. However, their status and career prospects have improved, as has that of vocational and technical teachers. Career advancement within the teaching profession is parallel to that of other professionals employed by the government. The same level of preparation leads to the same level of advancement. Young men now find advantages in joining the profession.

8. *The implication of the changing role for pre-service and in-service training of teachers* (The most interesting part of this section is that, in the selection of future teachers the academic standard is held to be over-stressed. By 'academic standard' is meant 'examination results' since these are decisive in deciding at what level, if any, a student will be trained. It could be argued that the over-crowding of the syllabuses, often with subjects not usefully studied at the school level, leads to a cramming of textbook information that militates against high academic standards, which imply a creative approach to learning, an ability to evaluate and relate information.)

9. *The problem of teacher-educators* The Ministry recognizes that the provision of teacher-educators of high quality is a key problem in teacher education. The standards are set, but at present very difficult to apply, owing to the shortage of suitable candidates. The Ministry is doing its best in the circumstances, trying to involve the staffs of the training institutions in research in the fields of curricula and method. Special programmes for training educators are carried out by the joint efforts of the universities and the Ministry. Before appointment for training primary school teachers they need at least six or seven years of successful teaching at preparatory and secondary schools (notably none in primary schools!) plus a university degree and diploma in education. They receive 25 per cent more salary than colleagues working in other institutions. The Ministry concedes that not only the problems of shortage in staff but the question of where and how to qualify and train such personnel have not been solved. (It appears that five years' minimum experience in primary schools with the freedom to experiment with modern methods, group and individual teaching, which can be done, even with classes of forty children, remedial teaching of reading and number and an accent on courses in child development would be more valuable than experience in subject teaching at preparatory and

secondary level. During the period when attempts were being made to introduce the modern approach into the formal, subject-orientated, English primary-school system, 'discovery' courses were arranged by the Ministry of Education, attended by groups of inspectors and teacher-educators who temporarily became 'primary school pupils'. The situation was not without comedy, especially when dignified officials, entering into the spirit of the venture, tried to 'express themselves' by distorting their bodies in response to various kinds of music, and toured London underground stations to gather information for an environmental project, as an alternative to watching coots for hours by a Wimbledon pond. However, the message was communicated: all were agreed that to be not merely instructed but educated involved active participation in the information-gathering process, opportunity for creativity and a closer understanding between teacher and pupil.)

10. *The need for continuing training* This section of the paper consists of a summary of the needs and provisions for the initial and continuous process of education for Egyptian teachers with emphasis on the complexity of the problems and the hope that clarification would result from the international conference on education, for which the paper was prepared.

Adult education

Egypt has accepted the opinion of the Third Regional Conference of ministers of education and ministers responsible for economic planning in the Arab States, held in Marrakesh (January 1970) that

> Efforts on behalf of adult education and literacy based on the new concept of 'functional literacy' and 'life-long education' and conducted by modern methods and techniques should be reinforced and extended as an important and integral part of national plans for educational development.

Until 1946, adult education was provided only by agencies outside the government, but in that year the idea of 'popular culture' was born, and government 'Institutions of Popular Culture' were opened initially in Cairo and Alexandria, but later in all the governorates. At first the concept of a popular university was favoured, but perhaps under Russian influence, the idea of 'culture palaces' emerged. The government, which since 1952 has always been willing to experiment with educational schemes from overseas, East or West, has now had time to assess her needs in adult education, both in terms of formal education and the dissemination of her culture. The importance attached to both these aspects is seen in her mobilization of every ministry, the Arab Socialist Union, trade unions and all the corporations in the public sector to take part in the literacy campaign, and the development of a cultural policy by the Ministry of Culture, which not only integrates the work of all the other cultural agencies, but initiates its own research and acts as a guardian for the conservation of Egypt's rich cultural heritage.

Literacy

Illiteracy is the legacy of a feudal social system associated with an agricultural economy supported by cheap labour. In a population which increases by about a million babies in a year, where education is compulsory only in the legal sense, and 'dropping out' during the early stages is tolerated owing to the large classes, while poverty and ignorance fortified by tradition makes the education of females a wasteful luxury, in some people's eyes, it is not easy to gather reliable statistics. The absolute number may increase while the percentage decreases so that, unless the basis of comparison is very clear, the fact, for example, that it is estimated that there were 7·3 million of illiterates in 1907 but 12·6 million in 1960 may be misleading. It is not surprising that, as Magdi Wahba (1972) states, 'Periodically since 1925, illiteracy has been regarded with a mixture of despair and frantic activity.' The latter, which increased in momentum in the wake of the Revolution, with its ideal of social democracy, became less frantic and more efficiently organized with the passing of the new literacy law of 1970 (No. 67) which tried to avoid the difficulties of the previous law (No. 110, 1940) by defining illiteracy and classifying illiterates. An illiterate was held to be a male or female between the ages of eight and forty-five years not participating in organized study and who had not previously reached the level of the fourth primary class.

For the purpose of the campaign, illiterates were divided into two groups, the first of which were to be given priority. These were about a million workers in the public sector of industry and government departments. The intention was to have the sector of the population literate by 1976. Each organization was split up into units so that responsibility could be shared, although the organization was legally obliged to give facilities and was answerable to the government. This part of the campaign was financed by profits made from industry and the budgets of various government departments. All workers were informed that their promotion depended on acquiring a literacy certificate by 1976. The response from both teachers and taught has been enthusiastic and the campaign is deemed to be highly successful in achieving its object.

The second, larger group is the population at large, a much tougher proposition, since it includes fellahin (peasant) women with large families and no motivation or time to change their way of life, often with husbands who are only interested in getting more money. In 1970, a Higher Adult Education Council was formed under the chairmanship of the Minister of Education to represent ministries concerned with production and services, including vocational trainee organizations, labour unions, the Arab Socialist Union Central Committee and the ASU Feminist Committee. Its task was to devise an integrated national plan to be supervised by central authority under the auspices of political organizations. President Sadat himself charged the local branches of the ASU with the duty of exposing the dangers of illiteracy and of co-operating in the task of its elimination. The ASU, whose main function is to watch over the welfare and interests of the masses, regarded the campaign as a vital humanitarian and social scheme. By 1972, through the organizations in the governorates, the ASU had made lists of the level of literacy of all the members of the families in the various neighbourhoods. Meanwhile the Higher Council in Cairo approved the establishment of a similar Higher Council for the Education of Adults and elimination of illiteracy in every governorate. No organization escaped involvement, since these councils, chaired by the governor, included the ASU secretary, five members of the People's Council, representatives from the Teachers' Association, workers' Trade Unions Federation, the Ministries of Education, Higher Education, Social Affairs, Manpower, Culture, Treasury, Public Health, Industry, Land Reclamation and Interior, the Director of Statistics and the Director of Education in the governorate.

It is not proposed to itemize all the activities and contributions of this vast army of officers in a war against illiteracy only second in importance to the war to regain Egypt's lost territory. A few examples will illustrate the single-minded response of the country's leaders in all walks of life to the challenge of the Minister of Education, who said in 1970,

> If we could live any kind of life with this stigma in the past, we
> cannot occupy our position in today's world – the world of
> modern science, advanced technology and the tremendous
> intellectual and political conflicts – without eradicating illiteracy
> and arming the people of our Arab nation with the weapons of
> the age.

By 1972 the agricultural workers' trade union were already carrying
out a year's plan for combating illiteracy among agricultural labourers
in 1,500 villages. Activities had begun in 420 villages in Dakahlia, 443
villages in Sharkia, 30 villages in Menufia and 60 villages in Minia,
Fayoum and Beni Suef. Teachers in the villages who had attended
fifteen-day training courses for teaching adults, participated with the
co-operation of one labour instructor for every five teachers. In 1973
(and since) the Cairo governorate has arranged for university students
to work as teachers in literacy campaigns during their summer vacation.
Two students were entrusted with the job of teaching each of the
twenty-four classes in Cairo. In the same year the governorate of
Menufia decided to open 245 anti-illiteracy classes in the squares and
cities, with the aim of educating half a million illiterates in the governorate. Also Law 76 (1973) made it compulsory for all graduates from the
university or an institute of higher education who do not join the army
to spend a year in community service, including literacy teaching, after
training for one month in classes organized by the Ministry of Education all over the country. Although help has also been sought from
private organizations and individuals, the main burden of the campaign
falls on the teacher, whose role was decided at a meeting of the Higher
Council in 1972. Financial and moral incentives were to be offered in
the form of a premium of £E 1 for every pupil to every teacher whose
pupils distinguished themselves in their studies, priority in promotion
and secondment to Arab countries and the possibility of being honoured
on Science Day, as well as a medal if they instructed ten persons outside
the literacy classes. There were also to be sanctions for 'negligent'
teachers who would be barred from secondments abroad and from any
privileges such as teaching at the services classes, where teachers receive
premiums for extra work, and, on top of this, a cut of one month's
salary by 50 per cent if his pupils had poor results owing to his negligence. (*Egyptian Gazette* 29 March 1972).

In her campaign, Egypt has been greatly helped by the Sers el-Layyan Educational Centre funded by UNESCO to handle educational problems confronted by Arab countries in general. Founded in Egypt, which was one of the first countries in the Middle East to face the literacy problem, on a recommendation of the first conference of education and Ministers responsible for economic planning in the Arab states (Beirut 1960), it aims at studying, analysing and finding solutions for educational problems within the framework of overall national development planning.

In the field of literacy, Sers el-Layyan has much to offer. Regular conferences are attended not only by delegates from Arab countries, but by workers in the field from any part of the world, who exchange experiences and have access to the latest audio-visual aids. It is here that experts are trained for three months in order to be able to organize courses for teachers in their own countries. Demonstrations are arranged in the local villages, curricula discussed and a vast amount of literature printed and distributed, including textbooks.

To pinpoint the urgency of the literacy problem, 1971 was selected as Arab Literacy Year. Egypt has not only received but contributed much to the value of the Centre. Its Director at the time of writing was an Egyptian and it was the Egyptian Minister of Education who stressed that the new message of the Centre lay in providing all the Arab countries with leaders of functional education, to turn literacy projects from mere teaching of the three R's to linking education with production and public services. In practice this meant providing functional literacy classes, that is, training people to read in their own specialization, whether it be in the home, the factory or on the land. Thus, reading would become part of the process of learning technical skills, giving an incentive to increase production and linking literacy to economic development. In Egypt the two main projects for functional literacy were carried out experimentally in the clothing industry at Mahala and the sugar factory at Howamdya. It was an expensive venture because a whole series of books had to be printed which included technical language not suitable for general use in classes. Also it was necessary to find personnel trained for teaching who were also able to train workers in the skills required for their jobs. However, the principle of relevance to real life and interests found expression in the publication of different sets of readers for use in an industrial or rural environment and with bedouins or women. More recently the Centre is experimenting with lesson courses on cassettes which can be used without the presence of a teacher in the home or at work, in conjunction with graded readers. These appear to be very successful both because of the novelty and the pleasure derived from knowledge of results. Their usefulness in village classes appears to be less appropriate or effective: the pupil does not get the benefit of a stimulating class lesson or of individual programmed learning.

Fundamental and workers' education

Experience has shown that literacy classes do not fulfil the educational needs of adults whether they are 'drop-outs' from primary schools or people who have never been to school. The reading lesson is now part of a group of lessons which may include practical subjects like sewing for women and sport for men. The search for incentives is particularly important for women who form the largest group of illiterates. Many projects are under discussion or being tried out. An example is the 'Productive Family Project' emanating from the Ministry of Social Affairs. Women first have dressmaking lessons at a centre, then, when they are proficient, are given material to use in their own homes. After learning to master a sewing machine, they are given one to take home. Instruction continues in the Centre which distributes and sells their products. Another suggestion is to license pedlars in the streets, the licence being a reward for gaining a literacy certificate.

Egypt is gradually increasing adult education at every level in accordance with the principle of continuous education. Evening classes range from extra-mural university courses to vocational-technical evening schools. Mosques, churches and clubs are encouraged to organize voluntary classes and increasing use is made of radio and television, as well as correspondence courses. There are also part-time courses for workers at different levels. An excellent example was seen in Cairo, where the Higher Institute for Co-operatives was visited. The 15,000 students who occupied the building in shifts for a four-year period were being taught largely by visiting professors from Ain Shams University, who only accepted expenses. The curriculum included religion, commercial and managerial studies, accountancy and business administration, the main aim being to supply suitable leaders for the 8,000 co-operatives throughout the country. Currently the fourth-year students were making a survey of the governorates to evaluate the co-operative movement in Egypt.

On the other hand, the important function of clubs in adult education can be illustrated by the activities of the Science Clubs, which participated towards the end of 1976 in the sixth international conference for science clubs sponsored by *al-Ahram* newspaper in collaboration with an international club body. These clubs, which are on the increase, help to make science understandable to the ordinary citizen, helping him to keep pace with the modern world.

TABLE 6 *Comparative statistics for the teaching staff in the general and technical education in 1973–74 comparing with 1974–75*

Stage of education	School year and (+) or (−)	Male	Female	Total
Primary	73/4	42,151	51,351	93,502
	74/5	49,183	51,718	100,901
	Difference	+7,032	+ 367	+7,399
	Percentage	+ 1·67	+ 0·7	+ 7·9
Preparatory	73/4	19,108	9,809	28,917
	74/5	20,242	10,673	30,915
	Difference	+1,134	+ 864	+1,998
	Percentage	+ 5·9	+ 8·8	+ 6·9
General secondary	73/4	10,378	4,242	14,620
	74/5	10,859	4,306	15,165
	Difference	+ 481	+ 64	+ 545
	Percentage	+ 4·6	+ 1·5	+ 3·7
Technical secondary	73/4	13,748	3,017	16,765
	74/5	17,363	3,354	20,717
	Difference	+3,615	+ 337	+3,952
	Percentage	+ 26·3	+11·2	+ 23·6
Teacher training schools	73/4	1,422	960	2,382
	74/5	1,603	1,070	2,673
	Difference	+ 181	+ 110	+ 291
	Percentage	+ 12·7	+11·5	+ 12·2

(*Source:* by courtesy of the Ministry of Education, Cairo.)

5

Higher education

The role of higher education in finding solutions to Egypt's problems

The following pages will indicate that higher education in Egypt faces many problems but also that they receive prior attention from the government which looks to its intelligentsia for solutions to all the obstacles in the path of its rapid transition from an agricultural to an industrial state, independent and viable.

Politicians and educators alike stress the vital role to be played by the universities in building up the modern state. President Sadat himself set the pattern for public speeches on this subject, when, in 1971, he spoke of his concept of the university and its mission:

> The university is a complete unit with its professors, students and workers who seek the shortest way to the building up of the modern state. . . . Our universities have to work out their regulations in the manner that suits them best for the sake of the greater objective of building the state of technology and faith, so that every citizen may feel his true, active and realistic participation. . . . University men have a great trust placed in their hands for the coming generations. . . . Change has already begun, and you are entrusted with preparing this generation. . . . Every one of us should have his equal share of responsibilities so as to achieve what we want for our homeland, security, safety and welfare for every citizen and the realization of all our dreams and aspirations.

Sadat's Cromwellian approach ('Trust in God and keep your powder dry') is not just rhetoric; the Egyptian 'Utopia' is to be built on a base of science and technology which can only be taught at the required level in the universities and institutes of higher education, which are also the sources of the manpower vital to its achievement.

The scope of higher education

Higher education in Egypt is in the process of expansion and re-organization both with reference to administration (see Chapter 3), entry requirements, rationalization of subjects offered by the different universities, balance of provision for academic and applied courses and geographical distribution of institutions. Basically the classification includes courses provided at a post-secondary level, whether they take place in a higher institute, college or university, thus excluding at present the secondary teacher training schools which draw their students at the preparatory (middle) school level, combining secondary level teaching with professional training. Theoretically these students study for two years at a post-secondary level, but it is unlikely that their academic level at the end of their first three years would qualify them for entrance to a university if they so desired.

TABLE 7 *Comparative statistics for the students who were registered in the faculties, higher institutes and training institutes for commercial and industrial technical (73/4–74/5)*

Stage	1973/74			1974/75		
	Male	Female	Total	Male	Female	Total
The four universities	—	—	232,448	—	—	268,280
The higher institutes affiliated to the Ministry	31,426	11,500	42,926	36,074	13,613	49,687
The higher institutes not affiliated to the Ministry	20,717	7,883	28,600	—	—	—
The training institutes for commercial technical	10,431	6,527	16,958	—	—	19,570
The training institutes for industrial technical	—	—	8,733	—	—	10,446

(*Source:* by courtesy of the Ministry of Education, Cairo.)

According to Qubain, in 1966 there were four state universities (Cairo, Alexandria, Ain Shams, Assiut) and about forty independent state colleges and higher institutes besides the religious university of al-Azhar and the American University in Cairo, which is a private enterprise. Expansion has been rapid in the last ten years: the 1976 review of the Supreme Council of Universities speaks of eight universities in addition to al-Azhar and the American University (now recognized by the Egyptian government), the new additions being Tanta, Zagazig, Mansoura and Helwan. These eight comprise one hundred and five faculties and institutions. Of the new universities, three had been branches of older universities, while Helwan is a technological university incorporating higher institutes of technology. Thus they are an expression of the two main trends in higher education; to provide universities in the governorates to relieve the congestion in the older cities while providing courses relevant to local needs, and to up-grade technical education by making the higher technical institutes part of the university system.

Scientific planning, research and organizations

No account of higher education in Egypt whether in universities or institutes makes sense unless viewed in the context of scientific planning and research. Until recently, it was a free-for-all provision, turning out graduates as on an assembly line in far greater numbers than could ever be absorbed in appropriate occupations, and taking up far more than its share of the national budget. In the last few years, Egypt's determination to harness all her resources, including manpower, to transform herself into an efficient, modern, industrial state, is becoming effective; expansion in higher education is still taking place, but at least it is now subject to decisions based on overall planning and research into the country's needs. It needs research not for the sake of adding to the number of PhDs in the country, but for helping to solve the problems that beset industry, agriculture, medicine and other aspects of life in Egypt itself. For example, in 1973 the Minister of Agriculture's seminar on 'Cotton marketing today' needed scholars able to discuss scientific research papers on modern trends in cotton marketing and export and scientific solutions for related problems. The new aluminium complex at Naa Hamady, the project for the development of Safaga Port on the Red Sea, the mine design centre for handling mining affairs in Egypt, including the construction of roads, transport and housing projects related to mining, the new industrial city to be constructed west of Alexandria and all the other projects in hand demand planning at every stage based on scientific research, its discussion and assessment.

Since the Revolution, planning and research have been so closely related that the expansion of the former has almost implied expansion of facilities for the latter. The Supreme Science Council founded in 1956 was concerned with scientific policy whose functions and objectives were defined in Law No. 5. These were:

1. the progress and development of scientific activities, norms and standards;
2. making surveys of the needs for specialists and devising schemes for meeting these needs;
3. keeping track of the progress of science throughout the world and creating facilities for Egyptian scientific workers;
4. organizing on unified criteria the assessment of grants and awards for stimulating research, both pure and applied. (Cited in Qubain, 1966)

In the same year national planning in Egypt was started by the National Planning Committee which was founded as an advisory body to the President of the Republic. Its terms of reference were:

1. the study and preparation of national, comprehensive plans for economic and social development with a follow-up and evaluation;
2. studying the general economic and social course of development in the years before 1960, using the statistical and recorded information available;
3. to translate the directives of national planning, as formulated by the political authorities, into action at the national and regional level. (Imam Selim, Under Secretary for Planning)

Both these bodies had advisory functions only and both were directly responsible to the President. The National Planning Committee became the Ministry of National Planning, split into twelve main divisions composed of experts and researchers with the task of keeping the Ministry informed of the situation in their specific fields. According to Selim, there are also many study groups attached for analysing and appraising developmental projects, preparing records showing the year-to-year activities of the different sectors of the economy and making a continuous study of the structure of the economy in the past and as projected. Meanwhile the Council for Scientific Research was abolished by the Ministry of Scientific Research, established in 1961, and eight specialized scientific councils developed its functions. A further development came with the creation of the Academy of Scientific Research and Technology in 1971, now the centre of scientific research in Egypt, carried out in the institutes attached to it. These include specialized research institutes, such as the Atomic Energy Organization and the main research organization in Egypt, the National Research Centre.

According to Moussa (1974), the president of the National Research Centre, the main functions of the Academy are:

1. the support of scientific research and the application of modern technology in all fields included in the programme of economic and social development;
2. the formulation of the policies which ensure the linking at a national level of the scientific and technological organizations with the principal trends of the scientific and technological research which serve the national development plans;
3. the formulation and co-ordination of research projects related to national problems, financing them and following up their execution;
4. co-ordination of the major research projects affecting the national economic and social plans, which are executed in the different institutes or departments;
5. participation in the study of the scientific and technological aspects of the major development projects, and, when necessary, recommending the establishment of new research institutes;
6. encouraging basic research as a means of building up research personnel, and supporting research schools working in the modern fields of science;
7. dissemination of information concerning the possibilities of exchange in international modern technologies;
8. participation in the development of science curricula;
9. developing incentives for scientific workers;
10. organization of scientific publications and the popularization of science;
11. supporting scientific societies and encouragement of holding scientific conferences;
12. developing international relations.

Two years after the foundation of the Academy, Dr Abdul Aziz Hegazy, Deputy Prime Minister and Minister of Finance, Economy and Foreign Trade, speaking at the first conference held in Egypt by the Central Agency for Organization and Administration, on the organization of scientific research, reminded his listeners that it was not an end in itself, but a means to an end: the objectives of scientific research must first be defined and a national strategy should be drawn up for scientific research priorities. He stressed that human and material resources should be properly used to serve the targets of economic and social development and that the best remedies for loss and waste in all sectors should be found through scientific research. He gave us an example that the scientific research on waste in the wheat crop as a result of bad storing had shown that the loss amounted to £E 7,000,000 a year and that this could be avoided in the future by establishing stores at a cost of £E 35,000,000. Stressing the importance of scientific documentation, he called for a national library or scientific documentation centre to help overcome the problem of financial shortage.

The Academy had begun its work by making a survey of the research conducted in Egypt during the previous ten years as well as drawing up lists of names of scientific researchers, to be circulated among the various departments of scientific research. Its first director, Dr Mustafa Kamal Tolba, and the Academic Board included in their first plan of scientific research such basic issues as the problem of lost and wasted resources, the rebuilding of villages, the association of rural electrification with environmental pollution, family planning and scientific publications.

The universities

Organization

The organization of universities is controlled by Law No. 49 of 1972 and subsequent adjustments made annually. The following is a summary.

Under the general administration of the Supreme Council of Universities, each university is internally governed by a university board with a president at the head, a deputy head for educational affairs and students, a deputy head for higher education and research, a deputy head for branch affairs and a chairman for university internal affairs. Colleges are organized by a board chaired by the head, a deputy head and a college scientific council, while faculties have a similar structure. (It may be noted that there is a scientific council at every level.)

Law No. 49 covers hundreds of items and sub-items concerned with the affairs of members of the teaching board, teachers and assistants; teaching, examinations, student affairs, higher education and research (general laws, conditions of acceptance for BA and BSc degrees, course work, examinations and transfer); higher studies; attendance, training and coaching and general lectures; student services; scientific degrees and diplomas granted by the universities; discipline; and the financial system. A full coverage is not possible here, so a few items have been selected from the original document, followed by important amendments since 1972. A short account of the main universities will then be followed by more details of two of the largest universities, Cairo and Ain Shams. Finally, a few of the faculties are described in more detail.

The range of university studies is shown in the list of faculties (sometimes called colleges or institutes) which are entitled to award degrees and diplomas. Some can be found in all universities while others, as indicated, are attached to a particular university. The order is taken from Law No. 49.

1. Art faculties
2. Law faculties
3. Commerce faculties
4. Science
5. Medicine
   (a) Faculty of medicine
   (b) Higher institute for nursing
6. Dentistry
7. Pharmacy
8. Engineering
9. Agriculture
10. Veterinary agriculture
11. Teacher training
12. Economics/political science (Cairo University)
13. Arabic language and Islamic studies (Dar el-Uloum), i.e. 'House of Sciences'
14. Mass communication and journalism
15. Faculty of antiquities
16. Institute of African studies and research (Cairo University)
17. Institute of statistical studies and research (Cairo University)

18. Institute of cancer (Cairo University)
19. Higher institute of community health (Alexandria University)
20. Institute of medical research (Alexandria University)
21. Girls' college Ain Shams (most faculties represented)
22. Linguistic faculty (Ain Shams)

General rules are laid down for the handling of university finances, including the keeping of accounts, records of purchases, insurance and expenditure on scholarships and awards of various kinds, but an allocation for the year having been made by the Ministry of Finance, the university, advised by its various committees, is free to make its own financial decisions.

Entry to Egyptian universities is based on the results of the secondary school certificate for the current year. As more than 100,000 students are involved, acceptances are dealt with in stages. In 1975, for example, 18,000 students (approximately) were admitted during the first stage, leaving about 90,000 students to be distributed during the remaining stages. Minimum marks for admission are announced by the Ministry of Higher Education at each stage, after which those who qualify may submit an application to an admission office. In 1975, for example, the minimum total of marks for first stage admissions into universities and higher institutes was set at 320 marks for the scientific section and 195 marks for the literature section, representing the original total mark plus the mark achieved for advanced level answers. Out of the 18,000 students of both sexes qualifying, about 11,600 were from the science section and the rest from the literature section. It will be seen that there is a marked difference in the standards required for scientific and arts courses and that most able students elect to study sciences at the secondary stage. Candidates holding equivalent certificates receive a different treatment, their total marks having to be 36·5 per cent for the scientific section and 69·6 per cent for the literary section. The scientific bias is again shown in the distribution of places by faculty. In 1975 101 faculties and institutes admitted both specializations, 100 admitted only holders of the scientific certificate, while only 2, namely Dar el-Uloum and al-Azhar literary departments, admitted the literary section only. Naturally the first-stage applicants take all the available places for prestige subjects so that choice becomes more and more limited for those admitted in the subsequent stages. For example, in 1975, first-stage students on the science side took all the places available in the faculties of medicine, pharmacy and dentistry, while those from the literary section took all the vacancies in the faculties of economics and political science, mass communication and commerce at Cairo, Ain Shams and Tanta (external) Universities and the Higher Institute for Foreign Trade, as well as the faculties of art at Zagazig and education at Mansoura. By the time the fourth stage is reached, vacancies are being filled in agricultural institutes, technical institutes, higher physical training institutes, technical training institutes, specialized institutes and al-Azhar University.

With so much of the daily routine of university life being subjected to legal decisions, amendments to Law No. 49 (1972) are largely a tidying-up process; for example, Item 139 (Law No. 54, 1973) concerning the qualifications of university assistants, states that all contradictory items in Law No. 49 are to be cancelled and that the new law is to be published in official newspapers and to become effective upon publication. Other adjustments are also concerned with the conditions of service of teachers in the universities. In this matter, Egypt is much stricter than many countries, showing a great anxiety to maintain high standards of scholarship. Thus a PhD degree is a prerequisite for a teaching appointment and the training of university teachers a matter of concern. Law No. 11 (1974) states that to be appointed as a professor the person should have occupied the post of assistant professor at a university subject to Law No. 49 (i.e. one of the state universities) for at least five years and should have had his PhD for at least ten years and his BA or equivalent for at least eighteen years. At the other end of the scale, professors who have reached the retirement age (sixty) may remain as sabbatical professors of personal status until the age of sixty-five unless they do not ask to stay on. This period is not considered for pension, but they receive a payment equivalent to the difference between salary and pension plus the pension. Reflecting the shortage of senior professors, the Minister of Higher Education may even, if a chairman of a department agrees, appoint to a vacant post a professor in the 'sabbatical' category above, after he has passed the age of sixty-five years (Law No. 83, 1974). Within two months it was seen to be necessary to make even further concessions, so Law No. 120 (1974) shows willingness to appoint assistant professors lacking five years' previous experience, reduces the period of eighteen years from BA to thirteen years, and from PhD to five years if the post has been advertised in a regional newspaper, and, if the vacancy is for a professor, requires an advertisement in another regional university.

Other adjustments are concerned with the establishments of new universities from existing colleges. For example, Law No. 18 (1974) formed the Zagazig branch of Ain Shams University, while Law No. 70 (1975) is wholly concerned with the organization of the new technological University of Helwan. A motion from the President of the Republic would be needed to determine the locations of the colleges and institutes of higher education which would form the core of this university, as well as the technical institutes and colleges which the university might establish in the future. Meanwhile, members of the teaching staff, assistant professors and assistants of the colleges and institutes involved whose qualifications did not fulfil the requirements of Law No. 49 (1972) at the time of issue of Law No. 70, were given seven years in which to qualify. Otherwise they would be transferred to other posts in the general structure equivalent to the posts held, according to a motion from the Minister of Higher Education, after the University Board's recommendation. The university head and deputy heads should have filled the posts of professors for at least five years at these colleges and institutes of higher education, but the Minister of Higher Education would assume the role of head of the university until the administrative and financial bodies had been established within the period of time ending in December 1975. Finally, BA degrees or their equivalent given by the university would have the status of other university degrees.

The motion mentioned above finally came from the Prime Minister, (No. 924, 1975). Details are given both as an example of re-organization adopted by Egypt in her attempt to attract high-grade students to technical and technological education, and to highlight the importance of Helwan University as the first technological university in Egypt, which in time is likely to be the focus of technological education in the Arab world. As the instructions to implement this motion were not issued to the Minister of Higher Education until October of 1975, it must be assumed that work is still going on in the various colleges and institutes while adjustments are in progress at the administrative level. The University of Helwan is to consist of:

Faculties of technology at Helwan and Mataria;
Faculty of agricultural sciences at Mushtuhur;
Cairo faculties of fine art, commerce and business administration, social services, tourism and hotel management, physical training for

boys, physical training for girls, musical training, art training, home economics, postal studies;
Alexandria faculties of fine arts, physical training for boys, physical training for girls, cotton sciences.

The same motion instructs the Minister of Higher Education to implement the incorporation of the High Institute of Nursing and the Institute of Physiotherapy into the faculty of medicine at Cairo University, the faculty of engineering and technology to the Elmenya branch of Assiut University, the faculty of engineering and technology at Shabin el-Koum to Tanta University and the faculty of electronical engineering at Menouf to Tanta University. A further motion of the Prime Minister (No. 376, 1973) is followed up by a reminder in 1976 to the Minister of Higher Education that the plan to incorporate the Technological Institute of Shubra into Ain Shams University as a faculty of engineering must be implemented. The logical outcome of these and similar changes will be a return to one Ministry of Education to cover its present responsibilities, while the Supreme Council of Universities covers the former functions of the Ministry of Higher Education.

The four older and well-established state universities are mainly concentrated in Cairo and Alexandria. It is proposed to give more detailed information of two of the largest, Cairo University which is the oldest, and Ain Shams University which is a more modern institution. The others will be mentioned briefly.

Cairo University

Between 970 AD and 1908 there was only one university in Egypt: al-Azhar, which serves Islam as a world centre, as well as being a university with a network of institutions serving its various religious and educational objectives. At the beginning of this century there was a growing demand for a national university with a more practical bias, so funds were raised and the small Egyptian University was officially inaugurated in 1908. With expansion, especially in the physical sciences, advanced mathematics, political economy, the setting up of faculties of arts and philosophy and the development of social studies and feminine studies, its potentiality for developing modern studies was recognized. The *Egyptian Gazette* reports in 1913 that

As soon as Ibrahim Pasha Neguib, Director-General of the Wakfs, was appointed Vice-President of the board of directors of the Egyptian University he submitted to that board a report in which he recommended:

1. the suppression of the literary sections because it is not as necessary as other studies for which there is a greater need in the country;
2. the creation in its place of a scientific section for the instruction of engineers, mechanics and other practical sciences;
3. the recognition by the Government of the diplomas given by the university so that the holders may be accepted in the Government service.

However, within ten years it was decided to found a state university, using the Egyptian University as a nucleus of the faculty of arts, and this came about in 1925. Starting with four faculties, arts, science, medicine and law, by 1960 it was well into the process of assimilating independent schools of higher learning and splitting up faculties that had outgrown their organizations. Also the Khartoum branch had become established in 1955 with three departments (later faculties) of arts, law and commerce. At present it has fifteen faculties and three graduate institutes (listed under Law No. 49 (above)) as well as the three Khartoum faculties. Details of the faculties will be found in Appendix 1.

Alexandria University

This University was a branch of Cairo University until 1938. Like other Egyptian universities, it has expanded rapidly and now covers most normal university studies. It is known particularly for its facilities for engineering, medicine and the social sciences. Engineering and medicine are discussed below. It is not possible to cover all the other exciting developments at this progressive university, so mention is confined to the most important current project of the Faculty of Arts, that is the establishment of the first centre for American studies in the Middle East, financed by American sources. The project involves joint research and interchange of faculty students. Already students from New York are attending courses concerning Arab society, Islamic thought, Egyptian civilization, the political situation in the Middle East, economic development problems and Arabic language. American postgraduate students will have the opportunity to join in field research undertaken by the anthropology department, including a two-year project agreed with the United Nations to study environmental changes and their effect on life in the western desert.

Ain Shams University

Ain Shams University, opened temporarily in northern Cairo in 1950, was established in Heliopolis, an ancient cultural centre, in 1954. By 1959 it included the following faculties and colleges: arts, law, commerce, science, medicine, engineering, agriculture, education and the University College for Women, as well as a number of branches at Zagazig and Shebin el-Kom, which have now been incorporated in the new universities. It is not proposed to give details of all the faculties which follow the pattern at Cairo University but to describe briefly some aspects of the Faculty of Education, the University College for Women and the Department of Sociological and Psychological Studies in the Faculty of Arts which have achieved a reputation. The university also has a Public Service Centre which organizes free studies to meet the requirements of society as well as general lectures and cultural programmes. It includes five departments: modern languages, literary, artistic and social studies, hygiene and preventive medicine, business administration, and child welfare. In 1967 a Middle East Research Centre was approved to encourage, publish, interpret and exchange research, particularly related to the Middle East, to collect documents, prints, maps, statistics and periodicals dealing with the Middle East and to issue scientific magazines concerned with current problems. At present it has three branches, concerned respectively with natural resources, political and economic studies, and the humanities. In 1968 a Scientific Computer Centre was established to make use of a computer donated by the University of California. A brief description of some of its more important institutions will be found in Appendix 2.

Assiut University

The University of Assiut was established in 1957/8 to serve the needs of Upper Egypt, especially in science and engineering, which became the first faculties. Agriculture was added to its offerings in 1959/60, medicine in 1960/1, veterinary medicine in 1961/2 followed by pharmacy and dentistry. Assiut has an exceptionally spacious campus, allowing for future expansion. Its tendency to follow the organizational pattern of American universities and problems posed by its aim to teach wholly in Arabic are discussed in the section on engineering.

Medical education

Medical education began in Egypt in 1824 with the opening of a College of Medicine and Veterinary Medicine. Thus it was the second institute of higher education to be opened in Egypt, having been preceded by the School of Engineering in 1820. It was incorporated with other higher institutes in the new Egyptian University (later known as Cairo University) in 1925. Since then, the history of medical education is one of expansion and prestige.

By 1827 Cairo Medical School had incorporated seven hospitals, including three among the most famous in the Middle East: Kasr el-Aini, al-Manial, the Children's Hospital and Institute of Infantile Paralysis plus Shubra Hospital for Women and a School of Nursing.

The Alexandria University included a Medical School in 1942/3 with four hospitals which were incorporated in 1955: the Central University Hospital, al-Hadra Hospital, the Paediatrics and Women's Diseases Hospital and the Children's Hospital, besides a School of Nursing and a Higher School of Nursing.

Ain Shams has had medical education since 1950, incorporating a Children's Hospital which includes women's diseases and two general hospitals. More recently, medical schools have been opened in the Universities of Assiut and al-Azhar and branches have been opened by Cairo University in Mansoura, Alexandria University in Tanta and Ain Shams University in Zagazig.

Dentistry, pharmacy and veterinary medicine started as branches of the medical schools but, as they expanded, they broke away and became independent faculties or colleges. The most recent and important expansion of medical educational facilities has been the establishment in 1974 of a Regional Training Centre for Medical Record Science at the High Institute of Public Health, University of Alexandria. This, the first Medical Record Centre in the Middle East, will open its doors to participants from any country and will serve all World Health Organization regions. It will particularly contribute to scientific and technological development in the health sector and health education in Egypt,

Arab and African countries by producing and supervising training in the use of modern educational audio-visual aids, organizing theoretical and practical seminars for instructors in the field of health services, collecting medical data, documenting it and disseminating it in the health centre, conducting studies to develop health instruction and training methods, giving advice to the authorities in charge of planning health education and training programmes, so that they may adopt the latest methods, and contacting and co-operating with other countries and similar centres abroad and with international organizations working in this field.

Another important medical project is the Nasser Medical Institute at Shubra planned by Nasser, who did not live to see its birth. According to the Chairman of the Institute, Nasser had insisted,

> that this institute on the land of Egypt should act as an open heart for all Arabs as an expression of Arab unity, for all Africans as an expression of African unity, and for all people as an expression of the unity of human action to realise prosperity, peace and security.

The finished project will consist of a medical research institute on the most up-to-date scientific lines to work in co-operation with the main laboratories for diabetes, blood analysis, biochemistry and vaccines as well as the parasite, bacteriological and pathological laboratories, the radio-active isotopes laboratories, the blood bank and the animal experiment department. It will also include a hospital to house 600 beds and a polyclinic for diseases of the digestive system, the blood circulation, nerves, skin, bones etc. Other departments would be included for radiology, physiotherapy and heart and kidney diseases.

During recent years there has been continuing effort to improve the quality of medical education. In 1971 there was still a shortage of specialists in spite of an additional 150 newly graduated, due, it was thought, to the great number who were continually being seconded to Arab and African countries. To fill the gaps, it is the policy of the Ministry to encourage and provide all possible facilities for doctors to obtain higher diplomas. In that year 600 doctors were admitted to higher studies at the universities and one hundred more doctors were provided with facilities to specialize in anaesthesia, which was the worst shortage in the hospitals. Workers in all fields of medicine were being provided with all possible opportunities to keep abreast of recent scientific discoveries and progress in the medical sciences. Medical programmes were to be provided by radio and television to help the doctors to complete their higher studies and sit for a diploma within a pre-scribed period. In 1972 long-term policies for the reform of medical education to fit the crisis conditions in Middle Eastern countries were reviewed in a 'brains trust' meeting of experts in Alexandria by the World Health Organization. The crisis was due to too few medical schools and qualified people to staff them, a dearth of material resources for clinical training, the irrelevance of many curricula to the actual pattern of disease encountered when doctors leave the academic world and start to practice and the poor incentives offered for work in areas where the need is greatest. Topics reviewed included,

> the multi-disciplinary approach to medical training, an educational concept integrating the whole range of medical sciences in a unified body of knowledge. By breaking down the artificial barriers between medical departments, this approach 'makes students think in terms of organs and systems, rather than subject matters,' as a WHO expert puts it.

In spite of integrated teaching of basic medical sciences in multi-disciplinary laboratories in some medical schools in the Middle East medical teaching had altered little in response to the changing patterns of medical care and its growing claim on the doctor's skill and know-ledge. Close-circuit television had proved its worth, but faculties of medicine needed affiliated health centres where doctors could be trained side by side with paramedical and auxiliary personnel, as leaders of a multi-purpose health team. WHO had already contributed to medical education by providing assistance to twenty-one medical schools in the Eastern Mediterranean Region through teaching and advisory staff as well as equipment and supplies. (*Egyptian Gazette* 28 March 1974).

The theme was taken up by the Minister of Health in 1973 when he ordered the appointment of a special technical committee of university professors and leading specialists of the Ministry to consider the im-provement of postgraduate training programmes for interns, to prepare them for working in rural areas as general practitioners. Emphasis would be laid on rural environmental diseases, training in first aid to victims of accidents, cardiac, pulmonary and nervous complaints, family planning and the combating of epidemical diseases.

In 1973 emphasis was still on providing more specialists. The

Minister of Health approved a proposal to send 1,046 doctors who were working at the Ministry to the various faculties of the universities to obtain higher diplomas and doctorates as well as 100 of the technical workers at the Ministry's laboratories and 674 of the nursing staff to the health institutes and nursing institutes of the Ministry to obtain higher diplomas in these specializations.

The first conference on medical education in the Arab countries was held in Cairo in 1974, attended by representatives of twelve Arab countries. Medical education experts discussed 'The needs for research in medical education' and issued the following important recommendations:

1. Medical schools are urged to define their educational objectives for the purpose of:
   (a) development of appropriate curriculum content,
   (b) selection of the right methodology of teaching and use of alternative educational resources,
   (c) qualitative and quantitative selection of teachers and students,
   (d) adoption of effective techniques of evaluation,
   (e) design and proper use of physical facilities,
   (f) allocation of budget resources,
   (g) participation in the definition of health policy and structure of a health care delivery system,
   (h) definition of tasks of various types of health providers in the system.
2. To achieve such effective definition they are further urged to embark upon programmes of applied research on problems identified by the workshop.
3. Medical schools are urged to establish units, departments or centres consisting of a core of interested professors with expertise in educational planning and medical education research.
4. Dissemination of information between medical schools and medical educators and administrators should be facilitated as widely as possible.
5. All workshops, courses and other teacher training programmes should embrace a research approach. (*Egyptian Gazette* 16 March 1974).

All this effort to improve medical education was supported in 1975 by an agreement between the Egyptian government and the United

Nations Development Programme (UNDP) for the contribution of $302,000 worth of equipment to the new Egyptian Centre for Medical Aids and documentation discussed above, as well as scholarships for scientific training to instructors and technicians who would be engaged in the project for the following two years.

Discussions, seminars and conferences, national and international, are a perennial source of medical education in Egypt. It is proposed here just to give a list of topics selected over the last few years in order to illustrate their scope and depth, and to indicate some of the medical organizations that have developed in response to specialized interests. In 1971 the Egyptian Scientific Conference on Urology of the Egyptian Society of Urological Surgeons had its attention drawn by the Minister of Public Health to the problems of bilharzia, which reflected badly on the national economy and hampered development plans. Alexandria's Diabetes Welfare Association chose World Health Day for organizing a symposium for several hundred medical students on diabetes in normal daily life. The Cancer Researches Institute of Cairo in collaboration with the Faculty of Medicine of Alexandria University held a three-day symposium on cancer to discuss fifty-six new research papers. At the sixth conference of the Union of Faculties of Medicine in Africa, organized by the University of Ain Shams, African medical curricula were studied, while an Arab League Narcotics Conference discussed the planning of drug addiction clinics in the governorates. The second Orthopaedic Surgery Conference in Cairo attended by three hundred doctors representing twenty-five countries was followed by seminars on wartime surgery organized by the Scientific Activity Committee of the Medical Association and sponsored by the Egyptian General Pharmaceuticals Organization. In 1972 the Bone Surgery discussions continued and in 1973 the African Conference on Nervous and Mental diseases resumed its meetings in Cairo. In 1974 the Egyptian Medical Association organized twenty-four seminars on various specialized branches of medicine over a period of three months and members were encouraged by the offering of an increase of scholarships from 400 to 1,170 for higher study over a period of two years (5 per cent of the medical research students on government grants were reading for a PhD). The first Dermatological Conference in the Middle East, which reviewed rare skin diseases, also took place in 1974.

Egyptian doctors, like Egyptian teachers, have been academic ambassadors for their country abroad, as part of a cultural co-operation package deal, as for instance, in Malaysia in 1971 or as visiting professors within, for example, the framework of the WHO programme for the exchange of professors, or as individuals seeking posts that will enlarge their experience or provide research facilities not yet available in Egypt. Perhaps the most renowned of the last is the Egyptian who became one of the most prominent heart surgeons in Britain. By their agreement to take part in the celebration of the golden jubilee of the Egyptian Medical Association in 1970, the many world-known professors and famous specialists who contributed to the scientific programme representing the International Federation of Medical Associations, medical research centres and the faculties of medicine in various countries, were testifying to the esteem in which Egyptian medicine is held in a world-wide context.

Engineering education and training

Engineering has the distinction of being the oldest faculty subject in the modern universities, having been taught in the College of Engineering, founded in 1820, which was incorporated in Cairo University in 1925. By a roundabout route Ain Shams also acquired a Faculty of Engineering which had its origin in a school for training plant managers and supervisors, founded in 1839, which later became a school of arts and industry, a college in 1946 and a faculty in 1950. In Alexandria University according to Boktor's undated table, engineering about 1962 commanded the largest number of full-time staff. Assiut University started with a Faculty of Science and a larger Faculty of Engineering to meet the needs of Upper Egypt.

In the mid-fifties, the need for practical engineers in all fields became so great that specialized institutes were widely established. In theory, the courses and degrees were equivalent to those at universities but they were never accepted as such, since they were professionally biased rather than academically. Students were trained either to teach basic technical subjects at the school level or were absorbed by industry. Very few found their way into postgraduate courses or research. In 1955/6 a Higher Institute was established at Helwan to train teachers for industrial secondary schools. Others have followed, covering specialized subjects such as mechanical engineering, automotive engineering, electrical power engineering, machine engineering, vehicles, ship-building, petroleum engineering, and mining engineering. These

higher institutes have now been incorporated into Helwan Technological University.

Cairo and Alexandria each have eleven departments and Ain Shams
seven. The subjects cover mathematics and physics, construction
engineering, irrigation and hydraulics, architecture, public works, and
electrical engineering. A compulsory preparatory year is used for basic
mathematics and physics, engineering terminology and acquaintance
with instruments, workshop practice and handling machines, except for
students of architecture who have their own programme. All students
must spend at least their last summer vacation working in a plant or
establishment related to their field of specialization. Many get paid
work in West German or Austrian industries. This is valuable experience, as technicians and skilled labour are in such short supply in Egypt
that the graduate engineer must be able to handle machines and take on
practical jobs usually associated with a lower level of engineering
education.

Besides the general problems common to all institutions of higher
learning in Egypt, Assiut has had particular problems resulting from
the decision to make Arabic the medium of instruction. These are
discussed in detail in Chapter 2. A unique experience in the Engineering
Faculty has been the MASUA - Aid Programme in Engineering
Education under a contract with Kansas State University. American
visiting personnel included professors of mechanical engineering and
agricultural engineering and assistant professors of mechanical engineering and electrical engineering supported by a 'project co-ordinator', an
administrative assistant, an associate professor of mechanical engineering
and full- and half-time secretaries. In 1965, visitors included the Dean
of Engineering of Kansas State University to assess progress and
discuss future assignments and needs with Assiut University officials and
contract personnel, while the Egyptian Dean of the University toured
MASUA (Mid-America State Universities Association) universities in
the USA and attended the World Congress of Engineering Education
in Chicago.

The very detailed reports made of this project cannot be discussed
here. In spite of the great difficulties involved in transplanting an alien
faculty using the medium of the American language in an Arabic-
medium university, it was an interesting experiment in comparative
education. The programme appears to have been far too ambitious, but
progress was made in pin-pointing the problems. Unfortunately the

war in 1967 brought the venture to a close before a full assessment could be made.

In pursuance of the aim to link scientific studies with the needs of industry, Ain Shams University made an agreement in 1971 with the Egyptian General Electricity Organization to participate in the training of senior engineers and to improve postgraduate research facilities for the organization's personnel. In return, the Electricity Organization would provide the Faculty's Electrical Engineering Department with equipment and staff. The Faculty agreed to conduct postgraduate courses for forty-five engineers, of which thirty engineers from the Organization would study for MSc degrees and fifteen engineers, including ten from the Organization, would study for DSc degrees. The university would gain all the equipment installed, whether imported or manufactured.

An interesting development, in line with Egypt's policy of identification with other Arab states, has been the affiliation of the Egyptian Engineers Association with the Arab Engineers Association. At resulting conferences held in Cairo, discussions have included matters of common interest to delegates from all over the Arab world, such as the co-ordination between electricity networks in Arab countries, the unification of the study of engineering in the Arab faculties of Engineering and Technical Institutes, road planning in the Arab states and the problem of water supply in the Sudan.

Science and technology

In every plan for every aspect of living in Egypt, the word 'scientific' has an assured place, signifying the enormous importance attached to this (for Egypt) comparatively new approach to the problems of the state. In her educational system Egyptians are aiming at training students not only with enough scientific background to be able to pursue scientific studies at a higher level but having the capacity to 'think scientifically' in any situation that confronts them. However, specialization begins rather early and science has become an 'élite' subject: only students reaching a certain level in the first-year secondary stage are allowed to study science to a school certificate level. The implications are discussed in the section on the social sciences.

However, a recent estimate is that 80 per cent of students in secondary general education are following science-maths studies and, for those who reach the next stage in the educational ladder, 27 per cent enrol in the sciences, engineering and agricultural faculties and 16 per cent in the health sciences.

Practical necessity has made applied sciences receive more attention than pure science, so that there has been a danger that much of the science taught in the universities would be more appropriately taught in technical colleges. However, with the establishment of Helwan University, which raises the status of technical education, there may be a shift of provision in these fields. The four older universities each have science faculties with five departments: chemistry, physics, botany, zoology, and geology. In addition, Cairo and Ain Shams have departments of entomology, Cairo and Alexandria institutes of Oceanography, Cairo has astronomy linked with the Institute of Astronomy and Meteorology and the Helwan Observatory. Chemistry at Cairo and physics at Alexandria are particularly strong. Ain Shams has a special department for bio-chemistry.

First-year classes in the science faculties of all universities tend to be overcrowded as there is no extra provision for the fact that, as well as being important in their own right, science subjects are a basic requirement for all students studying medicine, veterinary medicine, pharmacy, dentistry and, in Assiut, agriculture and engineering, which in other universities are provided for by the specialist faculty.

Science is essentially concerned with research demanding, even at the school level, well-equipped laboratories and expensive equipment, which Egypt can ill-afford. In schools it is possible (although not desirable), to economize by substituting demonstrations for individual participation, but at the university level, even basic laboratory equipment is complicated, expensive, in need of spare parts, and maintenance by competent technicians. Unfortunately it also needs to be purchased abroad, so must be paid for in foreign currency. The result is a critical shortage, which delays research projects, as well as making teaching difficult. Recognizing this, the Egyptian government arranged for a UNESCO-sponsored regional Seminar on Science Teaching Improvement to take place at Ain Shams University in 1971. Its aim was to stimulate the exchange of ideas and information between leaders of science education, to prepare teaching strategies and to discuss a regional plan for the establishment of a regional Science Teaching Centre for the Arab world. The event included an exhibition organized by the Ministry on modern methods of teaching science. Such seminars, led by experts in the field, are a factor in improving the quality of students even before they reach the university.

Another important feature of science in Egypt, is the stress made by the Minister of Scientific Research on the need to co-ordinate the various activities of scientific bodies. Sometimes the impression given in the West is that rivalry rather than co-operation governs relationships between research bodies and individuals. With her limited resources of facilities and experts to use them, Egypt cannot afford the luxury of duplication of equipment and effort, so teamwork is encouraged. For example, in 1972 three new research bodies were called upon to aid a development plan, a Permanent Tile Drainage Research Committee, a Scientific Council for the Food Industry and a Scientific Council for the Textile Industry. Members of the National Research Centre would be represented on each Committee. In the first, the Committee would determine the scientific content of the research to be conducted and form the research teams to co-ordinate the work of the Tile Drainage Authority, the Ministry of Irrigation and the National Research Centre, to combat the water hyacinth and other weeds, preparing detailed plans for related studies and employing the centre's soil, pests and organic chemistry laboratories in dealing with such problems. In the second instance, a Scientific Council for the Food Industry was formed with fifteen members of food companies headed by the Egyptian General Food Industry Organization. The Council, assisted by members of the National Research Centre, aimed at solving production problems, improving specifications and using Egyptian raw materials as substitutes for imported materials. Similar co-operation was effected between the Research Centre and the Scientific Council for the Textile Industry, whose members represented the spinning, dyeing, weaving and finishing companies headed by the chairman of the Egyptian General Spinning and Weaving Organization.

It appears that Szyliowicz's criticism (1973) that 'the able young scientist finds it extremely difficult to engage in productive research' is becoming less true, due to the work of the Academy of Scientific Research and Technology, although the high cost of scientific equipment in some areas will inevitably continue to drive them across the Atlantic, as happens with able British scientists. A physics conference in 1971, organized under the auspices of the Academy in conjunction with the Egyptian Society for Physics, attracted 150 research papers ranging from nuclear physics – both theoretical and experimental – neutron physics, reactors, plasma physics, crystals, metallurgical physics, conductors, magnetics, spectrum, bio-physics, electrons, to designs of scientific apparatus and electronic computers. Moreover, the President of the Academy emphasized that the modern state (of Egypt) cannot remain content with importing some of the products of science and technology, which is in line with another criticism of Szyliowicz. It is a tribute to the President and the Academy that within two years it was able to organize the seventh Arab Scientists' Conference, attended by scientists from Egypt, Iraq, Syria, Palestine, Saudi Arabia and Jordan. Out of 230 research papers, Egypt had contributed 70.

The theme of co-operation was taken up again in 1974/5 at a conference called by President Sadat of 400 scientists at home and abroad to discuss 'Egypt until the year 2000'. The chairman, Dr Mahmud Fawzy, called upon Egyptian scientists living abroad to share in the scientific research needed for the homeland's great development plans. Papers were concentrated on problems of social and economic development, including the possible use of atomic energy in the service of Egypt's plans. This account contains only a fraction of advances being made within the space of a very few years: the trend seems clear.

Agricultural education

There are faculties of agriculture in each of the Egyptian Universities as well as five Higher Agricultural Institutes. In 1961/2 there were 7,618 students studying agriculture in the universities and 2,828 in the institutes. With the increase since then of land available for cultivation there has been renewed effort to attract to this branch of science, students who after qualification will be able to apply modern scientific knowledge and techniques to raise the standards of the industry. Perhaps the most important and attractive means has been the distribution of new farming land to students successfully graduating from the university or institute. Recent amounts mentioned have been 2,600 feddans (acres) in 1973 and 33,500 feddans in 1974.

Advances in this field of education can largely be attributed to the efforts of the Society of the Graduates of Higher Agricultural Colleges and Institutes which celebrated its Golden Jubilee in 1971 at the fifth Agricultural Conference. The following are important recommendations made at this conference:

In the field of agricultural production
the establishment of farms, whose produce would be exported or
used in industries;
the establishment of model farms on the newly reclaimed land,
applying the system of mechanized agriculture;
increasing the number of centres for training on maintenance work
of agricultural machinery;
the change of the traditional rotation of crops applied to the newly
reclaimed land in order to increase its output;
the establishment of a special centre for experimenting with new
kinds of imported crops.
In the field of livestock production
the setting up of a higher council for the planning of livestock
production;
to be responsible to the Council of Ministers;
the increase of funds allocated for the development of livestock
production;
drawing up plans for developing industries which are based on livestock production and encouraging the private sectors and agricultural
co-operative societies to increase their livestock production.
In the field of land reclamation and exploitation
the enrichment of the soil of sandy areas to increase their productivity;
finding new markets for agricultural produce and the development of
the role played by agricultural guidance in the field of horticulture.

The conference also called for the promulgation of a new law on co-
operative production, and recommended the appointment of agricultural counsellors at the Egyptian embassies in the countries which
have economic and agricultural relations with Egypt.

In the same year, at the third Scientific Conference on Vegetable
Research held at the Faculty of Agriculture, Alexandria University, to
study the development of vegetable production and problems facing
vegetable research, the proposal was made to establish a scientific
society covering all aspects of this area of agriculture. The main task
would be to consolidate co-operation between the organizations concerned with vegetable production, such as the Ministry of Agriculture,
Universities, the Academy of Technology and Scientific Research and
research centres. The society would be based in Cairo, with branches
in all the governorates. Future research should be devoted to solving

vegetable production problems, in the light of directives from the scientific society.

Also in 1971 the first graduates of the new Agricultural Engineers Training Centre in Sakha completed their courses. These one hundred and thirty agricultural engineers had been trained to take over the work of agricultural supervisors at the agricultural co-operative societies. They would start work the following week.

In 1972, the Egyptian Botanical Society established in 1956, held its first conference with five botanists from the GDR, Hungary and Algeria as observers and lecturers. It discussed fifty-two research papers on the physiology of medicinal herbs, horticulture fertilizers, insecticides, the environment and the soil. The conference drew 150 Egyptian scientists representing the botanical departments at the Egyptian universities, research centres, and representatives from the Ministries of Higher Education, Agriculture, Land Reclamation and Irrigation. Included were a number of important papers on the effects of spraying vegetables, fruit and medicinal herbs.

Further expansion took place in 1974 when the first Egyptian conference on food science and technology was held at the Agricultural Professions Union to deal with linking agricultural industry with food processing industries, modern food industries, technology, economic nutritional problems in Egypt and how Arab integration in food supplies can serve overcoming them. This was a conference at very high level, attracting not only university professors and scientists from research centres, specialized international bodies and experts in the field, but the Ministers of Industry, Agriculture and Land Reclamation and board chairmen of the Scientific Research Academy, industrial organizations and companies.

The Federation of Arab Agricultural Engineers (incorporating the Egyptian engineers mentioned above) also held a conference at the Agricultural Professionals Association in 1974, attended by representatives from the Arab League, the Arab Organization for Agricultural Development and the UN Food and Agricultural Organization. Egypt's main contribution was a study of her co-operative set up; the amalgamation of planning and training departments of similar sectors to avoid duplication of efforts, which called for the establishment of a Higher Council for Co-operatives to ensure that co-operative activities are performed in line with general policies established by the representative governments.

The activities above, which have been initiated within a very short period of time, are not exhaustive; they are meant to exemplify Egypt's regard for applied scientific research as, to quote Dr Emad Eddin el-Sheshiny (Vice-President of the Academy of Scientific Research) 'one of the elements of national wealth whose aim is to increase national production and bridge the gap between under-development and development preventing the isolation of economic development from scientific progress.'

Cultural borrowing

In addition to her own increasingly large provision for higher education, especially at the university level, Egypt relies a great deal on cultural borrowing of different kinds to raise her manpower to a level of efficiency that will eventually make her self-sufficient. For convenience, one can roughly divide the cross-cultural experience, which plays a vital part in the modernization of Egypt into three main categories: academic missions abroad, which always take place at the postgraduate level, cultural accords, which are expressed in a variety of activities and often include the provision of training programmes, and the secondment of Egyptian teachers to other countries.

Academic missions abroad

Egypt's record for cultural borrowing and exchange, both incidental to her long history of foreign occupation, and the deliberate policies of her government from Mohammed 'Ali onwards would make her an ideal centre for comparative education studies. There is nothing haphazard about student missions in modern Egypt: they occupy the attention of several ministries, including the Ministry of the Interior, the Ministry of Youth, the Ministry of Finance, and, above all, the Ministry of Higher Education, which has overall responsibility, and the Ministry of Manpower as well as the Arab Socialist Union. Every care is taken to ensure that the student is of the right calibre, that his studies will benefit himself and the country, that he is well prepared before he leaves, understanding what is going on in his country and the role that he will play as a student to the people in his host country. It is also ensured that he will be cared for during his absence and be able to take part in discussions at home. On the basis of experience, rules and practices are regularly revised.

Typical of the kind of preparation given to students about to study abroad is a fifteen-day seminar arranged in 1970 by the Nasser Socialist Youth Organization in collaboration with the Ministry of Higher Education. It was opened by the Secretary General of the Arab Socialist Union, accompanied by the Ministers of Higher Education and Youth Affairs as well as the ASU Secretary for Youth. The session's programme for the 700 students included political meetings with the ASU Secretary for Organizational Affairs, a Deputy Premier, as well as the Ministers of Information, Higher Education, Youth Affairs and Wakfs (Religious Affairs). The students could not be in doubt about their importance as representatives and ambassadors for their country.

In addition to the seminar, the students were also expected to attend lectures on foreign affairs, world public opinion and the role of students and student organizations abroad. They also studied 'political organizations, the inevitability of a socialist solution, the fields of struggle for victory and the Palestinian issue'. Egyptian Cultural Attaches at embassies abroad, as well as students just returning after completion of their studies abroad, together with a number of experts, delivered lectures on the history, geography, the nature of economic and social systems as well as the conditions of everyday living in the various countries to which the students were expected to be assigned. The students would also visit industrial landmarks, the High Dam and historical sites. (*Egyptian Gazette* 19 April 1970)

Apart from missions abroad directly financed by the Egyptian government many are financed by friendly powers who offer scholarships to students selected by the government. If, for any reason, the scholarship is discontinued before the student has completed his studies, the government takes over the financial responsibility. The scope of such scholarships and the range of countries involved is indicated by the following examples, which are not comprehensive. As part of a French offer in 1971 to finance and set up a number of tourist projects, agreement was reached to train ninety-nine men and women hotel students at French hotels on Corsica. All training expenses were borne by the company and periodic reports on the progress of trainees were sent to the Minister. In the same year a total of forty-eight scholarships were offered by the French government, thirty-six of which were for teachers, two for French language instructors and ten other long-term scholarships for teachers of French. (In the same offer, the French Ministry of Education agreed to send twenty-six French teachers to teach in government schools in addition to the twenty-three teachers already in Cairo, and to co-operate in teaching modern mathematics through secondment of French teachers and organizing training courses in Cairo for Egyptian teachers, to open experimental classes and prepare textbooks in French.) During 1971 there were also more than 600 students from Egypt studying in the German Democratic Republic and the two countries were discussing the possibility of establishing schools, similar to the Shubra Kheima Mechanical School in other parts of the country. The Federal Republic of Germany has never lagged behind: seventy-three holders of Master's degrees from Egyptian universities in the fields of science, engineering, arts and agriculture were offered postgraduate scholarships in her universities. Still in 1971, the Alexandria University agreed to despatch a number of research students on school missions to the Soviet Union, Poland, Czechoslovakia, the GDR and Britain to study for a doctor's degree. In 1972, the Uppsala University in Sweden reached an agreement with the Ministry of Higher Education to increase to forty its scholarships given to graduates of science in Egypt, mainly in chemistry and physics. By 1973 the Manpower section of the Ministry of Higher Education had investigated the precise shortages in education so the trend was to use academic missions to fill precise gaps. A plan was designed to reinforce the teaching staffs of the universities, higher institutes and the National Educational Research Centre. Of 500 research students or assistant lecturers to be sent abroad to obtain PhD degrees, 284 were to be given to candidates from provincial universities and the Ministry's higher institutes. The missions were distributed as follows: 74 science; 78 engineering and technology; 46 agricultural and veterinary medicine; 98 medicine, pharmacy and nursing; 73 law; 97 education and the humanities; 34 arts and general studies. At the same time a group of physicians were to be sent to the Soviet Union to have their qualifications up-graded. In 1974, the United Kingdom signed a new accord on technical co-operation which would formalize the advisory and consultative services already operating. These include the Moharrem Bey Technical Training School in Alexandria where British experts are co-operating with their Egyptian counterparts to raise the standard of technical education, and help being given in the fields of English language training, agriculture, mining and medicine, as well as the provision of seventy scholarships a year for Egyptians to study in the United Kingdom. In the same year an Egyptian-American group discussed the exchange of technical and scientific assistance to include the granting of scholarships for Egyptians to study museums in the United States while a corresponding number of American experts would be conducting preliminary research on Egyptian institutions.

By 1974, Egyptian students abroad had become a distinct organization ready to hold a conference in Cairo to discuss means of establishing closer relations and constant contact between Egyptian students studying abroad and the homeland, and the problems faced by these students and means of overcoming them. This was following the October War, and their representatives had already sent telegrams of support to President Anwar el-Sadat, President Hafez el-Assad of Syria and Field Marshall Ahmed Ismail, War Minister and Commander-in-Chief of the Armed Forces. A political statement at the end of the meeting said that the representatives of Egyptian students abroad believed in the 'inevitability of adopting the ten principles contained in the October Working Paper which was presented by President Sadat in his meeting with us to face the challenges of the future scientifically and effectively'. (*Egyptian Gazette* 21 April 1974)

Cultural accords

The Ministry of Higher Education is also responsible for signing cultural accords with foreign countries, the end of a process which usually includes receiving visitors, advisers and other personnel and visiting foreign countries, to explore possible areas of co-operation in the form of direct aid or projects of mutual benefit in the fields of education or training. Over the five-year period, 1970–5 accords have been completed every year, with, perhaps, a significant increase in 1971, after the accession of Anwar el-Sadat and in 1974, after success in the October War. It will be noted that the areas covered are wide-ranging, many including further offers of scholarships and that any suitable offer, whether from East or West is acceptable, provided that the help is unconditional.

It would not be appropriate here to give an exhaustive account of cultural accords, but it is necessary to know enough of their scope in order to understand not only the important contribution they make to education in modern Egypt, but to discuss problems arising from or accentuated by this peaceful form of 'foreign intervention'. The following information which was collected from 1970–5, mainly from the *Egyptian Gazette,* will it is hoped, be sufficient for the above-mentioned purposes.

1971/2

Soviet Union: The plan provides for broader co-operation between the Academy of Sciences of the USSR and the Ministry of Scientific Research, through the exchange of scientists and publications, specialists for joint work on the restoration of ancient manuscripts and documents and the study of ancient Arabic manuscripts. The number of Soviet teachers and specialists at institutes of higher learning and of Russian language teachers at the Cairo Higher School of Foreign Languages and other educational establishments to be increased; exchange of companies of artists and soloists; a Soviet director to direct a Soviet play for the Egyptian theatre; a delegation of the planning body of the Ministry of Education to be sent to the Soviet Union for training in methods of drawing up educational plans and how to follow them up; teachers to be sent to the Soviet Union for training in the field of teaching sciences and mathematics and the use of audio-visual aids; the Soviet Union to send experts to Egypt for training Egyptian teachers in modern educational systems. *Poland:* The two-year agreement provided for the development of co-operation in the fields of science, art, means of mass communication, artistic research and youth organizations, exhibitions, artistic groups and delegations of university students would be exchanged between the two countries. (Poland also signed an economic and industrial protocol to co-operate in a number of heavy industry projects included in the five-year plan for 1970–5.) *Czechoslovakia:* The country would co-operate in the establishment of a secondary school specializing in the teaching of chemistry and geometry; four teachers of geometry and six others in chemistry would be sent by Czechoslovakia to teach in the proposed school; the country would also help to set up two schools, the first to train technicians in chemical and allied industries, and the second to provide courses on precision industries; Czechoslovakia would provide both schools with the necessary equipment and technical staff and would arrange for exchange of techniques and for teacher and student-training missions; two biologists arrived in Alexandria for a four-month stay in Alexandria for consultations with their counterparts in the Institute of Oceanography and to acquaint themselves with the studies and researches conducted by the Institute. (Czecho-slovakian experts and technicians also helped to establish the units of a petrochemical plant in Alexandria.)

Chad: The five-year agreement provided for the promotion of relations in the fields of university education, sports and arts; co-operation in teacher-exchange; facilities for students on educational missions; equivalence of educational and academic degrees; exchange of television and radio features, technical and artistic writings and scientific research; agreement that the geography and history syllabuses in each country should contain sufficient material to avoid misunderstanding.

Rumania: Co-operation in the field of scientific research and co-ordinating the exchange of technical expertise; a medical delegation.

United Kingdom: One-year accord to strengthen economic, technical, educational and social co-operation between the two countries; training Egyptians in Britain and sending British experts to Egypt to give advice in questions of development; supplying Egypt with equipment and textbooks related to development projects; twenty-five-year loan; seminar on Arab-UK cultural ties, concentrating on co-operation, especially regarding scholarships offered by Britain to Arab professors and students.

Somalia: Secondment of teachers.

German Federal Republic: Discussions about problems and measures concerning the academic and scientific links between the two countries; visit of well-known ophthalmologist for two weeks to deliver lectures, participate in study groups and perform eye operations in the Military Hospital, Maadi.

Bulgaria: Co-operation in the sphere of youth welfare; exchange of youth delegations, experts and cultural publications; friendship weeks.

Italy: Scientific co-operation on basis of exchanging data and documents pertaining to research work, exchanging scientists and technical scientific research workers; holding seminars and carrying out joint research work; possibilities of extending co-operation in the field of maritime sciences, fisheries, observatories, subterranean water, water pollution, water desalination, agriculture hygiene, the cultivation of arid areas, food preservation, documentation, scientific information of maintenance of antiquities, space research and nuclear power.

Syria: Week of cultural exchange programmes, including book fairs, exhibitions of applied arts, repertory companies and leading orchestras; co-ordination of publications; exchange of theatrical ensembles, folklore art troupes, texts of plays; and joint film production.

Indonesia: Delegation to discuss cultural co-operation.

Iran: Visits to consolidate co-operation in the sphere of agriculture.

German Democratic Republic: Exchange of expertise and data pertaining to planning and administration of education; exchange of scholarships, dramatic troupes; and film weeks.

Austria: Visit of 700 medical specialists.

Saudi Arabia: Promoting co-operation in the spheres of culture and information.

France: Discussion of matters relating to the strengthening of cultural and scientific relations between France and Egypt.

Five States: Five new agreements signed for technical co-operation with Hungary, Poland, Yugoslavia, Bulgaria and the German Democratic Republic, in the fields of planning and development of manpower to serve production: these countries to provide £E 9,000,000 for the project to cover the cost of training Egyptian personnel in these fields; GDR would participate in a series of seminars, to study agricultural guidance and its effect on the agricultural production and the application of modern technological system to agriculture. Bulgaria would participate in a series of seminars which would deal with small and food industries. Egypt was now holding a series of contacts with the Soviet Union, the United Kingdom, Italy, India, Austria and Iran as part of the efforts exerted for promoting friendly relations of technical co-operation with foreign countries through joint seminars and exchange of experience. The central authority was studying the possibility of concluding a number of contracts with the United Kingdom, Yugoslavia, Hungary, the GDR, Poland, Sweden and France for establishing centres for training personnel engaged in the field of livestock and vegetation production.

Reports of other cultural agreements made in the years 1972–6 include continuation of the co-operation in previous years as well as with countries not yet mentioned, such as Sudan, Iraq, Uganda, Malta, South Korea, India, Sierra Leone, Spain, Pakistan, Denmark, Hungary, and Libya.

The secondment of Egyptian teachers abroad

In 1975, according to the Minister of Education, Egypt seconded more than 20,000 teachers to Arab and friendly countries, according to a statement to the People's Assembly in January, 1975.

Although the cultural agreements between Egypt and her friends include exchange elements, perhaps it could be fairly said that, owing to vital need to modernize her educational and training systems as quickly as possible, the balance of advantage has remained in her hands. It is equally true that developing countries in the Middle East and Africa have relied and are still relying on Egypt's teachers and experts to help them make the foundation of their own educational systems. Egypt's role as the undisputed centre of Islam, with al-Azhar's tentacles stretching to the Far East, Africa and India, the centre of education, with modern universities turning out graduates numerically out of all proportion to her immediate needs, the centre of literacy campaigns and the centre of the most successful bloodless revolution in modern times, is accepted, though reluctantly by her enemies, as a fact of life. Her teachers, ranging from university professors to primary school head mistresses could be found in countries as widely separated as Malaya, West Africa, the Trucial States, South Yemen and Sudan almost any time during the last twenty to twenty-five years. At the intermediate and secondary level they have been especially welcome in former colonial territories, where the departure of expatriate teachers has come about before an adequate local supply of teachers has been built up in sufficient numbers to meet both the growing demand for more and better education and the need for a local intelligentsia in newly independent countries. In the fifties in Aden, for example, they were in demand for teaching in the expanding intermediate and secondary schools and in teacher-training, especially in girls' schools, where a sudden demand created local shortages. The Egyptian government was motivated both intrinsically and extrinsically to encourage the export of teachers to ease her problems of population and need for foreign currency, as well as to identify with the needs and aspirations of the Arab and African world. The teachers who came to Aden were not only the best paid teachers in the Arab world (getting more than a professor in Cairo), but they drew a special overseas allowance from their own country and every year abroad was counted as two years' pensionable service. More recently, in view of the high salaries paid by the oil states for expatriate teachers, it has been necessary to organize the flow, especially at university level, so that an institution does not lose too many senior staff during the same period. Periodically, an assessment of Egypt's losses through secondment is demanded by some of her anxious educationalists.

In 1971 the Minister of Education approved new rules for secondment of teachers abroad, for both males and females, whether for services in other Arab states or friendly countries. Initial qualification would depend on fulfilling the prescribed conditions of specialization and financial grade in government service, followed by a special interview. Officials who had formerly been seconded for the full four-year maximum period for secondment would still be eligible for a second secondment provided that at least five years had elapsed since the termination of their first secondment. Unmarried women were to be considered as likely candidates for service abroad, but a married woman needed in each case the agreement of her husband for her to leave the country on her own. In the event of a couple being named as candidates they would be loaned for service 'to the country of least financial treatment', and if the husband's secondment were terminated, the wife's term of office would also be ended unless the husband agreed to her continuing alone. Divorced women had to enclose their divorce certificates with the application. Applications reached the Ministry of Education via the zonal directorates where they were put in order of merit. The candidates obtaining the highest marks in their reports and personal interviews would be named for secondment to the countries offering more favourable financial treatment. There would be an age limit of fifty-five years.

In these transactions Egypt has the unique advantage that she can offer teachers capable of using Arabic, French or English as a medium of instruction. The demand in Arab countries is likely to decrease as national teachers become more plentiful, and the trend in recent years appears to be an increased focus on Africa. In 1971 a cultural accord with the Democratic Republic of Somalia included provision for the secondment of 25 additional Arabic language teachers for service in Somalia's preparatory, secondary schools and teacher-training institutes in addition to the 269 teachers and the 4 professors already delegated to the country to conduct teacher-training courses. Arabic and religious textbooks to cover the needs of 5,000 students in preparatory, secondary and teacher-training institutes were part of the deal. Meanwhile a training course would be organized in Egypt to train additional numbers of Somali primary school teachers, and Egypt was ready to send her experts for the same purpose to aid UNESCO's efforts. In 1973 the President of the Republic of Dahomey welcomed Egyptian teachers to teach the Arabic language in Dahomey's schools and universities. It was an occasion when President Sadat's gift of twenty grants for study in Egyptian universities and institutes and twenty air tickets for performing the pilgrimage were handed over to Dahomey Moslems. In 1974 it was officially announced by the Minister of Education that all African countries would be supplied with the teachers that they needed in order to develop their systems and programmes of education, a decision that had been taken in appreciation of the moral support given by Africa during the October War of 1973. It was decided to organize a training programme for teachers of mathematics, science and social studies to be conducted in English and French enabling the trainees to instruct in either language when seconded to work in schools of African countries. The Minister issued a decree stipulating the conditions of applying for teaching posts in those countries. All teachers under forty who had not been seconded to other countries during the previous five years might apply. One African country which has relied on Egyptian educational aid for many years is the Sudan, which reviewed its links in 1974. A joint Egyptian-Sudanese technical committee for education and scientific research recommended the

TABLE 8 *Total number of teaching staff in faculties and higher institutes in the year 74/75*

Stage	Teaching staff	Out of cadre	Assistant professors	Lecturers	Total	Notes
Universities	4,977			7,522	12,499	
Higher institutes affiliated to the Ministry	993	129	85	1,244	1,441	Approximative statistics
Al-Azhar University	—	—	—	—	—	—

(*Source:* by courtesy of the Ministry of Education, Cairo.)

exchange of technical experience and the standardization of education between the two countries. Plans were made for extending Egyptian support to the Khartoum branch of the Cairo University and the Islamic University of Omdurman as well as giving more openings for the admission of Sudanese students in the Egyptian universities and higher education institutes. The report on the recommendations also called for co-operation in the fields of scientific research, and in research works conducted on rice crops, the study of environmental conditions in both Lake Nasser and the Nubian Lake, vegetable and fruit export, besides co-operation in research work being conducted on endemic diseases. (*Egyptian Gazette* 17 March 1975)

6

Other agencies of education

The government sector

Training courses in other ministries

Egypt looks to training programmes at every level to raise the efficiency of individuals and organizations, so the national plan for training aims at defining responsibilities so that each state organization understands what is required. For some years now, postgraduate students have flocked to management courses in the universities; for many of them it will be part of their responsibility to know the available human and material resources at their disposal and the volume of investments required to carry out their responsibilities in the national plan for training. This matter is considered so important that in 1971 Dr Abdel Aziz Hegazy, Minister of the Treasury and chairman of the Central Agency for Organization and Administration inaugurated an agency-sponsored conference of administrative training. It was attended by five hundred directors of training departments in the various sectors of the state, on both central and local levels as well as high officials in the field of administration. Time was spent on discussing relationships which should be defined between labour sectors and central institutes, and between those institutes and the Central Agency for Organization and Administration. A few examples of training programmes in some of the ministries will be given to illustrate the importance attached to these programmes to supplement the formal education provisions made by the Ministries of Education and Higher Education.

The Ministry of Manpower

The Minister of Manpower has a special interest in the expansion of vocational training. In 1973 he laid particular emphasis on apprenticeship schemes, vocational orientation, quick training and the measurement of skills. During the previous two years apprentices' training programmes had been applied to 4,840 boys, of whom most had been engaged for service with public and private sector establishments. Individuals who received vocational orientation services the previous year numbered 8,014 in the governorates of Cairo, Giza, Kaliubieh, Alexandria and Dakhlieh where vocational guidance plans are being implemented. Quick training services are designed to provide production needs of technical and vocational skills: 550 had also been trained in the previous year, of whom 439 were appointed to posts in the public and private sectors. The following year a comprehensive assessment of vocational training centres was carried out jointly by the Ministries of Manpower and Social Affairs.

The Ministry of Industry

Advance was made in this sector in 1971 when the Productivity and Vocational Training Department prepared a new plan for turning out highly trained personnel for industry. Under this plan sixty training centres would be established for holders of the preparatory school certificate. The new centres would be built over a period of five years during which 9,000 students would be accepted. This was in addition to the training centres already available and from which 3,000 workers graduate every year. The new plan also envisaged raising the standard of training through the use of the most up-to-date methods. A special training centre had been built for the petrochemical industries and for developing training methods to meet the needs of the industrial sector. It would help a great deal in providing highly trained personnel for the petrochemical complex to be established in Alexandria.

The Ministry of Communication

The Minister of Communication is responsible for the supervision of Post Office Schools and Telecommunication Schools.

The Ministry of Health

The Minister of Health is responsible for the supervision of schools for nurses, laboratory assistants and X-ray workers.

The Ministry of War

Military training has been of paramount importance in Egypt in recent years, but it was not introduced into secondary schools until 1971, starting with Cairo, Alexandria, Tanta, Giza and Assiut and afterwards spreading to the governorates. It was planned to build seventeen secondary military schools to be ready in 1972. They would be special boarding schools governed by a higher council. The name is rather misleading as military subjects would be taught only twice a week in addition to the ordinary curriculum of secondary education. Provincial schools would also be established but with external military courses only. Like other secondary schools, all these experimental 'military schools' would be under the Ministry of Education who would have military counsellors to advise him. The teaching would be done by ex-soldiers. In 1971 military training courses were also provided for 70,000 undergraduates at universities and higher institutes. Training, which is mainly for 'home guard' duties varies with the faculties, while the women students take courses in nursing and first aid at military and civilian hospitals. This preparation stood the country in good stead during the October War of 1973.

Professional military training is provided at the Military Academy, the Egyptian Armed Forces Technical Institute and the Air Force Academy.

The Ministry of the Interior

The Minister of the Interior is responsible for the training of police officers of various grades. Institutions include a police college and an institute of non-commissioned police officers and a police officers higher studies institute. To keep the force up-to-date, personnel are sometimes sent abroad for extra training.

The Ministry of al-Azhar Affairs

The fact that there is a Ministry of al-Azhar Affairs and that Islam, the declared state religion, thrives in a modern secular Egypt is a tribute to the diplomatic skill and religious sincerity of the revolutionary leaders. The Moslem Brotherhood, the political élite of Egyptian Moslem society, were convinced that the salvation of their country

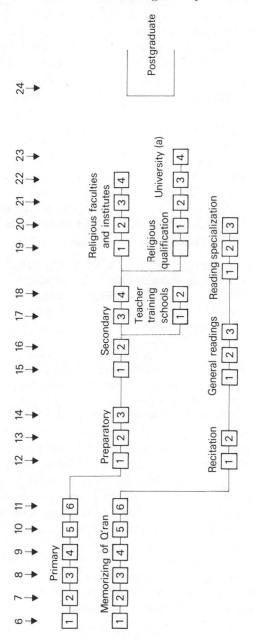

FIGURE 2 *Educational ladder in al-Azhar*
(*Source:* by courtesy of the Ministry of Education, Cairo.)

depended on a religious revival in the form of a domination by the letter of the Q'ran and other holy writings, the strict observance of Islamic law and practice and an educational system that basically meant memorization of the Q'ran, and at higher levels steeped the student in classical Arabic studies. In his famous book, *The Stream of Days*, Taha Husayn (1948), the blind Egyptian scholar, describes life at al-Azhar prior to the Revolution: the sterile teaching, the suppression of criticism or creative thought, the inefficiency and slackness and the emphasis on rote learning and passive acceptance of traditional interpretations of knowledge. With the increasing contact with the West and the growing emphasis on science and technology in modern living, it was plain even to the faithful that reformation in education was necessary at all levels. Scholars had, since the 1830s, fought a kind of rearguard action, defensive and negative, by claiming that western sciences are, in fact, Islamic sciences (Sharabi, 1966). In the words of Sharabi:

> This attitude provided the best justification for the process of borrowing from Europe. For by showing that in its essential structure European civilization was really nothing more than 'Arab civilization improved upon by new discoveries and inventions', it became not only legitimate to borrow from it but 'a duty to retrieve it'.

After 1952 Egypt adopted a western secular concept of government with the 'nation', that is, the 'masses' as the source of authority. Al-Azhar, which at that time consisted of three faculties, Islamic law, Q'ranic studies (creeds, ethics, etc.) and Arabic language and literature, fed by some primary and secondary institutions, was urged to establish relations with the Ministry of Education and bring its institutions into line with the governmental system. The sting of the political and religious separation of church and state would be removed by the continuing prestige attached to the university and its rector who was also the supreme leader of the Islamic world. As Minister of al-Azhar Affairs he would be appointed directly by the President and receive the second highest salary in the state.

The new relationship was defined in 1961 by Law No. 103. Boktor's (1963), selection from more than eighty articles forms the basis of the following points. Barriers between al-Azhar and other universities and higher institutions were to be eliminated so that their respective graduates would enjoy equal opportunities in education as well as work. This would be achieved by including in the courses a common core of knowledge and experience, with the proviso that Islamic and Arabic studies in al-Azhar be strictly maintained, and the educational certificates and university degrees in all the universities and higher institutions be unified. The new al-Azhar's functions were to be higher education and related research, and the transmission of the spiritual, intellectual and scientific heritage to Islamic and Arab peoples. The new law specified the colleges of which al-Azhar would be composed. They began with a number of colleges of Islamic studies in addition to colleges of business and administration, Arabic studies, engineering and industries, agriculture and medicine. Provision was made for increasing the number by order of the President of the Republic. By 1975 there were fourteen colleges or faculties and about 60,000 students. Boktor quotes the explanatory statement of the law for the apparent duplication of the faculties to be found in government universities:

These colleges should not be replicas of already existing ones in al-Azhar or in other universities. They should rather maintain, besides their general characteristic, the specific quality pertinent to al-Azhar, that is Islamic and religious studies, which should exist side by side with professional studies. This is by no means an innovation. Centuries ago great scientists in Mathematics, Chemistry and Medicine were also famous theologians, such as Avicenna, Tabari, Jabir ibn Hayyan, etc.

By the same law, Arabic would be used exclusively unless the Council of the university decided to adopt a foreign language for a specific occasion. Also both staff and students would be drawn exclusively from the Moslem community. The Council of the university would consist of the Director (Chairman), the Sub-Director, the Deans of the Faculties, a representative from the Ministry of Education, not more than three members from the Academy of Islamic Research and not more than three 'outside' members 'well-conversant with university matters'. Three degrees would be given, equivalent to the bachelor's and master's degrees in the other universities, and a 'Alamia' degree in higher Islamic or Arabic studies, equivalent to a PhD degree. Primary, preparatory and secondary schools already connected with al-Azhar would follow the pattern of the government schools, but with more emphasis on Islamic religion and Arabic.

The development of al-Azhar was very slow between 1961 and 1970, owing to the many practical problems arising from the law, but after 1970 the attention and very real support given by President Sadat enabled activity to be increased not only in Egypt but all over the world. Its budget is independent of the government, which supplies the money. Prior to 1970 this could only be spent in Cairo, but al-Azhar is now free in this respect. With the increasing demand for educational opportunities for Moslem girls has come the expansion of the Girls' Islamic Institute which is developing faculties that eventually will make it the equivalent of al-Azhar for men. Already it includes education, medicine, Islamic studies, Arabic literature, social studies, foreign languages (English and French) in addition to the first translation course in the country, offered as a present from France. Two other institutes affiliated with al-Azhar University are the Islamic Arabic Studies Institute, which offers legal studies, Arabic language studies and cultural and general studies in specialized branches. The other is known as the Language and Translation Institute, where most of the students are from Azhar secondary schools. An equivalent certificate to a BA degree is given after four years' study. An ambitious project is to establish branches of the university all over Egypt: some progress has already been made in Alexandria and the scheme includes Minia, Zagazig, Mansoura, Tanta, el-Fayum and Beni Suef. It is no longer necessary for students in al-Azhar University and higher institutes to have passed through the religious primary and secondary schools. They may qualify from the government schools, but the course is extended by a preparatory year which provides opportunity for the student to reach a required standard in Arabic and religious studies.

All this activity in the field of higher education has made it necessary to extend primary and secondary religious schools all over the country, parallel to the government schools, but with more attention paid to religious studies. This might appear to be a duplication of resources were it not for the fact that, with the increasing population and the increasing demand for education, schools from whatever source seem unlikely to become redundant. These institutes were the responsibility of the Ministry of Works but the demarcation between this Ministry and that of al-Azhar is not always clearly defined: even when they work under the same Minister, according to a high official of al-Azhar, they are still separate. In 1975 there were 300 government schools under the name of 'Azhar Primary Institutes', educating 70,000 pupils. The admission rules are relaxed, as these schools can accept pupils from six to nine years old and keep them until the age of nearly fifteen. In addition there are still about 4,000 Q'ranic schools maintained by funds from the Ministry of al-Azhar Affairs until they can be changed gradually into formal primary institutes. Pupils completing the general primary stage can be accepted by Azhar preparatory schools after passing a competitive examination in the Q'ran and in mathematics and writing at the fifth-grade level. Also blind pupils who succeed in learning the Q'ran off by heart and pass the oral examination may be admitted. Pupils at this stage study the same programmes and use the same textbooks as in general education plus intensive courses in all branches of Arabic language and religion. (Apparently there is no move to lighten the load carried by these children.)

At the secondary stage, Azhar schools differ in some respects from other secondary schools. Courses take four years instead of three and division into sections of study (literary and scientific) begins in the first instead of the second year. In the literary section studies are based on religion and Arabic language, which takes up half the timetable (twenty to twenty-five periods), thus preparing students to continue their education in Azhar Faculties of Legislations, Principles of Religion, the Faculty of Arabic Language and the Institute of Islamic Study. During the other fourteen to nineteen periods they study history, geography and citizenship, philosophy and psychology, English and French languages, art education and vocational studies as well as some science courses in the first year.

The scientific section consists of two branches: mathematics and science. In the mathematics branch students spend fifteen to nineteen periods a week studying Arabic language and religion and the rest of the time, mathematics (which is stressed), science (physics, chemistry and biology), citizenship, art education and vocational studies. In the first and second years courses in social studies (history and geography) are introduced. The science branch has the same curricula but more stress is given to science than mathematics.

Children can be admitted to the Azhar secondary schools if they have an Azhar preparatory certificate or a general preparatory certificate at the 60 per cent level. The latter must sit for a competitive examination in the Q'ran, Islamic studies, worships and relationships and Mohammedan biography at the preparatory level. Boys are not admitted after the age of twenty-five, while girls should not be more than twenty years. Girls are examined only in the Q'ran at both the primary and preparatory level. (This means that 'boys' can be thirty years old when they finish secondary school.)

Al-Azhar has its own teacher-training institutes which prepare teachers for the primary level. According to the Ministry of Education Report (1975), 'These institutes aim at preparing primary school teachers who have a general cultural background to enable them to understand children and their growth side by side with suitable religious education.' These general aims translated into admission requirements entail two years of Azhar secondary education with 50 per cent results on the final examinations in the science section or 60 per cent in the literary section, success in an entrance examination on the Q'ran, a maximum age of twenty-three years and an agreement to teach in primary schools for at least five years. The course, which takes three years, has scientific and literary sections. For a complete comparison with other primary teacher-training colleges the curricula are included here. Students in the literary section study: The Q'ran, its sayings and readings, its meaning and understanding, the sayings of the Prophet Mohammed, branches of the Arabic language which include grammar, linguistics literature, composition, readings and recitation, biography of the Prophet and stories from the Q'ran, handwriting and dictation, general health, education and psychology, methods of teaching and instructional aids, foreign languages, social studies, community services, physical education and art education. Students in the scientific section study the same subjects with science and mathematics in place of social studies. (Report, 1975)

Al-Azhar is also responsible for reading instructions, described as 'special schools for a unique kind of religious education which is not limited by age or standard of achievement or previous attendance at schools.' Its aim is to prepare a generation of people who learn the Q'ran, how to read it and write and how to recite it in different tones, to study the branches of knowledge which relate to the Q'ran and to the Arabic language, besides some general subjects and to equip students with educational knowledge which qualifies them to teach religion in primary schools and give readings in preparatory and secondary schools. The education in these institutions is in three stages: an equivalent preparatory stage with entrance depending on success in a written and oral examination in the Q'ran; a second stage of general readings and a third stage of specialized readings. In the first stage, to which blind pupils may be admitted, the students study notation of the Q'ran, linguistics, the Prophet's biography and sayings, grammar and composition, Arabic reading, handwriting and dictation, arithmetic, science and hygiene, art education and physical education. Blind pupils are exempted from dictation, handwriting, art education and physical education, but take recitations instead. A certificate is awarded at the end of the stage. The stage of general readings takes three years, covering the study of different readings of the Q'ran, pronunciation and stops, its meaning and understanding, Arabic grammar and usages, composition and rhythm, social subjects, arithmetic, science and hygiene. Success brings a certificate in general readings. For the specialized readings another three years are required covering readings of the Q'ran, uncommon readings, design of the Q'ran, notation and periods, subject matter of the Q'ran, history of the Q'ran books, meanings and understanding, Prophet's sayings, Islamic history, grammar and usages of Arabic language, literature and composition, rhetoric, practical teaching and Islamic Society. (Report 1975)

The educational functions of al-Azhar are not confined to Egypt; it has a unique international role as centre of the Islamic world through which it has ties from East to West, including many of the new states of Africa, Asia and Latin America. An independent budget covers its missionary functions. Besides sending teams to tour Africa and Asia at frequent intervals under the auspices of the Islamic Research Academy and providing places in Egypt for foreign students, it holds regular international conferences at the Academy to discuss matters pertaining to the education and welfare of Islamic youth. An example of the wide range of activities covered by the Ministry of Wakfs and al-Azhar Affairs can be seen in the report of its five-year plan made in 1971:

The Ministry of Wakfs and al-Azhar Affairs has formulated a five-year plan for the building of thirty more mosques in various governorates which would involve a total outlay of £E 4,029,000 apart from one hundred houses for Imams [leaders at prayer] in outlying districts. . . . [The Minister, Dr Abdul Aziz Kamel] went on to say that the Ministry's five-year plan also visualized the building of an Islamic and Q'ranic Culture Academy, comprising an Islamic library museum of the Q'ran as printed in the various ages, and a centre for study of Moslem society on the basis of the ancient documents preserved in the Ministry's archives. The five-year plan, the Minister said, also envisaged supplying Moslems in the Arab, African, Asian, European, North and South American states and Australia with some 116 sets of intonated Q'ran records, 6,560 books for the teaching of prayers, 20,700 copies of the Holy Q'ran in addition to 120,000 various books and magazines of Islamic culture. . . . Dr Kamel gave the number of mosques operated by the Ministry's own means at 3,558 to which a total of 2,884 scholars are attached. . . . 1,359 scholars of high qualifications from al-Azhar University had been seconded for service in private mosques which totalled 4,916. . . . On the Ministry's charitable activities the Minister said . . . £E 24,216 [had been given] in monthly payments to 879 University and Higher Institute students. . . . Dr Kamel said that al-Azhar High Council had approved the establishment of six Islamic culture offices under the control of the Islamic Research Academy in Nigeria, Indonesia, Upper Volta, and Arab Gulf Emirates, apart from a religious institute in Indonesia to be placed under supervision of al-Azhar. (*Egyptian Gazette*, 22 April 1971)

The Ministry of Culture

It is said that the label 'culture' has been used in anthropology with over one hundred different meanings. Cultural policy in Egypt appears to be concerned with what Honigmann (1959), describes as the three kinds of phenomena that make up 'culture': socially standardized actions, that is, actions modified by the process of socialization; socially standardized thoughts and feelings, closely involved with the acts; and socially standardized artifacts, that is man-made characteristics of the environment. A revolutionary government, committed to socialism, is naturally much concerned with changing the pattern of the society it governs. This is a matter not only for direct but indirect education guided by a conscious policy. As a first step, assessment needed to be made of the cultural level and the cultural needs of each sector of society. Two examples will suffice. Wahba (1972), describes how, in 1969, the Minister of Culture commissioned a team of sociologists to conduct a socio-cultural survey of an ordinary Egyptian village, el-Marazeen in the Giza governorate, with a population in 1966 of 4,323. Data included the illiteracy rate, health and education provision, social organization (local branches of ASU, agricultural and co-operative societies), home and social life, possession of radios, pictures, books. A more ambitious project taking place during the same period, which emanated from the National Centre for Social and Criminological Research aimed at assessing children's needs in Egypt, covering health and nutrition, food consumption, rearing methods, legal needs, educational needs, psychological needs, custody of children, employment, problems in all these areas and recommendations for their solution. (Further details are discussed in the chapter on 'Problems'.)

From such investigations seen in the political context of the National Charter and the Permanent Constitution there emerged what Magdi Wahba, Under-Secretary for the Ministry of Culture calls 'the elements of a cultural policy'. To illustrate how far this policy seeks to achieve a nice balance between a conservation of all that is best in the cultural legacy of Egypt and her general plan to fit the various activities into a democratic socialist transformation of Egyptian society, Wahba's 'elements' will be quoted at length:

To increase awareness of the continuity of culture in Egypt,
while strengthening links with humanistic values of other cultures;
to contribute to a sense of solidarity between the rural and urban
populations by the encouragement of common cultural action and
the affirmation of common cultural values;
to enable all citizens to enjoy the right to participate freely in the
cultural life of the community;
to ensure that the quality of cultural action should not be
sacrificed to the requirements of quantitative dissemination;
to create a situation of fruitful dialogue between the intellectuals
and the majority of the people;
to provide the intellectuals with a sense of self-fulfilment within
the community;
to ensure the patronage of the arts without creating a sense of
totalitarian oppressiveness;
to ensure that the alienation of the creative artist should not
be overcome at the expense of alienation of the public;
to create intelligible links between cultural and socio-economic
development;
to provide systematically for the training and encouragement of
agents, for both the creation and dissemination of culture;
to reconstruct a system of cultural values based on a progressive
humanism from a synthesis of national and universal cultures.

To translate such an ambitious statement of intent into practical plans of action requires the resources of ministries primarily concerned with cultural matters, such as the Ministry of Culture, the Ministry of National Guidance (Ministry of Information), the Ministry of Tourism and the Ministry of Youth, while other ministries contribute through their own cultural departments. The latter include the Ministry of Education, the Ministry of Higher Education, the Ministry of Scientific Research, and the Ministry of Wakfs and al-Azhar Affairs. This section will summarize the activities of the Ministry of Culture itself.

The Ministry of Culture, originally a Department of Culture in the Ministry of Education, later absorbed into the Ministry of Culture and National Guidance, responsible for the arts, literature and mass media, was re-organized by Presidential decree in 1971 to become both a service and development ministry. It had been placed under a minister who was also a Deputy Prime Minister, in order 'to demonstrate the importance which the state attached to long-term planning and the recognition of the role of culture on development', but a further development was the creation of a new post of Assistant to the President for Cultural Affairs, ensuring that cultural planning in its widest sense would be a top-level priority, involving all the agencies concerned.

The Minister, whose business it is to help and encourage such projects as the National Ballet Company, the cinema and theatre and all creative and artistic endeavour, is directly responsible for a number of miscellaneous cultural activities. These include archeology, fine arts, the Academy of Arts, foreign cultural relations, general and financial administration relating to pension schemes for free-lance journalists, and self-employed artists and writers, popular culture (including seventeen houses of culture in provincial capitals, twenty-five mobile caravans, two hundred village cultural centres and two pilot cultural centres for children), libraries and archives.

Besides these direct responsibilities there are three corporations under the authority of the Minister, namely the Publishing and Printing Corporation which is a semi-autonomous subsidized public service used for long-term projects, the Theatre, Music and Folk Art Corporation, another service organization which provides among other things, free concerts, especially interesting for young people, and the state cinema corporation run on strictly commercial lines, like a nationalized industry (a successful nationalized industry, as Egyptian films have great success, both at home and abroad). There is also a documentary film centre which is supported by funds from the commercial section. The thriving private sector may use the studios and laboratories but they remain the property of the state corporation which owns all the means of production.

The Minister of Culture is the President of the Higher Council for the Arts, Letters and the Social Sciences whose main functions are the supervision of extensive programmes of translations, the holding of international conferences and the selection of candidates for state awards and prizes. He is also the patron and chairman of the Academy of the Arabic Language.

Projects currently in progress at various stages include an eleven-storey building at Giza, which will house a museum of modern art, a gallery of the history of art in reproduction, the national film society (with two projection halls seating a thousand persons), a library of art books, a record library with a large auditorium and cubicles for individual listening, an arts centre for children, eleven artists' studios, two multi-purpose exhibition halls, a small theatre for experimental productions and a lecture hall. Other projects mentioned by Wahba include the Roman Amphitheatre at Alexandria, recently excavated by Polish archeologists, which is being prepared for productions from Roman comedies and Greek tragedies, the Solar Boat Museum built beside the Pyramid of Cheops, the Tapestry Centre displaying peasant children's tapestry and weaving from Haraneya, the Youth Orchestra, provincial museums, Son et Lumière at Karnak, Ancient Egyptian Drama productions and a Higher Institute of Art Criticism.

Wahba's detailed survey of state patronage and the training of cultural agents underlines the importance that the government attaches to the conservation of Egypt's cultural heritage, not only for the education of her own citizens but in trust for mankind:

> The migration of peoples and the cross-fertilization of the Egyptian ethos with a tremendous diversity of cultures and religious traditions have created an extremely rich fund of folklore and archetypical patterns of thought and sensibility, making Egypt, 'a vast open-air museum of civilizations'.

The Ministry of Youth

Constant references are made to the importance of the 'masses' in post-revolutionary Egypt. According to statistics, about 43 per cent of them in 1960 were under the age of fifteen years, so, allowing for the yearly increase of about a million babies, it seems possible that the term 'youth' could apply to more than 50 per cent of the population of about 34,000,000 in 1975. As they are constantly being told by their leaders, their employers and their teachers, the ultimate success of the Revolution in all its aspects depends on their loyalty expressed in their willingness to live or die working in the interests of their country. Their education in terms not only of their potential participation in the new economic and industrial modernization of the country, but also in the understanding and acceptance of the particular ideology underlying the structure of modern Egyptian society, is therefore vital to the government. For working youth, whose parents and grandparents are able to recall the 'bad old days' of class privilege the task of the Arab Socialist Union is made comparatively easy: they have a new, dignified status in society with the promise of a better economic future in return for today's hardships. For the intelligent élite in the universities and institutes of higher education, the potential leaders in the new society, the new scientific approach to knowledge and administration implies freedom to question and debate even in the sensitive areas of politics. The problems arising from this situation are discussed in a subsequent chapter.

The Ministry of Youth is the department of government which is dedicated solely to the task of taking care of young citizens whether they are workers or students, its terms of reference covering all activities that can be classed as 'welfare'. Its educational function is exercised indirectly, but in terms of 'total man' is very important. It keeps in touch with, influences and in many cases co-ordinates the work of all other organizations concerned with specialized youth activities, mainly by representation on decision-making committees. These include the Arab Socialist Union organizations, the ASU for Youth Affairs, the Socialist Youth Organization and the People's Assembly Youth Committee and the Department of Youth Affairs at the Ministry of Higher Education, with its own special Under-Secretary. These organizations work very closely together, with the ASU having, so to speak 'a foot in every camp'. Not so, however, with the students' own organization for their welfare. In 1975 Dr Rifaat el-Mahgoub, First Secretary of ASU Central Committee, announced that an ASU student committee would be formed at each university faculty (college), but that membership would be voluntary, elections following after those for the student union. 'The

ASU Students Committee at each faculty will form part of a general
youth congress at district level, while the youth governorate congress
will be formed at all district congresses.' The new youth organization
would have no units in universities and it would not be committed to
political action alone. Confirming that student unions would resume all
their activities, Dr Mahgoub said:

> There will be no differences between university student unions and
> ASU committees . . . with no guardianship from any ASU
> authority. . . . No restrictions will be imposed as long as the
> unions comply with the university's roles. . . . The relationship
> between political organization and student unions . . . is one of
> co-operation within the framework of national unity, a relation-
> ship not in conflict with a pluralistic cultural representation at the
> universities. (*Egyptian Gazette*, 16 September 1975, 3 October 1975)

The main function of the Ministry of Youth is to provide social
welfare, including sport and cultural activities, for the young up to the
time when formal education ends. It combines the functions of extra-
mural studies, the Boy Scout movement and is the authority in charge
of planning, preparing and supervising sporting events, sports clubs,
hobbies centres, and vocational training centres. Its activities are wide,
and decentralized as much as possible, bearing in mind the problems of
the young in rural areas. A documentary film unit attached to the
Ministry keeps a record of conferences and youth rallies which are a
growing feature, both nationally and internationally. In both instances
the Ministry of Youth seeks co-operation from other authorities. For
instance, in 1973 the Board of the Cairo Local Services Fund approved
the allocation of a £E 20,000 to eighteen small sporting clubs and
twenty-one youth centres in the metropolis. This was in response to a
plan made by the Minister in 1972 with the aim of maintaining a
balance between newly constructed establishments and on-going
projects

> The first part of the plan comprises investments for the completion
> and construction of new youth establishments. Total costs for
> these projects are estimated at £E 7,272,100. The second part of the
> plan deals with the costs of programmes and operational expenses
> such as programmes for students, workers and farmers, clubs and
> vocational training centres as well as the mobile service units and

the apprentices training centres and the training of leaders. Costs entailed in these projects are estimated as £E 19,698,225. The third part which entails £E 8,240,274, envisages the consolidation of the Ministry's Administration, the central bodies and the Youth Welfare Directorates in the governorates with the manpower required for the implementation of this plan. A responsible source at the Ministry of Youth was quoted as saying that the plan, which would incur £E 35,210,599, would take at least five years to fulfil its targets. He pointed out that the number of new youth establishments would be 700 units apart from present units numbering 2,500 serving 4,840,000 beneficiaries. This would represent some 50 per cent of eligible youth beneficiaries. (*Egyptian Gazette*, 21 November 1971)

The importance of youth leadership and its training has been the subject of rallies and conferences organized by both the Minister of State for Youth and the ASU Secretariat for Youth. These rallies, held in Cairo squares, bring together as many as 10,000 youths of all sectors, while even in the governorates attendance reaches 2 or 3,000. All are deeply concerned with the role of youth in modern Egypt, their speeches being followed, for example, by some practical gesture of help, such as the offer in 1975 to donate £E 10,000 of the funds for the relief of victims of torrential rains which swept Minia governorate. All provide opportunities for youth to confirm their solidarity with the government. A typical telegram sent to President Sadat reads:

The Student Federation seizes the opportunity of holding the seminar on the role of the Student Federation in the current stage to affirm that the students are the vanguard of the alliance of the People's working forces seeking a better future, the realization of democracy and socialism.

That was 1972 and a year later they had the opportunity of testing their sincerity during the October War against Israel. Through the action committees of their organizations, they organized civil defence, work in hospitals, etc. A report in 1973 spoke of the participation of 233,000 youths who took part in the battle and civil defence work, claiming that 127,000 donated blood, 19,000 took part in public service activities and 5,000 found other means of participating in the battle. Two years after victory over 20,000 youths, pledging full support to President Anwar

166

el-Sadat, marched from the stadium to Kubleh Republican Palace, demonstrating among other things, the efficiency of their training in national responsibility and solidarity.

In spite of currency problems, every year thousands of students leave Egypt for holiday travel, vacation work or overseas studies, known as 'foreign missions'. The responsibilities and work involved are, as in all other youth affairs, shared between the Ministry of Youth, the Ministry of Higher Education and the Arab Socialist Union. In each case a selection has to be made but the aim is to grant as many applications as possible. Those travelling abroad as tourists have to be willing to transfer £50 or more and are only allowed to stay for fifteen days. Most of those who travel for the summer obtain work through the Central Students' Travel Bureau attached to the Higher Council for Youth and Sports. Committees formed in each university and higher education institute select students on the basis of their advancement in studies as well as their participation in various cultural, social and sports activities. The Central Students' Travel Bureau supplies the committees with lists of more than three hundred organizations in thirty countries who provide work opportunities and accommodation for Egyptian students during the summer vacation. In 1973 about 13,000 students took part in the scheme. Nominations from secondary schools are processed by the general education section of the Ministry of Youth, who lays down certain rules:

> The nominee should master either English or French, or the language of the country to which he will go, he should be enlightened on the political and national achievements of the nation and issues of national interest; those who have hobbies and who have engaged in social sports, cultural and/or artistic activities are given preference, the age of the nominee must not exceed 25 and must not be less than 18 and a superior study record is a prerequisite for travelling abroad. (*Egyptian Gazette*, 17 May 1971)

To ensure that all these criteria are fulfilled, the ASU Youth Secretariat organize studies for the successful applicants twice a week for about six weeks before they depart.

Other opportunities for educational travel are provided by direct cultural agreements between Egypt and other countries. These include 'youth friendship weeks' arranged by the Socialist Youth Organization with friendly countries in the Eastern Bloc and 'youth co-operation accords' involving exchange of youth concluded by the Minister of Youth. A typical example would be the package arrangements by the Minister of Youth resulting from a tour of Sudan, Somalia, the Arab Republic of Yemen and the People's Democratic Republic of Yemen in 1961. In Sudan the agreement provided for the organization of tournaments in such sports as football, basketball, volleyball, boxing, wrestling, weight-lifting, and track and field games, exchange of information and technical publications, documentary films and an Egyptian offer of fifteen scholarships a year for training in physical training and social services. Similar agreements were made with the other countries.

Most important of all are the educational missions abroad, which are the direct responsibility of the Minister of Higher Education, as they involve formal education at the postgraduate level. As the Minister of Youth and the Arab Socialist Union are only marginally involved, these missions are discussed in the chapter on the Ministry of Higher Education.

Most recent developments centred on the general education of youth, covering formal and informal aspects include the formation of the first Arab Youth Federation with its headquarters in Cairo, in 1974. The seven founding members included Tunisia, Algeria, Palestine, Libya, Morocco, Mauritania and the Arab Youth Federation of Egypt. Linked with the Arab League, its aims cover the aspirations of youth in all Arab countries: greater participation in economic development projects, campaigns to eradicate illiteracy, studies of various Arab problems and their solutions, training for youth in educational and cultural fields, and, above all, the linking of Arab youth welfare programmes with economic and social development projects in Arab countries. President Sadat, who first suggested making a federation of Arab youth organizations, saw this as a natural step after success in the October war:

> He said that Arabs should discuss their problems in the spirit of
> the age, should learn how to argue and differ without resorting to
> diatribes and accusations . . . that the Arabs have a golden
> opportunity now which they must seize or perish: the Arab
> nation has plenty of brains, cadres, adequate material and human
> resources . . . youth were responsible for the task of improving on
> civilization. (*Egyptian Gazette*, 25 October 1974)

The private sector

Private schools

Since 1948 the trend has been to bring private schools, of whatever origin or kind, more and more under the control of the Ministry of Education. Before that date they had been completely independent and unsupervised, ranging from small, money-making establishments to schools subsidized by foreign communities and Christian churches, some of which became so well-established that they drew their pupils from all over the Middle East. Some of them were inspired by missionary zeal but many of them originated to serve the many foreign communities that settled in Egypt temporarily or permanently from the seventeenth century onwards. Boktor quotes an Arabic report which listed countries of origin as Greece, Great Britain, France, United States of America, Ireland, Canada, Germany, Switzerland, and the Netherlands. Each foreign school, being designed for its own nationals, followed the pattern of the country of origin in organization, language, content, syllabuses, method and examination of pupils. This caused no government concern until with the increasing demand for modern education and the growing importance of proficiency in foreign languages, the wealthier sections of the Egyptian population sent their children to be educated with their foreign neighbours. The children so educated not only learned to think and speak in a foreign tongue, often despising their own language, but knew more about the history, geography and literature of a foreign country than of their own land. In some cases it was also feared that proselytism was taking place between Moslem and Christian or Eastern and Western interpretations of Christianity. In 1948, a quarter of a century after independence, the Ministry of Education demanded that foreign schools should teach Arabic, history, geography and civics at the same level as in government schools. To comply with this regulation some schools appear to have added the government syllabuses to their own offerings so that, having done their lessons, in say, English, the children have had to cope with a number of periods in Arabic. As Arabic is a very difficult subject with many branches, the time-table became overcrowded and the school day very long.

During this period there was no actual antagonism towards foreign schools, as many government officials had received their education in them and were proud of the connection as well as grateful for the opportunities they provided in girls' education and in the learning of foreign languages. It is claimed, for instance, that co-education in Egypt began at the German School, Zamalek in the year 1900, twenty-seven years after its foundation. The excellent French convent schools produced a female intellectual élite during a period when Egyptian society favoured protection of its Moslem ladies.

After the Revolution, which held foreign domination and imperialism responsible for most of the country's problems, attention was drawn more sharply to the presence of foreign influence in education. After the Suez aggression in 1965 anti-foreigner feeling became very strong and large numbers of foreign nationals left the country. The government Egyptianized all British schools and all French schools except those sponsored by the Vatican. Instead of sitting for the GCE examination set in England or the French Baccalauréat examination, the pupils would be tested by a new local examination. Law No. 160 (1958), was designed to destroy the concept of a 'foreign' school in Egypt. All proprietors, directors and staff were to be Egyptians, except those actually engaged in teaching the foreign language, the state curricula had to be followed and the children prepared for the new secondary school certificate examination.

This was a political decision and, not surprisingly, there were educational complications that are still being sorted out. In 1963, Boktor commented:

> It has been suggested that if these schools were called language schools, and their school subjects dealing with national matters were taught in Arabic, there would be no objection if the rest of the subjects would be taught in a foreign language.

Personal experience in a 'bilingual' state school has indicated that where two languages are used in parallel classes, in one of which language A is the medium and language B is taught for two periods a day (and in the other vice versa), it is possible for fluency to be acquired in the second language, but that there is a retardation factor in terms of reading, writing and comprehension. This is especially true in the early stages. The original products of these schools were expected to read, write and think in the foreign language as if it were their first language; not all children can cope with two languages at the same level. In Luxembourg, where, for geographical reasons it is necessary for children to be equally skilled in three languages the problem has been seen more dramatically, as primary education in the past was entirely taken up with language teaching to the exclusion of other educational experience relevant to the developmental level, and backward children finished their education by knowing three languages inaccurately and little else besides. My point is that the question of how soon and how much foreign language teaching becomes an asset rather than an educational liability is a matter for comparative study in a modern educational system, which caters for children of a wide range of ability according to their developmental characteristics and needs.

Other problems have arisen as a result of using foreign translations of the textbooks used in the government schools, even in teaching the foreign language. This, according to the Press, has been a factor in lowering the standards of foreign language teaching. English teachers, for example, have complained that much of their time has had, on occasion, to be taken in explaining and correcting an English text which had originally been translated into Arabic for use in government schools and then re-translated into English from the Arabic version for use in the English school. In fact, the government has been much concerned to raise the standards of foreign language teaching in state as well as 'private' schools, a term which, since 1958, has covered all non-government educational institutions, including evening classes, correspondence schools, training schemes, language and commercial schools, indeed any private organization training for an occupation or providing cultural courses. Attempts to preserve but integrate the private sector to the satisfaction of all concerned have been increased in recent years. To this end, the Ministry of Higher Education in 1971 approved the re-organization of private higher institutions to ensure that they would be run in the best interests of the students. Owners were given one month in which to appoint full-time directors. Five members of the board could be appointed from the institute's teaching staff or staffs of similar institutions while the other five would be provided from among the experts in higher education and relevant public affairs, and a member representing the Minister of Higher Education. The Higher Institute Council under the Minister of Higher Education also approved a set of rules for such institutes to follow in accepting students, their system of study and examinations, the teachers' salaries and other payments, health and social care of students, on the same lines as in government institutions, thus ending a great deal of confusion. In the same year the Ministry of Education made the educational departments in the different governorates responsible for supplying the necessary teaching staffs and bring them up to the mark qualitatively. They were charged with making surveys of the available staff to meet any shortage based on the government child-teacher ratio. They were also to make studies on the efficiency and qualifications of staff in private schools and institutions and the effect of full- and part-time secondment on the work of teachers in their own schools and the schools to which they are seconded. The needs of the private schools were to be entered in the general estimates of demands submitted by the education departments to the Ministry each year. (*Egyptian Gazette*, 23 January 1971) By 1974 the government was ready to take further steps to safeguard the interests of children attending private schools. The Minister of Education met the Under-Secretaries Committee to discuss policy to be followed in the development of private schools to ensure their efficiency. Not only would permits be given for the opening of new schools, but the conditions attached included inducements to enter this business. The following details illustrate the present trends of private education in modern Egypt:

applicants for opening private schools should be very particular about the choice of building and the measures for approving the applications should be ready within a fortnight;
the Directorates of Education would be entitled to raise fees of private schools in cases of absolute necessity;
schools would be allowed to add 5 per cent of the total cost of books to their respective prices and expenses;
charges for examinations would also be increased to cover what was spent;
directors of Education would also be entitled to employ people in these schools until the age of sixty-five and to give pensioners permission to work in private education;
the trend was to exempt distinguished pupils who score 90 per cent of the total marks from the fees in the third year.

The Council of the Cairo governorate was quick to approve the private schools aid programme presented by the Ministry of Education. It would be applied to 169 private schools in Cairo, which would be allocated funds amounting to £E 181,000. (*Egyptian Gazette*, 14 May 1974, 19 May 1971)

The American University in Cairo

The American University in Cairo must be one of the most outstanding and successful missionary products in the Middle East; to those investors who are currently evaluating its worthiness for financial support its capacity to survive would be a reasonable starting criterion. Institutionally speaking, it can be said to have 'kept its head when all around were losing theirs', maintaining complete independence through a period of great political and social change, which saw the struggle for national independence, marked by riots of the masses against the classes whom it educated, a revolution followed by expulsion of foreigners, closure of its embassy, strong, anti-American feeling provoked by America's support of Egypt's greatest enemy and near financial ruin as a result of withdrawal of American aid following an economic recession.

To this record of survival can be added its developmental achievement characterized by remarkable expansion. From a modest 142 students in 1920 enrolled either in the Arabic medium secondary school or the English medium junior college it now educates more than 6,500 students at the post-secondary level. The courses cover a range of levels from non-degree to masters' degrees in science and arts. By usual university standards its numbers are small and its courses limited and highly selective, depending more than usual on the abilities and enthusiasms of current staff, whose successful recruitment during the vicissitudes outlined above has been a crucial factor in both survival and achievement. That it has managed to attract quality in both staff and students is indicated by the consistent practice of major American and European universities accepting AUC graduates of good standing into their own advanced degree programmes. In America, for example, they have completed their master's or doctoral programmes in such well-known institutions as Bryn Mawr, Cambridge, Chicago, Columbia, Cornell, Denver, Harvard, Indiana, Kentucky, New York, North Carolina, North Dakota, Oregon, Princeton, Smith, South Dakota, Stanford, Tulane, Utah and Yale as well as being accepted by the United States Veterans Administration. Some of them also make their way to universities in England, such as London, Oxford and Cambridge, and to the Sorbonne in Paris. The University holds memberships of the International Association of Universities, the American Council on Education, the Association of American Colleges and other college organizations, its degrees being authenticated by the Board of Education of Washington, DC, where the University is incorporated.

For the students themselves the most important development in the last two years must be the recognition of their degrees by the Egyptian government. Although AUC is a multi-national university, most of the students and 45 per cent of the faculty are Egyptian. For many of the students it is more important to be able to complete their higher studies in an Egyptian university than in London, Paris or New York, especially if they are studying a major, like psychology, for which there are no postgraduate facilities at AUC. Many of them owe their under-graduate studies to the award of scholarships or the self-sacrifice of parents unable to afford to send them abroad for studies at the MA level. AUC students already studying at Ain Shams and Cairo Universities have, in the first year of recognition, justified this move by the Egyptian government. For those working in teaching and other posts demanding university degrees, salaries will now be commensurate with qualifications.

This link with the government universities combined with President Sadat's new 'open door policy', which will be discussed at greater length elsewhere, has marked a new era not only in the history of the American University, but in the whole educational system of Egypt. It seems that almost overnight advantages of co-operation between the private and public sectors in higher education are not only being perceived with great clarity, but are being acted on without delay. Instead of overtly or covertly criticizing each other's educational offerings, each has directed attention and energy to ensuring that all Egyptian citizens, whether they attend the free state universities or can afford to pay the fees at AUC, get the chance of contributing to the public good.

Co-operation between public and private sectors has always been present, especially through the work of the Social Research Centre and at professorial level, as well as the Public Service Department, but a few examples from the AUC reports of the last two years will justify the comments above. In his review (1974–5) President Cecil K. Byrd of AUC states:

Common efforts in research and teaching outside AUC have
involved us with Egyptian organizations and in Egyptian problems,
research projects in family planning, demographic projection
analysis, and protein-calorie malnutrition continued as co-operative

174

activities between AUC and the faculties of Cairo and Ain Shams Universities, the two largest in Egypt. We helped these universities develop cultural programmes for visiting American groups coming to learn about Egypt and explored other areas of future co-operation.

He gives as an example of university-industry co-operation the signing of a research contract between AUC and the Egyptian Organization for sugar and distillation. The two parties will be working together to find solutions to the problems of the sugar industry. 'AUC also sponsored a conference on comparative economic planning to study the implementation of the "Open Door" economic policy.'

Other collaboration with Egyptian institutions comes from departmental reports. A few examples will suffice. In the Department of Arabic Studies arrangements have been made resulting from the collaboration of the Ministry of Higher Education and AUC, supported by the Ford Foundation, to offer a three-year programme of intensive English and MA studies to junior faculty members of Egyptian national universities in Arabic history and literature before they leave Egypt for their doctoral work in the United States, Canada or England. After preliminary English courses, nine were admitted to the English Language Institute for the academic year 1975–6. The University will gain by receiving graduate students who are the best in their fields in Egypt. In the materials engineering and physical sciences department the chairperson and her students have participated in a major study to determine the environmental impact of the Aswan High Dam on the Nile Valley, a project under the supervision of the Egyptian National Academy of Science, in co-operation with the School of Public Health of the University of Michigan. The English Language Institute also made what has been described as 'the most substantial training programme for upgrading English language teaching anywhere in Egypt' including among its students eighty-four Egyptian school teachers, about forty of whom were on scholarships from the Ministry of Education. Meanwhile the Department of Sociology/Anthropology/Psychology has been initiating contacts with Egyptian institutions to explore ways in which AUC staff and students could help strengthen the social sciences in Egypt. The resulting projects include co-operation with the Director of the Arab States Fundamental Education Centre at Sers el-Layyan and participating in a conference on 'The Informal Education of

Women and Social Development', co-operating in a field project in urban development with members of the social sciences department at Assiut University, and both planning and teaching a new social science programme at the Cairo Higher Institute of Nursing.

In line with the revolutionary doctrine that Egypt is an integral part of the 'Arab nation', the American University has lost no opportunity to collaborate with colleagues not only in the Middle East but in North Africa. The Social Research Centre, for example, has provided the first elected Secretary General of a new 'Organization for the promotion of the social sciences in the Middle East' which is hoping 'to lay the groundwork for the establishment of a professional social science association by the end of a two-year period.' The Computer Centre, which has been honoured by having its Director, Dr Salah Hamid, appointed by President Anwar el-Sadat to the National Council for Education, Scientific Research and Technology, designed an admissions and registrations system for the University of Riyadh in Saudi Arabia and provided a training programme of Riyadh personnel. At the same university advice on the feasibility of establishing a Social Science Research Centre was given by the Department of Sociology/Anthropology/Psychology, which is also making research and other links with universities and organizations both national and international, in the field of psychology, notably in Child Development. This list is far from exhaustive: it tries to answer the question, 'What is the business of a small, fee-paying private and foreign university in a revolutionary socialist state which offers free education at the university level?' It may also partly answer the question why the President of the Republic has announced his intention of opening a state private, fee-paying university!

7

Student welfare

Health services

The scope of children's welfare

When, in 1970, it was desired to associate the name of the late President, Gamal Abdul Nasser, with appropriate educational projects, the three selected on the basis of their priority in his programme were all connected with welfare of students and teachers. The first was a £E 10 million project arising from badly constructed and inadequate school premises, including about 50 per cent in Cairo and Alexandria, the second was an up-to-date club for students to be designed by the Faculty of Engineering and their technicians, which would give scope for political and cultural activity, and the third was Nasser's plan for teachers' welfare, reflecting his great appreciation of their devotion and loyalty.

It will be seen that the concept of 'welfare' is wide in Egypt, which continues to plan a welfare state in spite of the need to demand sacrifices in personal comfort for many years to come, in order to finance long-term beneficial plans for the country. Student welfare can be viewed as the first and most important stage in an overall plan to give every one of Egypt's millions of citizens the opportunity for healthy physical, mental and social development. The overall plan, of which school health is a part, has been described by the Minister of Public Health as requiring three stages; the first being based on the establishment of health centres in the villages and cities. At that time (1973), 600 had been established in the cities and 1,800 in the villages. There were 4,500 practitioners serving in these centres, charged with preventive as well as curative work, including care of mothers and newly born babies. Family planning and school health are included in the responsibilities of these centres. Every centre in the cities serves about 25,000 of its inhabitants, and in the villages, 5,000 to 10,000. The centres are intended to ease the pressure on hospitals, so that specialists can give more time and effort where it is needed. The second stage is the establishment of new, specialized clinics or the development of out-patient clinics of the hospitals into specialized polyclinics, to which incurable patients could be sent for treatment. Every one would serve six health centres or around 150,000 persons. Three sections would be added to them including public hygiene, child care and school health. The third part of the plan was the development of training centres in all the university hospitals, such as the one already functioning in Kasr el-Aini Hospital, Cairo. The Director of the School Health Department of the Ministry of Health stressed the importance of preventive medicine, especially as it affected the problem of handicap among pupils.

Ministries involved in student welfare, using the term in its broadest sense, include Public Health, Education, Youth and Social Affairs aided at times by the Ministry of Housing and Local Government, and always a matter of interest to the Arab Socialist Union which has a special responsibility in community welfare.

The pre-school child

The Ministry of Education no longer makes provision for the pre-school child. In theory the first primary class at least is a kindergarten-type of educational provision, but, in spite of special teacher-training courses for those interested in teaching young children, it in no way resembles the modern infant school. At present the Ministry of Social Affairs is trying to provide a much-needed service for children whose mothers go out to work. With the increasing demand, the Ministry recognized that, to prevent abuse of the child, baby-minding establishments labelled as 'nurseries' or 'kindergartens' need very strict control. This is likely to be more possible in the establishments run by the Ministry itself than in a mushrooming private industry. The First Child Welfare Conference, held in 1971, was, in fact, organized by the Arab Socialist Union Secretariat and the General Assembly of Nursery Homes and Kindergartens in Cairo. Inspired by a recorded speech by President Nasser, entitled 'Childhood: maker of the Future', in which he emphasized the importance of developing child welfare programmes, in the interests both of women wanting to go out to work and the health, well-being and cultural advantage of the children themselves. Already 130 nursery homes and schools had been built in Cairo as a result of the joint efforts of the Arab Socialist Union and the executive bodies of the government. The aim of the conference was to discuss how child welfare systems could be developed, and the role played by such nurseries and kindergartens in securing a better future for children. The Ministries of Housing and Local Government and the Cairo Government Council offered to add £E 10,000 to the same amount already contributed by the ASU. More than a million children were benefiting from these organizations and it was hoped that similar provision would later be made in rural areas.

In 1973, the Planning Committee of the Ministry of Social Affairs reviewed the family and child welfare provided already and discussed the means of developing social welfare services which would include the establishment of nurseries in all sectors and districts, according to strict laws safeguarding the children's interests. Emphasis was made for arranging training courses for the personnel of nurseries; executive bodies should co-operate closely to provide the various kinds of needs of children under six years old. The Minister reviewed the Ministry's policy in the field of social research and recommended that all social programmes and projects should be scientifically evaluated and that the considerable number which had been conducted in the Ministry since 1953 should be re-examined to find out if they could be put to practical use.

Another child welfare project of interest to the Ministry was the acquisition of a 3,000 square metre site for the Social Service Association for the district of Bulac, a very poor, crowded area of Cairo. The project, which was funded by various sources, was directed to providing social services for the local families.

Student health services

The health of schoolchildren and students is the business of a special section of the Ministry of Public Health, which supplies medical facilities to supplement those provided by the medical centres in the cities and villages. In 1971, Unesco agreed to co-operate to extend school health services to the capitals in all the governorates. The plan was to establish 135 units, each covering 10,000 students. They would be set up in one of the new primary schools in the capital and would include a dentist, a school physician and a number of nurses. The plan was extended to include clinics at every teachers' institute. In Cairo, where nine school health units had been supplied, and in Alexandria, where there were six health units, equipment had been provided by UNICEF.

Besides the routine examination of the school population, the Director of School Health initiates special studies related to special health problems. Examples of these are two studies made in 1971. The first is a diabetes test given to about 3 million schoolchildren attending primary and preparatory schools. Preliminary results indicated that a high proportion of children were suffering from the disease, so that not only were follow-up studies necessary to find means of combating the disease, but that the number of school medical units equipped to treat diabetes would need to be increased. Another study, made in co-operation with the Ministries of Youth and Education, set out to discover the proportion of foot deformity and its causes among 6,000 pupils at various stages, attending schools in the governorates of Cairo and Menufia. It was found that 50 per cent of the pupils suffered from flat feet, among whom 2 per cent were incurable. Foot deformity was attributed partly to the unhealthy conditions of school buildings and overcrowding of classrooms which forced children to sit in unnatural conditions.

In 1974 progress was made in the provision of students' and teachers' hospitals. In both cases intensive care units were supplied to relieve the pressure on the only such unit in Cairo. Also in the students' hospital three surgical operation rooms are being equipped: for eye surgery, ear, nose and throat surgery and gynaecology, while in another hospital six rooms have been reserved for patients receiving treatment for nervous disorders. In Alexandria, improvements in health care also include the development of a students' hospital. The provision is still modest when related to the size of the student population, but a framework has been provided so that the provisions for child and student health programmes can be progressively improved as more money becomes available.

Student housing

The provision of university education has only recently been extended to the governorates outside of Cairo and Alexandria, so the rapid expansion of higher education has brought thousands of students to the main cities, which are already overcrowded with landless peasants. The problem has been so acute that the Ten-Year Plan (1970–80) included housing projects for every university. The Final Report in 1972 stated that twenty-one blocks of flats were to be built for 5,384 male students from outside Cairo for the universities of al-Azhar, Cairo, Ain Shams, and Assiut and six for 2,586 female students of the same universities, most of which would be completed and handed over in the following academic year. The Ministry of Wakfs (Religion) had made available £E 1,300,000 for the al-Azhar student housing projects and £E 7,060,000 had been appropriated in the General State Budget for Housing: for al-Azhar £E 3,500,000, Cairo £E 1,150,000, Ain Shams, £E 880,000, Assiut £E 280,000 and Alexandria £E 1,250,000. In each case student representatives were made members of the boards of the housing units: more than a thousand of them were elected from the 'University City' at Giza. The Governor of Giza stated his readiness to grant areas of land to any other governorate interested in building hostels for their students coming to Giza to study at Cairo University. Not surprisingly, one of the first concerns of student members of the Board was a solution of the transport problem to and from Giza to the universities.

School meals

During the discussions at the Modern Education Conference held in Cairo in 1971, it was agreed that some of the health problems among primary school children were the result of malnutrition. A strong recommendation was made that school meals should be provided at all stages of education. Subsequently the Minister of Education decided to form a higher committee for the implementation of food programmes for primary school children in the countryside. The committee was charged with making an all-year-round project and to co-ordinate with various bodies to anticipate and find solutions for problems attendant on the agreement of the World Food Programme to supply meals for pupils in rural areas. The Director of Nutrition at the Ministry of Education was made an executive director in the Programme, to be assisted by a team of experts from various departments, who would attend to accounts, administration and organizational aspects of the Programme. He would also be concerned with the response of the pupils to specific food items of the World Food Programme and the substitute provided for those items detested by the children. Finally, he would arrange for an extension of the Programme to nurseries and an evaluation of the project at the end of its first year.

Two years later a joint project by the Ministries of Education and Health to provide 2 million pupils with school meals over a period of five years was launched with the financial and expert assistance of the World Food Programme. Initially Egypt's contribution was $4 million, annually. In the first stage, half a million pupils in the 6,000 primary schools in rural sectors of the governorates, including all of Upper Egypt except Giza and the three Lower Egypt governorates of Beheira, Kafr el-Sheikh and Menufia, would take part. The Ministry of Health, with the co-operation of UNICEF (which during this period was also engaged in raising the standards of infant feeding), conducted a health survey before the execution of the project, including clinical researches and experiments to facilitate the study of nutritional problems and a fruitful evaluation of the project. The Ministry of Health was responsible for health supervision over the personnel to be engaged, and the places where stocks of food would be kept. World Food Programme experts and officials would remain available for any kind of assistance throughout the period. More recently, help with school meals contributing to the feeding of Egyptian primary school children has been promised by the Catholic Relief Body. Under an agreement with the Ministries of Education and Trade and Supply, this body will donate 12,074 tons of flour and 6,037 tons of flour mixed with soya for the feeding of about 700,000 primary school children in the governorates of Giza, Caliubia, Gharbia, Sharkia and the Canal governorates, later to be extended to Dakahlia and Damietta, bringing the total recipients to 100,000. The Ministry of Education will provide local foodstuffs to complement the meals and will bear the cost of bread-making, as well as providing £E 62,500 for expenses of the Catholic Relief Body, which will have the agreement renewed annually for five years provided that it agrees on the quantity and content of foodstuffs. (*Egyptian Gazette*, 18 November 1976)

Health education

The various ministries involved in student welfare, including health, are well aware that side by side with improvements in the social services it is necessary to educate and encourage students of all ages to achieve mental and physical health. This is done by direct education in the schools and colleges, by training courses for those who work with children and young people and by publicizing through the mass media the fruits of conferences and research. Below are a few examples of what Egypt has been attempting in these fields.

Hygiene was not a part of the curriculum of primary schools until 1953, when, according to Boktor (1963), it was added with economic and social courses, but no doubt personal cleanliness had always been encouraged. When making new plans for health education in 1971, the Minister of Education in agreement with the Minister of Public Health decided to concentrate on four main fields: nutrition, cleanliness, safety and the welfare of handicapped pupils. However, the psychological welfare of pupils, especially of the disabled, was also included and 'protection against deviation'. With the assistance of the World Health Organization and UNICEF a training course was organized for headmasters of primary schools, directors of teacher-training institutes and science teachers with the aim of developing health education in Egyptian schools. This was followed up a year later by six school health courses of three weeks each arranged by the Council of Education Directors in Cairo for 840 primary school teachers, with the object of spreading health awareness among their pupils. The courses were supervised by School Health Departments in Cairo as part of a project which included comprehensive medical check-ups on all the pupils in the governorate.

At a higher level, two more medically oriented courses will indicate the trend: the first organized by the Ministry of Youth for Physical Training instructors and school health physicians, and the second, a seminar on school health held at Cairo Faculty of Medicine, organized by the Minister of Health for 85 school health doctors and assistant directors in the governorates. The first conference concentrated on the detection of cases of physical deformities among secondary school pupils. Papers given by experts in bone surgery from Cairo University dealt with both the early detection of physical deformity, its impact upon students, medical rehabilitation and physiotherapy, and the role of physical training instructors in detecting the instances in schoolchildren. The medical seminar aimed at raising the scientific and technical standing of doctors working in the field of school health and guidance, but it was also attended by some technicians from the Ministries of Youth, Education and Social Affairs, as well as house health care nurses and women of the Red Crescent Organization. The agenda, which covered the interests of all the participants, dealt with the following topics: health problems of pupils at the first stage of education, health education in the school curriculum, the role of the teacher in making the pupils health conscious, means of improving health education in the schools, the importance of co-operation between both the governmental and the private bodies in the field of school health, the role of women in the Red Crescent in promoting school health services, the role of the social officers in the health care of pupils, heart diseases among pupils, auditory weakness and its causes, nutrition of pupils and its importance in their growth and dental diseases and the means of protecting pupils against them. (Source: *Egyptian Gazette*)

School psychological and social services

Introduction

Psychological services for children and young people today are the joint responsibility of the Ministry of Education, which is in charge of Special Education, the Ministry of Social Affairs, which maintains Institutes and Offices offering social services, and the Ministry of Health, which employs the psychiatrists, psychologists and social workers who run the clinics. During recent years each ministry has expanded its services independently, so that, in spite of efforts to organize joint committees of all organizations concerned with student welfare in school and university, there is some overlapping of function and a unified and controlled system has not yet been completely achieved.

Commenting on his survey of Egyptian education, Boktor (1963) states:

> Nowhere . . . has there been any reference to the important
> subject of counselling and guidance, whether educational,
> occupational, social or personal, for the simple reason that it does
> not exist. Any consideration of the behaviour of children and
> adolescents in relation to their background and early treatment is
> rarely tackled in the schools. This results in losing a substantial
> proportion of the potential benefits of educational effort.

He continues to describe the areas in which qualified psychologists are not only desirable but essential: delinquency and truancy, examination failure, counselling and guidance, tests and measurement, vocational guidance, sex problems, etc. An Egyptian physician (Sabry Girgis, 1967), supports the educationalist. Speaking of the early private psychological clinics opened in Egypt, he says,

> However, if we compare the speed in which clinics are opened
> and need of pupils and students for them, we find that they do not

correspond, which led to the specialization of certain public psychological clinics to direct part of their activities in the treatment of pupils and students. . . . With the fast changing society and the increased pace and tensions, it has become a must to propagate psychological health services in the domain of pupils.

He then pleads for co-operation between the clinics with all those responsible for children, parents and teachers and organizations such as social services for schools and delinquents, explaining the difficulties of operating such services:

The clinics here start their work without any previous preparation or exploration of the environment, out of caution and because of bad feeling existing towards such clinics, and it is only when they start to work and produce results that people start flocking in, and the social workers can then be accepted in the houses of the pupils they are studying or examining.

At the time that he was writing, 75 per cent of children referred to these medical clinics were for school failure, bed-wetting and epilepsy and a very few for emotional disturbance.

In 1977 it is possible to speak of an embryonic school psychological service as envisaged by Boktor (1963), and Girgis (1967), although, according to Tawadros (1974), whose information is the most up-to-date available, the lack of sufficient qualified professional psychologists makes the use of para-professionals inevitable in the immediate future. According to Tawadros (1974), the present psychological services have two sources: the psychological clinic attached to the Institute of Education (Colleyet el-Tarbiya) of Ain Shams University and student School Health Clinics at Helmia, Geziret Badran, Kubri el-Kobba, West Cairo, el-Dokki, Alexandria Students' Hospital and Assiut, which have psychological units. Apart from these services, counselling and guidance can be obtained from the School Social Services which have office facilities in every educational area.

Education and training

In Egypt, education in psychology has until recently been offered as an adjunct to other studies, such as education or the social sciences, so, although some of the senior psychologists took first degrees in psychology abroad or qualifying courses for higher degrees, most of them were educationalists who later studied for educational psychology doctorates in Great Britain or America. Ain Shams University awards degrees at bachelor, master and doctorate level, but very few in psychology in the last category, as the present policy is to send the most able graduates abroad to obtain their doctorates.

At Ain Shams University, for example, there is a Department of Sociological and Psychological Studies in the Faculty of Arts, and a Department of Educational Psychology in the Faculties of Education and in the University College for Women, while at Cairo University there is a Department of Psychology in the Faculty of Arts offering degrees at the three levels as well as a Postgraduate Diploma in Applied Psychology, and some elementary psychology is taught in the Higher Institute of Nursing. A similar pattern is followed at other Egyptian universities. Recently private students have been able to obtain a more concentrated and widely based education in psychology at the American University in Cairo, which is recognized by the Egyptian government, but for higher degrees in psychology students must study either at the government or overseas universities. Many students are sufficiently proficient in three languages, Arabic, French and English, to be able to take their higher degrees at European, English or American universities or to study under Piaget in Geneva.

Training facilities do not yet match educational opportunities. Ideally, in the clinical team, the psychiatrist has a bachelor's degree in medicine and surgery, a diploma in psychiatry, and training in the mental health clinics, with emphasis on the psychology of childhood and adolescence; the social worker has a BA in social work and one year's training in the field of mental health, while the psychologist has a BA in psychology, a diploma in clinical psychology and one year's theoretical and practical training in the field of mental health. Owing to the shortage of qualified psychologists, it appears that the social worker is liable to have her responsibilities increased (this is discussed below).

Counselling

This function appears to be shared by personnel at all levels from social worker to psychiatrist. With different emphases, each of the three ministries is concerned with solving the personal and social problems of Egypt's children and youth: in their dealings with individuals they are exposed to general problems which may warrant the kind of investigation that leads to legal action. The sifting process which ultimately leads to decisions on behalf of the individual or society in general begins with the interview designed to gather information about the client and make a preliminary assessment of the personal and general nature of his problems. Because the time of the more highly qualified personnel must be reserved for handling cases requiring skilled treatment and supervisory and training duties, initial interviewing and counselling devolves on the social worker.

The study of counselling began in 1956–7 in the College of Education that was later incorporated into Ain Shams University, with the co-operation of the Ministry of Education Department of Training. Participants were selected from the following categories:

1. Social workers in schools with the diploma of the Higher Institute of Social Work;
2. Teachers working in schools who had qualified for a BA in psychology or sociology, or in education and sociology from the Institute of Education or had graduated from the Teachers College.

Conditions for acceptance were grades of at least 'Very Good' in the last two years of study followed by at least two years' teaching experience in schools. Two hours a week are devoted to each of the following courses:

> Social guidance
> Educational psychology
> Mental health and students' problems
> Cognitive development
> Counselling
> Library and discussion

The training also includes a month's continuous practice in a secondary school under the supervision of personnel from the College of Education. In the first year twenty-one males and ten females were selected.

In a pamphlet from the Ministry of Education Department of Youth Care for Boys (Social Work), the psychologist's (or counsellor's) duties in the school are listed as follows:

1. to participate in the distribution of pupils when they are admitted and then at the beginning of every new year;
2. to help pupils to decide between subjects where a choice is available;

3. to help pupils participate in different activities according to their interests and capacities;
4. to make psychological and social surveys of groups of pupils in order to study specific general and individual problems, such as absenteeism and retardation;
5. to allow the psychologist one period a week in which to be in direct contact with the pupils, to facilitate understanding of them and their problems;
6. to arrange special hours when the psychologist would be available for advice;
7. to organize meetings with parents.

According to Makarius Tawadros (1974), the present psychological services have two sources: the psychological clinic attached to the Institute of Education of Ain Shams University, and Student Schools Health Clinics, including psychological units at Alexandria Students' Hospital and Assiut University. Apart from these services, counselling and guidance can be obtained from the school social services which have office facilities in every educational area.

Clinics

Ain Shams Clinic The psychological clinic of Ain Shams University attached to the Department of Mental Health is considered to be the leading clinic of its kind in Egypt; in fact it is unique. Its original modest aim was to treat problem children and other pupils in the schools and experimental classes attached to the Institute of Education. Consultations developed between the clinical personnel, teachers, and, very occasionally, the parents of the child. These discussions, dealing with educational, health, psychological and social characteristics of the child, were recorded as a means of diagnosis on which depended treatment and follow-up. As the work in the clinic developed and increased, the records became very important, needing organization and a full-time staff. Expansion of staff and facilities in time made it possible to accept cases of pupils and students from schools at all levels of education, institutes and universities. No fees were charged.

The clinic is interested in receiving patients suffering from mental retardation, backwardness in school subjects, enuresis, bad habits and difficulties in social adaptation, speech defects, adolescent neurosis and examination failure. In rare cases it accepts the parents because of their effect on the child, differing in this respect from British Child Guidance Clinics, where the child is treated in a family setting. Other activities of the clinic are the training of students at the postgraduate level, the training of social workers to help staff the psychological clinics and carrying out experimental research on methods of treatment. It is also engaged in preparing tests of intelligence and personality and their standardization.

The cases usually come from official sources, such as medical organizations, offices of social services in the educational areas, delinquency offices, psychological clinics in the hospital attached to the Faculty of Medicine of Cairo University, the children's parents and from schools, notably those for the mentally retarded. The 1974-5 Report on this clinic suggests means of making its services better known to university students and school pupils. It draws attention to the positive contribution that it wishes to make to mental health and suggests that, to be effective, a psychological service should include a guidance centre in each university and in at least one secondary school in each educational district, co-ordination between treatment services and social planning, and a role in family guidance.

Currently, except at the head, the team is completely feminine. The Director, who is the President of the Department of Mental Health, is assisted by a psychologist in the field of psychometrics, a psychoanalyst, a social worker, three women full-time helpers, a part-time psychiatrist, a part-time speech therapist and a secretary. It is noted that, as recommended by Makarius Tawadros, the team includes a psychometric expert but no educational psychologist, which seems odd, as a properly qualified and trained educational psychologist would be able to cover all the psychometric work required besides having much else to offer a clinic that provides a service for the school and college population.

Apart from the services already mentioned, mostly centred around emotional and social problems, the clinic is able to diagnose and treat epilepsy and schizophrenia or pass the patients on to a medical authority. Besides guidance, analysis and speech therapy, play therapy is used, but no mention is made of other therapies, such as drawing and drama. Diagnosis and treatment are decided after the weekly meeting of the team of specialists.

School health clinics These clinics are an integral part of the School

Health Service, so are the responsibility of the Ministry of Health which organizes them and employs all the personnel. It is planned to open these clinics in all the educational zones in Egypt. At present there are four serving schools and universities in the four geographical zones of Cairo. As they are concerned with all aspects of health of state school children in the district, the psychiatric unit which is designed to provide the usual psychological services is less important than if it existed in its own right. Indeed one psychologist claims that, apart from the clinic in West Cairo they occupy only one room 'stuck along with the rest of the expansive health services'. The West Cairo clinic occupies seven rooms and commands a complete team of specialists who serve about 300 schools in the district. Its terms of reference are wide:

1. the diagnosis and treatment of mental and nervous illnesses in the three scholastic stages, as well as in the university;
2. the direction of parents regarding the best methods of raising their children in a healthy manner, protecting them from mental illness (this involves arranging meetings with the parents through the school as well as interviewing parents of patients);
3. the training of all workers in the field of child and adolescent mental health, instructing them on the role of the mental health clinic in the school;
4. the carrying out of research based on the cases that are referred to the clinic.

These cases, referred by school social workers, hospitals, institutes, special schools, psychiatric adult clinics, auditory centres, parents and centres for mentally retarded children, include mainly:

1. school retardates;
2. mentally defective children (educable and non-educable);
3. nocturnal enureses;
4. behaviour disorders;
5. emotional disorders;
6. organic disorders;
7. epilepsy;
8. neurological troubles;
9. psychosomatic disorders;
10. psychiatric disorders which may be: neurotic or psychotic.
Schizophrenia is the main illness in adolescents.

The child is interviewed by the social worker, tested by the psychologist and examined by the psychiatrist, each of whom writes a report which is discussed at a conference of the staff for diagnosis and treatment, the assessment being re-evaluated after about three months.

School social services offices

In 1949 the Ministry of Social Affairs for the first time recruited social workers to co-operate with the school authorities to organize and direct school activities. Experience led to the realization that there was an urgent need for a new organization trained to cope with the problems of individual students that were too complicated to be dealt with easily within the school surroundings. As a result, the first office for school social work was opened on an experimental basis in the scholastic year 1953–4, in co-operation with the Institute of Social Workers in Cairo. A number of graduates from this institute took extra courses in order to work in the new office that dealt with special problems individually. The success of this experience encouraged the Department to open new independent offices in Cairo towards the end of 1954, in Port Said in 1955, and in Alexandria in 1955. By the end of 1957 the Ministry had undertaken to build offices for social work in schools in each of the four educational zones in Cairo. In 1958 another one was opened in Damanhour.

This policy led to a decrease in the number of social workers visiting schools and a steady increase in the number of pupils seeking direct help from the offices. Meanwhile the offices keep in constant touch with the school, supervising activities within their competence. When special care is needed in cases such as mental retardation or intensive psychological care, the offices refer the pupils to the clinics, which in turn, either give the necessary treatment or direct them to suitable institutes.

The main duties of the school social workers, as defined by the Ministry of Education, can be summarized as follows:

1. Each social worker has a specific number of schools in the district which he or she has to visit periodically.
2. When a case comes to the office it is registered in a special file and then given in the charge of a social worker with the permission of the director of the office. The investigating social worker is then

responsible for visiting the school, interviewing the parents and the social worker who referred the case and acquainting herself with all the aspects of the problem.

3. The social worker can meet the pupil at reasonable times in the school or in the office to get to know him from various aspects:
   a. his personality and attitude towards his problems;
   b. his school history from his reports;
   c. the relationships between him and his friends and teachers, from his and their point of view;
   d. family background;
   e. the child's and his family's medical background;
   f. the child's previous experiences and how he spends his leisure time, as well as his ambitions for the future.

4. After establishing ties of confidence, the social worker should, with the agreement of the pupil, make future appointments with him and his family.

5. The social worker will discuss with the director of the clinic or the psychologist the individual cases and the best methods for their treatment.

6. A report must be made on each meeting that takes place, and a summary of each case at least every two months as well as a final summary. The school must be notified about decisions concerning the case.

7. The social worker makes his plan for the week every Wednesday, and, after its approval by the director, it can only be changed with his permission. The Department of Youth Care in the zone is given this plan on Thursday. One social worker is always to be on duty in the office to receive cases.

8. On the fifth of each month the social worker gives his director a monthly report of his work, which is then incorporated in the director's own monthly report of the work of his office. Two copies are sent to the Youth Care Department of the Ministry of Education and another remains in the zonal office.

9. At a monthly conference, the social worker presents specific cases that he finds of interest to discuss, and the director as well as the psychologist also have the right to select cases and to suggest the kind of treatment necessary.

10. All the office staff meet once a week to discuss their work and make suggestions. These meetings are recorded in a special file.

Among the main problems faced by the social worker are (according to the Ministry of Education):

1. Social problems, e.g. where the pupil cannot adapt because of family conditions, such as the death of a member of the family, divorce, family quarrels, harshness of parents, which all prevent him from developing normal healthy relations in school with teachers and other pupils.
2. Economic problems, e.g. the child cannot present himself in proper clothes, or is unable to buy necessities for school or participate in school activities because of the low financial status of his family.
3. Health problems, e.g. poor eyesight and hearing or other common illnesses prevalent in Egypt and prevent the continuation of education.
4. School problems, which lead to his playing truant or stealing books and other school property, or poor work, lateness and negligence.
5. Psychological problems, e.g. shyness, low self-confidence, speech defects, mental retardation, deformities that may affect the personality.

This classification differs only in arrangement to the classifications provided by the individual offices. The Social Services Centre in Abbassiya, Cairo, for example, finds two main categories of problems: behavioural and financial, related to the behavioural problems or cases in need of financial help to continue their education. Under 'Educational Problems' it includes truancy, lateness, deliberate destruction, weak standards, specific weakness, repeated neglect of teacher . . .

It will be seen that, in some respects, these offices overlap the work of the psychology clinics, but that the terms of reference are wider.

In order to maximize its efficiency and help as many children as possible, the Abbassiya School Social Services Office tries to co-operate with as many different organizations involved in child care as possible by exchanging visits. It regards the most important as:

1. the schools, including all sections and levels in the area of East Cairo;
2. the office for social education at the Ministry of Education;
3. the offices of the Arab Socialist Union;
4. police stations and delinquency courts and other organizations belonging to the Minister of the Interior;
5. the Centre of Social Affairs in East Cairo and the attached offices for

family guidance and societies of social activities connected with students or their families;
6. offices of Adoption and Immigrants in the Ministry of Social Affairs;
7. health units and hospitals;
8. the Psychological Health Clinic in el-Kobba; and
9. clubs and centres for general services, and youth centres.

Juvenile court committees

In 1966 the Egyptian government proposed to conduct a national survey to assess the needs of her children at all stages and from every aspect as a basis for planning child care programmes. UNICEF was invited to co-operate with the project, which would be centred at the National Centre for Social and Criminological Research in Cairo. Part of the data, collected in the period 1966–9 concerned the needs of juvenile delinquents and neglected children. The detailed study was made by the Legal Sub-Committee of the research, who interviewed juvenile court judges, district attorneys, police officers and social welfare workers.

The Final Report (1974), states that 'there was almost unanimous agreement that broken homes (mainly on account of divorce) and poverty were the two major causes of delinquency, followed by neglect, bad company, ignorance and finally the influence of the mass media, especially the cinema and television.' There appeared to be a lack of co-ordination between the efforts of the juvenile courts, juvenile police, the Ministry of Social Affairs and various institutions which care for juveniles and delinquent children. The shortcomings of the service were laid bare in detail: the personnel involved, the institutions, the court procedures and the fate of the children. Briefly, not only were the personnel in most of the institutions unqualified for their jobs but also 82 per cent of the judges and most of the juvenile affairs officers had not had relevant training. The children were treated as if they were adult criminals, not being provided with separate waiting rooms at court, being taken to and from the courts in open trucks, fingerprinted, photographed and recorded both in the crime records and the newspapers, the whole procedure lacking privacy. The institutions to which many of the children were committed mostly lacked sufficient financial resources, educational and recreational facilities, playgrounds, workshops, as well as sympathetic and interested adults to look after the children. All the personnel involved recognized their inadequacies; the judges recommended the inclusion of a committee to aid the juvenile courts, consisting of a psychologist, a social welfare officer and educationalist and other specialists, and that the Family Court should be used, with sessions held 'in camera'; the police officers asked for training and the social workers for financial aid for the poorer families and social facilities for the juvenile delinquents who should be followed up after leaving the institutions.

The Egyptian government did not wait for publication of this report: by 1970 a new draft law was approved amending existing regulations for juvenile delinquency, which, in future, was not to be considered as 'a criminal phenomenon calling for deterrence' but as 'a social problem warranting care, reform and preventive action'. The new law included the provision of a guardian for the delinquent, who would not only take care of him, but himself would be liable to go on trial if his charge misbehaved again. The object was to reform rather than punish the offender, so control of his behaviour was necessary. If he escaped from an educational or training institution, instead of treating him as 'a waif or stray' which would put him in the criminal category, he would be regarded as 'vulnerable to perversion'. Rebellion against parents is considered a form of delinquency best treated by giving the rebel special duties such as vocational training or admission to an educational, rehabilitation or medical treatment institution. The new law also abolished corporal punishment, considering that the cruelty and humiliation involved might encourage the juvenile to commit further crimes. The court judges were given the right to use their discretion in treating the offender, such as handing him over to a suitable family or forbidding him to frequent places like bars and amusement centres where he was likely to commit a crime under the influence of drugs or strong drink. (*Egyptian Gazette*, 3 November 1970)

The new law was followed a year later by a plan put forward by the Minister of Social Affairs to establish twenty rehabilitation centres for juvenile delinquents in a number of governorates, as part of the new Ten-Year Plan. The project would enable delinquents to receive education up to university level, and adjust them to lead a normal life in society. This project, which was expected to cost £E 5 million, included the training of disabled and handicapped delinquents so that they would be able to earn an honest living. Indeed a fine project for the attention of the School Psychological Services!

Special education

In Egypt the need for special education in separate classes or schools has not yet been fully felt: when education is in short supply, the fittest are likely to be the ones who survive. The physically weak and under-privileged tend to die from 'summer diseases' or other ailments before reaching school age, the mentally weak cannot pass the examinations attached to the educational ladder, while those who cannot see the point of going to school, or are needed by parents to contribute to family earnings, just drop out of school, unwept for and probably un-noticed by the teacher struggling with a class 'bursting at the seams'.

One of the recommendations at the Marrakesh Conference (1970), was that 'particular attention should be paid to the education of the culturally underprivileged and to handicapped as well as gifted children.' In Egypt the culturally underprivileged are catered for in schemes for adult and literacy education, while the educational ladder has taken care of 'gifted children' since fees were abolished, although there must be wastage as long as some children are denied a sound primary educa-tion. Nevertheless, mindful of the need to nurture all the available talent in the interest of Egypt's progress in modernization, the Department of Special Education at the Ministry of Education is experimenting with 'advanced classes' for able children at the primary level. This is not just a matter of 'streaming': the children appear to be receiving the kind of 'enrichment' experience comparable in some respects to that provided in some countries for the underprivileged. Moreover, if they respond at the primary level, the same special treatment is available in the vocational school, the preparatory (intermediate) school and at the secondary level. The last appears to correspond to the British 'A' level classes, but at the earlier levels has interesting features described in a pamphlet from the Department of Special Education at the Ministry of Education under the heading of: 'Results of Research on Special Education of Advanced Children'. The following is a summary:

1. Plans are to be both long-term and short-term, to include the pro-vision of capable teachers and advanced curricula, social care, preparation of apparatus, laboratories and suitably equipped libraries; organization of scientific clubs and visits to museums and exhibitions; attention to sport and health care.
2. Providing special classes for gifted children in special schools rather than allowing them to be with older children in an ordinary school,

so that their personalities and physical development will not be adversely affected, as well as catering for individual differences in intelligence and abilities, and providing scope for competition in such classes.

3. Providing social care by the encouragement of bonuses.
4. Co-operation between teaching organizations and parents to supervise the pupils' behaviour and to facilitate school tasks.
5. Developing curricula in all branches of knowledge and providing the recent scientific apparatus in teaching, and giving the children the chance of selection and experiment in what they are learning.
6. Providing adequate library facilities so that the pupils can read independently, making their own summaries.
7. Making use of leisure time by encouraging different hobbies.
8. Giving the advanced pupil (boarders) more physical tasks, such as arranging his bed and room to help him relax and socialize.
9. Getting him to prepare charts and posters; organize competitions and parties and encourage scientific research; increase trips and excursions.

According to the latest statistics there are at present 156 of these special classes for highly intellegent children: 111 primary, 30 vocational, 9 preparatory (intermediate) and 6 secondary.

Since the establishment of preparatory schools in 1957, 'Practical' schools have been provided for pupils in 'Schools of Light' for the Blind, 'Schools of Hope' for the deaf and dumb and 'Schools of Thought' for the mentally handicapped. This vocational training was intended to help handicapped children to earn a living as technical workers in factories. Depending on the nature of the handicap, they were trained in the following industries: brushes, brooms, carpets, blankets, leather, light mechanics, knitting and sewing, typing, metals, plumbing, building and painting, carpentry, car electricity and oxygen welding. The more recent trend is to enable the children to follow the normal general education curriculum, using methods appropriate to the handicap and allowing extra time to cover the courses. With the increase in special schools and classes, the categories of 'handicap' have been extended to include, for example, 'partially sighted', 'maladjusted', 'delinquent'. Provision is also made for the more highly intelligent handicapped child. Previously, if he were blind, for example, he had been sent to the mosque for an education which sometimes led to employment as reciter of the Q'ran. The enormous potentiality of the handicapped child has been exemplified dramatically in Egypt by the blind Egyptian scholar of international repute, Taha Husayn, who became a distinguished Minister of Education. Now about forty handi-capped students graduate each year from the university, and, in 1974 about a hundred handicapped boys and girls were successful in gaining a school certificate (Thanaweyya 'Amma), arts section from secondary schools.

There are some schools for the handicapped which combine primary, preparatory and secondary education. One such, a boarding establish-ment for the blind, was visited in Alexandria, where 145 are taught by eight blind and eight non-blind teachers under a headmaster from the Taha Husayn Secondary School for the Blind. Some of the teachers had received eight months' in-training at the Ministry of Education Centre in Cairo. The school is well known, so pupils are brought for a medical examination at the age of eight years. They are tested for sight, memory and intelligence, the last consisting of an IQ test in the process of being standardized, in a psychological clinic. They study the same subjects as other children up till the end of the first secondary year, after which they concentrate on literary subjects, including two foreign languages. Typing and reading in braille are part of the curriculum and extra curricular occupations include basketry, such as chairs and brush-making as well as rug-making crafts. Music is of course very popular, lessons being obtainable for piano, violin, xylophone, accordion and local instruments. Some of the boys continue their education at special music schools, while others go to the university, where they are admitted to the Faculty of Arts with exemption from the normal regulations.

In the same city a pioneer school for the deaf was visited. The headmistress had trained with a specialist in 1942 and had started the school as a private venture, relying on charitable sources. Later it was taken over by the Ministry of Education, the three teachers having received in-training. In this particular school there were 305 children being taught in 29 classes (23 primary and 6 preparatory) by 34 teachers, all with hearing. All are specially trained, some in Cairo but others on a month's course, held locally. Boarding facilities are provided only for little children and those who come from afar. The Ministry supplies everything, including facilities for carpentry and needlework. No special reading books are available but children in the sixth primary class reach the fourth-year standard. Microphones and loud speakers are provided and the children are taught to lip-read with the aid of mirrors. After they leave school they mostly take craft jobs found by their parents.

As the number and variety of special schools in Egypt increases, statistics are becoming available but they are still rather confusing and inadequate, differentiating more precisely between the different types of physical handicap but not so clearly between mental retardation, maladjustment and delinquency. This is due to the inadequacy of the psychological services which, in the present circumstances, have to be manned largely by para-professionals. However, progress is marked by laws and decrees, such as:

Law of Primary Education No. 213 issued in 1956, making primary education compulsory for all children (implying a right for handicapped children to receive it).

Law No. 6 issued in 1962 that excuses handicapped children from continuing their education in normal schools (thus making it necessary to make special provision).

Decree No. 64 issued in 1957 that only excuses children whose IQ is less than 50 from continuing their compulsory education.

Decree No. 156 issued in 1969 which was followed by a statute defining the trends in special education.

As a rare source of information this last is worth a summary. Children with an IQ of below 75 instead of 70 were to be allowed in these schools, which in future would keep them until the age of seventeen instead of sixteen years. The class/teacher ratio was to be raised to one-and-a-half times that at the primary school, and to one teacher for seven pupils in the vocational primary schools for the handicapped, for which provision would be made in a separate budget. Not only had the inspection of Special Schools become the responsibility of a Special Education Department in the Ministry of Education, but, in all the governorates advisory councils had been formed for studying and making recommendations for the education of the handicapped. The study plans and curricula had been revised and new textbooks published to be used in the schools for the blind and partially sighted, and the preparatory vocational schools for the deaf and retarded. Also in-service training programmes were being organized to help the teachers of special education in their field, and to alert them to modern methods of teaching the handicapped.

In 1973 a further progress report was made. The Advisory Council for Special Education had, in 1971, been exhorted to co-ordinate the different efforts of governmental and private bodies concerned with the handicapped not only to give every child his right for an education, but to enable him to return as fast as possible to the community of normal persons. Teamwork was advocated in the various directorates to achieve this object and the Board of Under-Secretaries of the Ministry of Education decided from 1971 to exempt the fully or partially handicapped pupils from the conditions of both age and total marks when admitting them to preparatory and secondary schools.

In the attached table of Special schools and classes for 1974–5 it will be noted that schools for maladjusted are not included. It appears that, in the first Five-Year Plan, the Ministry of Social Affairs was made responsible for organizations for children whose special problems might make them a social liability. These are grouped under a title which has been locally translated as 'Organizations of Thought Education'. Because of the variety of the provision, the list is given in full:

1. Home for thought rehabilitation in Alexandria for mentally retarded boys, supervised by the Society of Social Rehabilitation in Alexandria.
2. Organization of Thought Education in Tanta for boys, supervised by the Society for Social Rehabilitation in Gharbia.
3. Organization for Thought Education in Minia for boys, supervised by the Society of Family and Children in Minia.
4. Thought Education Organization in Helmeyet in Helwan, for girls.
5. Organization for Social Care, Cairo, for girl delinquents.
6. Unity of Thought Education, Giza, for boy delinquents.
7. Training Centre in Mataria, Cairo: Society of Thought Development in Mataria, Cairo.

It can be seen that the term 'special education' is used to cover the needs of children with widely different problems originating from physical, emotional or intellectual characteristics and their interaction, as well as social factors. The Minister of Education is well aware of the inadequacies of the provisions for these children. He points out that the total of boys and girls enrolled in primary education is not less than 4 million, and that, according to statistics, about 12·5 per cent, that is, half a million of the handicapped children are at the primary level. Special education at present takes care of about 7,000 of them, that is, 1·4 per cent and the Ministry of Education has not managed to reach the rest. His aim is to raise the quality of the services that he is able to offer, and this can only be done by increasing the services and number of the fully trained psychologists available for diagnosis, treatment and consultation. Meanwhile it is necessary to train a para-professional group of helpers as has, indeed, been done among the social workers. At present the provision can be seen as a 'first aid' service aimed at getting the unfortunate child into a special group as quickly as possible, in order to get a quick diagnosis, and then keeping him just long enough to teach him a special skill that will enable him to face life with some degree of confidence.

In Egypt the full significance of individual differences in her school population will come when compulsory schooling is supported by sanctions and the leaving age raised to the adolescent level. The Ministry of Education has wisely begun the framework for building up a service that will be needed to cope with the many special classes and units not only for slow learners and backward children but for the educationally subnormal who always form a percentage of a large child population. With changing social patterns there is likely to be an increasing instance of maladjustment and delinquency. There is an urgent need to give every teacher the skills required for grouping children in the lower classes in order to give them sufficient individual attention to be able to diagnose correctly their educational problems. This is difficult but essential in large classes, where the lazy, the shy and the child who needs spectacles, as well as the maladjusted and the delinquent, can lag behind the rest of the class for different reasons, requiring different treatment. The potential role of the psychologist in all this activity is discussed below in the section on 'prospects'.

Research and prospects

It will be noted that at all levels personnel involved in the Egyptian psychological services are urged to engage in research. For example, according to the Ministry of Education pamphlet, one of the main duties of the Office of School Social Work is listed as

> gathering general information which will be useful as a basis for
> new research and possible hypotheses which will help recognize

TABLE 9 *Special schools and classes in Egypt: 1974/5*

Stage	Kind	Schools			Classes		Pupils		Staff
		Schools	Sections	Total	Classes	Total	Pupils	Total	
Primary	Blind	11	0	11	11	71	92	573	111
	Weak sight	2	9	11	3	24	15	193	30
	Deaf, dumb	16	6	22	36	250	344	2,381	335
	Hospital	2	2	4	3	19	30	239	20
	Mentally retarded	23	27	50	58	262	439	2,242	317
	Total	54	44	98	111	626	920	5,628	823
Vocational	Blind	1	1	2	2	6	14	35	14
	Dumb	1	10	11	7	32	178	326	39
	Mentally retarded	1	17	18	21	48	221	425	60
	Total	3	28	31	30	86	413	786	113
Preparatory (intermediate)	Blind	4	0	4	5	15	57	190	43
	Weak sight	1	0	1	2	5	20	72	10
	Hospital	1	1	2	2	5	37	86	0
	Total	6	1	7	9	25	114	348	53
General secondary	Blind	4	0	4	5	15	63	195	27
	Part blind	1	0	1	1	5	26	66	12
	Total	5	0	5	6	20	89	261	39
Total		68	73	141	156	757	1,536	7,023	1,028

more of the pupils' problems in the schools and present practical solutions, which in turn aid the formation of a general policy for the treatment of such problems.

The Ministry clearly distinguishes between 'fact-finding' and scientific research which can only be achieved by specialists, such as psychologists with the necessary training and education. In his Report of the Psychological Committee, (1973), of the 'Assessment of Children's Needs in Egypt', a joint project of the Egyptian government and UNICEF, Tawadros reviews important Egyptian studies carried out at the doctorate level prior to the project. He finds that most of the studies have been concerned with adolescents and their problems. They include:

Ibrahim K. Shehab: *Personal and Social Problems as defined by Egyptian Adolescents* (1953), PhD thesis, Columbia University.

Samuel Makarius Tawadros: *Spotlight on the Egyptian Adolescent* (1957), in Arabic.

Ahmed Z. Saleh: *Enquiry about youth problems* (1959).

Moustafa Fahmy: *Application of Egyptian version of Mooney check-list in Cairo secondary boys' and girls' schools* (1959).

Mohamed A. Ghali: *Bases on which Adolescents rate each other in Egyptian Secondary Schools*. MA thesis, Cairo.

Nagig I. Ibrahim, Mohamed E. Ismail and Roshdy F. Mansour: *How we Rear our Children*, Social Research Centre, American University, Cairo, (1966), in Arabic.

A. A. El-Koussy: *The Characteristics of Rural and Urban Adolescents in Egypt*, paper presented at 16th International Conference of Psychology, Bonn, (1960).

More recent investigations, including those in the project above (Report 1973), concentrate on the secondary school child, although the full project covers the needs of children from babyhood onwards. Studies of younger children appear to be more concentrated in the Department of Anthropology, Sociology, Psychology of the American University in Cairo, where N. Ciaccio is preparing a UNICEF manuscript, 'Planning for Children's Services in Egypt' and (in collaboration) a manuscript on 'Child Development in the Arab World.'

In spite of the many urgent preoccupations with its expanding educational services and the frustrations arising from external pressures necessitating a war economy, and internal pressures arising from the rapid expansion of her population, Egypt has made solid advances in the development of health and social services for her school and college population. Egyptian experts know their problems well enough and seek answers to them by internal experimentation and discussions with external bodies like UNESCO in order to benefit from their experiences in other countries.

As in many countries, the medical profession is reluctant to relax its traditional domination in the field of mental health, so, in the clinical teams outside the university, it is the psychiatrist who is responsible for supervision of the work, both medically and clerically, including the diagnosis and treatment of all the cases. It is he who advises the responsible authorities on how to deal with the child. On the other hand, the social worker is obviously the backbone of the psychological services: it is she who works closely with the psychiatrist, has close contact with the troubled child and his family, as well his teachers, and, when the team is incomplete, covers the testing which falls to the lot of the psychologist if one is employed. (It was a psychologist who, when interviewed, offered the observation that 'in Egypt it is the psychiatrist and the social worker in the clinic who do all the work'.)

Psychiatrists in Egypt are in short supply, so could be fully occupied with mentally sick children requiring medical treatment, social workers have been supplying a service in the schools which might be the envy of some of the industrial centres in Western society, but, with the rapid expansion of the school population in communities that are increasingly using the social services, it is vitally necessary that they should not be burdened with responsibilities for which they have neither been educated nor trained in depth. Students of psychology in Egypt are increasing in number annually, notably in the American University in Cairo, so manpower shortage will be solved in the foreseeable future. It appears that the time is ripe for a rationalization of the functions of the three ministries which contribute to the psychological services, and the planning of a secure career structure that would attract the most able of the country's students of psychology to a school psychological service that would provide a status equivalent to that of a psychiatrist and a satisfying job that would make full use of their education and training. With her interest in educational systems in other countries, Egypt might well exchange her experiences with the International School Psychology Organization which brings together world experts with mutual benefit.

8

Plans and trends

Trends

Open door policy at home and abroad

President Sadat's declared 'open door' policy appears to be the spearhead of present and future developments in Egypt, both at home and in her relationships with the world at large. This is strongly indicated in the October Working Paper (1974). Conscious of her geographical position at the centre of the world and at the meeting place of all routes, Egypt has nothing to gain by secluding herself like an Arab lady in purdah, and endless possibilities to gain from exploiting her largely untapped human and physical resources within the country and her unique opportunities to benefit from the experiences of both East and West.

At home this policy will be achieved by the social transformation of the country, aimed at satisfying the personal and social aspirations of all its inhabitants. In what is called 'a comprehensive project for drawing up a new map of Egypt', village life is to be revived in reconstructed old villages and new settlements supported by new economic activities in an electrified countryside, which will allow large population groups to enjoy a settled productive life outside the large cities, while the development of strong local governments, managing their own budgets, will ensure a fair return for provincial enterprise.

In November 1976, Egypt committed herself in three areas, social, educational and political, to ensure that all Egyptians, wherever they live and whatever their status and occupation, will benefit from what is hoped to be a growing prosperity following the modernization of industry and agriculture. Social legislation, which provided £E 166 million for annual pensions and indemnities in 1976, would increase the amount progressively to cover 'all those able to earn their livelihood whether through work or property' by 1980 (*Egyptian Gazette*, 11 November 1976). The drive behind urban migration from rural areas would be reduced and manpower problems partly resolved by the establishment of eleven new university colleges in the governorates of Ismailia, Gharbia, Sharkia, Dakahlia, Menufia, Fayyum, Beni Suef, Assiut, Suhag, Qena and Aswan. Decentralization would no longer be a talking point but a fact; without delay, authority would be transferred from the central government to governorate departments. In view of the active role that governors would play in the future solutions to the governorate's problems, by, for instance, mobilizing available human and material resources, following up local projects, developing youth clubs and centres and controlling agricultural and irrigation agencies, governorate leadership would need to be constantly evaluated.

This ideal is not to be achieved by a communist-type uniformity of economic and social structure but by diversity within unity. Thus the national economy will be supported by three sectors: the public sector, responsible for basic projects, which is the primary and most effective instrument of development, in spite of its shortcomings; the private sector, characterized by its utilization of individual creative initiative 'guiding consumption through creating production spheres in which savings can be directed' and the co-operative section which keeps alive the traditional crafts and brings modern methods and machinery within the reach of peasant farmers.

Educationally, 'open door' is applied to state schools and universities by the abolition of fees, which ideally makes it possible for a child, boy or girl, from any sector of society to climb the educational ladder. This freedom is reinforced by the maintenance of a private sector in education, with a wide range of schools, basically fee-paying but generous with scholarships, by the formal recognition of the fee-paying, independent American University in Cairo with mutual benefit and the decision to establish a state fee-paying (in hard currency) university to serve the foreign community but, above all, the children of expatriates.

The freedom of the individual, which already extends to the Press, is expressed most dramatically in the emancipation of women, who have come out of their seclusion to take a vital part in building up the new Egyptian society. Article XI of the Constitution stipulates that: 'The state ensures a co-ordination between the duties of women towards their families and their work in society. It also ensures equality between men and women in the political, social, cultural and economic aspects of life without violating the provisions of Islamic Law.' This kind of social change is a slow process which legislation can aid, but not enforce

Level	Number of institutions			Number of teachers			Teacher–pupil ratio			Enrolments			Average size per school	
	Public	Private	Total	Public	Private	Total	Public	Private	Total	Public	Private	Total	Public	Private
Pre-primary	—	284	284	—	1,787	1,787	—	—	—	—	52,611	52,611	—	240
Primary	8,941	841	9,782	88,677	4,825	93,502	1:42	1:41	1:42	3,719,240	199,156 (5%)	3,918,396	415	240
Preparatory	1,561	913	2,474			28,916	—	—	1:38	893,799	205,492 (19%)	1,099,291	570	225
Secondary general	393	207	600	12,917	1,703	14,620	1:20	1:40	1:22	254,421	69,182 (21%)	323,603	650	335
Secondary technical														
Commercial	182	157	339	6,988	—	—				149,451	42,688 (22%)	192,139	820	270
Agricultural	51	—	51	2,055	—	—				36,539	—	36,539	715	—
Industrial	107	2	109	2,041	—	—				92,369	280	92,649	860	140
Teacher training (five years)	61	—	61	2,382	—	2,382				278,359	42,968	321,327	510	—
Secondary (all types)	794	366	1,160							31,288	—	31,288		
Higher education (MOHE)										564,068	112,150 (17%)	676,218		
Technician training (two-year courses)	32	—								25,029	—	25,029	780	—
Higher technical institutes	31	—		2,451						42,926	7,000[4]	49,926	1,390	—
Universities (including al-Azhar)	8	—								259,000[3]	—	259,000 32,000		
Literacy programmes	71	—				6,004				326,955	7,000	333,955 219,920[2]		

(*Source:* by courtesy of the Ministry of Education, Cairo.)

[1] Ministries of Education, Higher Education and Universities only.

[2] Only 9,310 females; average attendance is given as 80 per cent.

[3] Close approximation as enrolment figure used for al-Azhar is for 1971/2.

[4] Includes all post-secondary private education.

in all aspects of family life, but the achievements of Egypt's female intelligentsia and the expansion of girls' education give promise for the future.

In the political field the democratization of society extends the freedom of the individual to a point where it is considered that the society itself would be at risk. Supporters of the one-party state (who are the vast majority of Egyptians) think in terms of the need for political unity in time of war, of national security, and, viewing many of the wastages and absurdities of party government, frankly consider that their own system is superior in many respects. However, it is noted in the October Working Paper that

> today the people's demands and aspirations are increasing, and their awareness of the need to call to account the public sector, public utilities and public services is growing, because the state since the Revolution – and the social services it has introduced – has placed itself in this new position of responsibility on behalf of society. This is one of the important factors of the transformation which took place, for he who makes himself responsible also exposes himself to criticism.

It is recognized that, in the absence of a political opposition, there must be a politically acceptable vehicle for different approaches to the country's problems. So, since 1975 there developed the concept of 'forums' to step up Arab Socialist Union development. It would soon be known whether these would quieten the fears of those seeking safeguards against the possibility of abuses by a single-party organization, but they were calculated to enable the leader to reach sound decisions based on the will of all the people and not just dictated from the top. The nature of the forums was itself still a matter for debate in which members of professional associations, workers' trade unions, the universities and all groups in the society were taking part.What emerged suggested that the multiplicity of forums was not meant to provide 'just facades for new leaderships looking for a role' but opportunities to discuss in a democratic way differences of opinion concerning application, not differences in ideology and objectives. It would be legitimate to pinpoint contradictions in statements of policy and to offer solutions but it was hoped that the forums would spring from 'the political practices and attitudes concerning the issues that crop up and not formed by virtue of an administrative decision.'

In the event, the 'forums' became a pilot study for the establishment of a party system of government. Only about a year after their experimental introduction, free democratic elections were held on the basis of the three political trends within the ASU, namely, the Right, Left and Centre. The results was an overwhelming victory for the Centrists (the moderate element), the Right gaining 12 of the 342 elected seats, the Left only 2, while 48 seats were gained by Independents. A highly delighted President Sadat quickly followed with an announcement that the government recognized that the country was now ready for full, democratic party government, for 'democracy is worth whatever violence may occur in its practice. It is democratic action that keeps opportunists away.' The only alternative was 'dictatorship, tyranny and the domination of centres of power over the people.' The Revolution had developed full circle: created to destroy a corrupt party system, it survived to inspire what was hoped to be a new party system based on freedom, stability, security, democracy and the rule of law. The political door was the last and perhaps the most important to be opened.

The 'open door' policy is not confined to home affairs, but guides and controls Egypt's relationships with the outside world within all spheres of contact. As a nation that prides itself on lack of fanaticism, it seeks help from both East and West, strong ties with the rest of the Arab world and lesser ties with the African continent, while depending on international bodies like United Nations Organizations and the World Bank for advice, encouragement and financial support, when national resources are inadequate. However, Egypt is determined not to fall within spheres of influence, regarded as the most lethal danger that can threaten a country. President Sadat says that:

> On the contrary a country like Egypt is today capable of extending international lines of co-operation into various directions and of utilizing all the opportunities afforded by the new international situation, well aware that our own strength as well as our Arab ties and African relations and our affiliation to the non-aligned nations movement are basic weapons in our hands for the protection of our interests and rights, enabling us to prevent any agreement that could be reached at our expense.

The Arab League and ALECSO

Of the relationships mentioned perhaps those with the Arab world are the most interesting and the most significant. While the outside world watches with horror one of the worst civil wars taking place in the Lebanon and speculates on the next Arab territory to receive attention from President Gadafy of Libya, Egypt regards political unity as an ultimate aim. The reality is that the danger from Israel has, for the first time, brought Arab countries with widely different political and social systems to join ranks effectively, agreeing on definite actions. To quote Sadat,

> The battle has proved to the Arabs the value of their natural resources and wealth, underlining this value not merely for conversion to money but as a necessary weapon for negotiations with all parties and as a means of facilitating the fast-moving pan-Arab progress.

The League of Arab States was not a post-revolutionary movement, since it produced its first Charter in 1945, but its 'Cultural Agreement' approved by its first council and subsequent developments had and are having a continuous influence on the course of education in Egypt. The early recommendations of this committee were largely educational: the exchange of teachers, professors and students, the encouragement of cultural and sportive excursions, the establishment of educational institutes, the unification of scientific terminology, the strengthening of the bonds between libraries and museums, the implementation of co-operation between scientists, writers and men of letters and art and the establishing of common legislative trends among the Arab countries.

A natural outcome was the establishment of ALECSO, an Arab League version of UNESCO and 'a successful step towards the implementation and deepening of the common Arab endeavour in the fields of education, culture and science'. Its charter was ratified by eight member states in 1964 and it held its first General Conference in 1970. By 1971, ALECSO had absorbed the Cultural Department, the Arab Institute of Manuscripts, the Arab Institute of Research and Study, the Arab Regional Literacy Organization, the Permanent Arabization Centre and the Office of the Permanent Delegate of UNESCO. It is not proposed to detail all the activities of this dynamic organization which is now composed of fifteen member states, but the extent of its services to Arab education can be appreciated by a glance at its programme of projects for the year 1972–3. Among the main items are listed 15 in co-operation with local, regional and international unions, organizations and centres, including convocation of conferences, seminars and committees for the study of educational problems facing the Arab states, or for the study of a common educational problem, of interest to the Arab world as well as covering the question of encouraging research in the educational fields; 12 cultural projects based on selected topics of vital interest and importance in the fields of language, literature, heritage, antiquities, arts and social sciences, carried out through conferences, committees and seminars, supported by research and special studies; 13 scientific projects to strengthen and co-ordinate Arab scientific relations, 18 projects under the title of Documentation and Information; 6 projects for the Institute of Arab Manuscripts; 8 projects for the Institute of Higher Research and Studies; 6 for the Arab Regional Organization; 4 for the Permanent Arabization Centre and 6 'diverse projects' to be discussed by ALECSO for future implementation. Egypt takes an active part in this vast network of cultural exchange, her professors and educational experts making valuable contributions. In view of the capability of funding ALECSO from Arab oil resources, the possible trend is that Egypt will become increasingly involved with this organization, which is in harmony with so many of her declared aspirations and policies.

The search for an ideal system of education

For Egypt to profit fully, educationally speaking, from the influences of foreign occupation, her wide experiences of cultural exchange, educational missions abroad, membership of ALECSO and advice from UNESCO and other international bodies, it would be necessary for her to carry out a vast and complicated experimental exercise in comparative education, or, as suggested by one UNESCO mission, in conjunction with her own National Committee for the Reform of Education in Egypt, to say 'a plague on all your systems' and create an entirely revolutionary system of her own, transforming her educational institutions into 'People's Learning Guidance Centres'. Theoretically this would be the best solution, but, at this stage of Egypt's educational history, the problems it created might outweigh the ultimate advantages. So, she soldiers on, gradually modifying her institutions to meet her national needs, but meanwhile formulating the principles that guide her decisions.

The most fundamental and oft repeated of these was expressed by the Minister of Education at the Third Regional Conference of Ministers of

Education and Ministers Responsible for Economic Planning in the Arab States in Marrakesh (1970), 'Egypt is dynamically searching for a uniquely Egyptian solution, rather than waiting for others to present a ready-made educational pattern to be implemented.' For example, her Management Training Programmes benefit from the Eastern Bloc when the aim is to organize courses for future executives on collective farms, and comprehensive education may be a part solution to break down the prejudice against technical education, but Egypt has no intention of importing, 'franchise' – style Swedish or German systems of comprehensive education or, say, a Yugoslav system of industrial education. Each innovation must be tailored to fit not only the technical and industrial needs of the society, taking into account all the problems previously discussed, but must be compatible with the Egyptian way of life.

Conservation is, for Egypt, equally as important as innovation, especially in cultural matters, beginning with her concept of Egyptian national character. This is not merely a nationalistic sentiment, but a sincere belief that she has something worth preserving and a firm resolve to exclude unwanted influences as far as possible. In the words of the October Working Paper, 'Egypt has been open in general to the world around it, assimilating all that is new and useful . . . it has been receptive to all that is new, remodelling it and reshaping it, and adding to it its own Egyptian character.' The Egyptian citizen is regarded not only as the means of achieving progress but 'the guarantee for us to move forward and adopt the latest techniques of the age in all fields, without fear of losing our identity, breaking away from our genuine character or abandoning the virtues in which our people have always taken pride and honour'. These values and virtues are variously described as national cohesiveness, constructive skills, love of peace, loyalty and, above all, faith free from fanaticism. In short, according to Sadat 'Radical change does not necessarily mean a complete severing at the roots from the national, spiritual and civilizational heritage of our people.'

With this in mind, Egypt, appealing for help in her quest for an ideal educational system, does not ask UNESCO's experts to propose goals 'but to suggest a strategy for attaining those nationally postulated' (UNESCO 1972). Nor does she feel obliged to accept the strategy in the form of a package deal, believing that 'no expert or group of experts can formulate such a complex subject as a country's national policy of education within a very short time.' The descriptive reports provided by consultants to some developing countries are not required by Egyptian experts who know the situation and problems but, having already attempted to find answers to the questions raised, appreciate working with a UNESCO mission in order to benefit from the organization's experiences in many countries. As stated by the Minister of Education (1975), 'Egypt wants to have a liberal outlook to the world and follow an open door policy, thus trying to find the most suitable, a unique solution for Egyptian society.'

Expressed plans (1976–80)

Egypt's leaders hope that by the year 2000, by careful planning and efficient use of manpower, her industrial, social and economic measures will have brought about the revolution envisaged by her politicians poets and philosophers. Meanwhile, the restraints of a war economy, (£E 5,000 million in direct military expenditure and a similar amount from direct losses and losses of profit because of the aggression between 1967 and 1974 and, according to preliminary calculations, more than £E 3,000 million yet to be spent on the rehabilitation of the areas directly affected), as well as a population which is only just beginning to respond significantly to family planning, make it essential to achieve as much educational advance as possible with every five-year plan. Below are some of the more important projects to cover, roughly, the years 1976–80. Some of them will be financed by the national budget, while others, it is hoped, will attract international funds.

Primary education

Projects for primary education are related to two long-term plans: the implementation of compulsory primary education in 1980, and the upgrading of all primary teacher-education to two or three years at the post-secondary level, eliminating the old secondary teacher-training schools. It is estimated that the annual requirement for teachers, now about 10,500, will expand to about 12,000. To provide the estimated new places for the period under review, the Ministry of Education proposes to expand the existing provision and to construct nine of the thirty-five new type teacher-training institutions which will be required to complete the whole operation.

Bearing in mind the overall social plan for the countryside, it is planned to develop at least three of these institutions in developing provinces such as the North-West Coastal area (probably at Mersah Matruh), one in a desert-oasis or newly reclaimed area (possibly the New Valley), and one in a predominantly rural environment. As there is little post-preparatory education in these areas at present, these three schools will be modified versions of the present secondary teacher-training schools. The trainees will receive basic training in the crafts, cottage industries, activities of the region, literacy and adult education teaching techniques, with some specialization, basic instruction in remedial work and diagnostic and general testing practices, additional training in modern school organization and teaching method and techniques, e.g. team teaching, group teaching, handling multiple-grade schools, use of mass media, preparation of teaching aids, etc. Practical experience would be obtained in the school workshops and the primary schools.

These new teacher-training centres would have appropriately equipped workshops, laboratories, audio-visual centres, a library and an annex primary school for 480 pupils (twelve classes). It is hoped that closed-circuit television facilities tied in with adjoining primary schools will be feasible. Each teacher-training school would have a maximum of about 800 boys and girls, five groups of thirty-six during the three secondary years, and five groups of twenty-five during the professional training years. This would make the combined output of the three schools about 600 annually. There would be dormitory accommodation for about 400–600 at each school and housing for twenty to twenty-five teachers at each. The schools would function as teacher resource and development centres for the region, by making in-service training available during vacation periods and providing for short teacher seminars or workshops during the school year. The staff (with a teacher-pupil ratio at 1:16) would preferably have had primary school teaching experience or be given a period of exposure to it, and all subject teachers would need to have had professional training. In addition, special intensive training courses may be organized for them.

Intermediate education

Plans for intermediate education are very long-term, as they cannot be implemented fully until the compulsory stage is extended to eight or

TABLE 11 *Secondary education plan period projections*

Year	General	Industrial	Commercial	Agricultural	Primary teacher training	Total	Technical 5-year courses
1975–6	360,000	108,000	243,000	40,200	32,600	783,800	4,200
1976–7	375,000	116,000	260,000	43,400	32,500	826,900	6,100
1977–8	382,000	127,000	292,000	47,200	36,000	884,200	8,500
1978–9	385,000	142,000	306,000	52,500	38,800	924,300	11,200
1979–80	386,000	158,000	332,000	57,800	41,800	975,600	14,200
1980–1	386,000	171,000	356,000	61,400	44,400	1,018,800	17,300

(*Source*: by courtesy of the Ministry of Education, Cairo.)
All figures rounded.

nine years. Perhaps it is premature to talk about detailed plans, since the operation will probably not take place until the last decade of the century, but an experimental 'Eight-year School' is already functioning (see pp. 88–9) and important discussions are being conducted with reference to the nature of the organization of a combined primary and intermediate school of the future. Recently the Ministry of Education has been making intensive studies concerning the reorganization of secondary education, seeking alternatives to the present system which provides two main types, technical and general, with two different concentrations, arts and science sections in the general secondary school (details are given below). One of the schemes suggested would assume the reorganization of pre-secondary schooling into a comprehensive system embracing the compulsory combined primary and intermediate school of the future.

Secondary education

The Ministry of Education, considering that the secondary system in Egypt is in urgent need for reorganization, set up a national committee of twenty-five experts to assist the Minister to find new, suitable alternatives to the present system, which favours the general secondary pattern and puts obstacles in the way of technical students wishing to study at the universities. Some kind of comprehensive education appeared to be the answer. In 1975, the Minister of Education invited a multi-disciplinary team (known as the Unedbas Mission) to visit Cairo to survey the existing secondary educational situation in Egypt and to discuss, in the light of world experience, possible future trends and plans.

The Egyptian authorities were keenly interested that such plans should not only increase the efficiency of their schools but meet the real needs of the country: their own serious attempts to solve their problems had met with a limited success, but had not yet been able 'forcefully to set secondary education in Egypt on the road to innovation'. The team suggested various experimental projects reorganizing some of the present schools more on comprehensive lines, such as unifying the first-year course of study in both technical and academic education to facilitate transfer from one to the other, to break down traditional barriers between the so-called literary and scientific branches and to introduce practical subjects in the general secondary school, to revise higher education admission regulations to make it accessible to technical students, to strengthen ties between vocational and secondary schools, making transfer possible and combining neighbouring types of secondary school into 'comprehensive complexes'. More innovative experiments could involve relating education and life experience so that the educational experience could be shared with uneducated youth outside the school. These experiments should be located near or within new settlement patterns or remodelled areas (Unedbas Mission Report: 1975).

Meanwhile Egypt's experiments during the period under survey will include a project comprising the construction and equipment of three new comprehensive secondary schools and the conversion of two existing secondary schools to conform to the comprehensive pattern. (At the onset it must be made clear that the term 'comprehensive' here does not mean non-selective: entry into secondary schools will inevitably remain highly selective for the foreseeable future, in spite of the increasing provision each year.) The aim is to provide a school that will embrace secondary technical programmes (industrial, agricultural, commercial, etc.), so that all secondary pupils stand an equal chance of

TABLE 12 *Ministry of Education: The technical training Institutes (five year courses) which are to be established in 1976–80*

Location	Specialization
Cairo	Wool and allied textiles
Alexandria	Petrochemical industries
Port Said	Shipbuilding and marine engineering
Kaft-el-Sheik	Tractors and agriculture machinery
Suez	Petrochemical industries
Mansoura	Tractors and agriculture machinery
Tanta	Wool and allied textiles
Guiza	Electrical equipment of industrial enterprises
Souhag	Electrical equipment of industrial enterprises
Aswan	Electrical equipment of industrial enterprises

(*Source:* by courtesy of the Ministry of Education, Cairo.)

TABLE 13 *Curriculum of the agricultural teacher education course*

I *Common course* (*Years 1 and 2*)

Year 1

First semester

Subject	Number of weekly hours		Credit units
	Lecture	Practical	
Chemistry (inorganic)	2	4	4
Physics	2	2	3
Botany (general)	2	4	4
Zoology (general)	2	4	4
Mathematics	2	—	2
Economics (general)	2	—	2
English	2	—	2
Total	14	14	21

Second semester

Subject	Number of weekly hours		Credit units
	Lecture	Practical	
Chemistry (organic)	2	4	4
Soils	2	2	3
Botany (applied)	2	4	4
Agricultural accounting	2	2	3
Statistics (general)	2	2	3
Rural sociology	2	—	2
English	2	—	2
Civics	2	—	2
Total	16	14	23

TABLE 13 *continued*

Year 2

First semester Subject	Number of weekly hours Lecture	Practical	Credit units	*Second semester* Subject	Number of weekly hours Lecture	Practical	Credit units
Biochemistry	2	4	4	Microbiology (general)	2	2	3
Genetics	2	2	3	Agricultural cooperatives	2	—	2
Crops	2	2	3	Plant physiology	2	2	3
Agricultural economics	2	—	2	Animal production	2	2	3
Agricultural engineering	2	2	3	Agricultural extension	2	2	3
Horticulture	2	2	3	Food and dairy processing	2	2	3
Entomology (general)	2	2	3	Rural sociology	2	—	2
Civics	2	—	2	Animal physiology	2	2	3
Total	16	14	23		16	12	22

TABLE 13 *continued*

II *Course specialization (animal production) – Years 3 and 4*

Year 3

First semester

Subject	Number of weekly hours		Credit units
	Lecture	Practical	
Physiology of reproduction	2	2	3
Sheep and goat husbandry	2	2	3
Poultry husbandry	2	4	4
Animal nutrition	2	2	4
Economics and marketing	2	—	2
Educational methods	2	—	2
Psychology	2	—	2
Principles of education	2	—	2
Total	16	12	22

Second semester

Subject	Number of weekly hours		Credit units
	Lecture	Practical	
Dairy cattle	3	4	5
Animal feeding	2	2	3
Animal health	2	2	3
Animal production economics	2	—	2
Principles of education	2	—	2
Educational methods	2	2	2
Teaching practice	—	4	2
Curriculum	2	—	2
Total	15	14	21

TABLE 13 *continued*

Year 4

First semester

Subject	Lecture	Practical	Credit units
Animal breeding (basis)	3	—	3
Beef cattle	2	2	3
Wool technology	1	2	2
Poultry feeding	2	2	3
Poultry physiology	1	2	2
Agricultural education methods	2	—	2
History of agricultural education	2	—	2
Teaching practice	—	4	2
Total	13	12	19

Second semester

Subject	Lecture	Practical	Credit units
Animal nutrition	3	4	5
Animal breeding	2	—	2
Poultry breeding	2	—	2
Fish	2	—	2
Farm management	2	2	3
Vocational guidance	1	—	1
Psychology	2	—	2
Teaching practice	—	4	2
Total	14	10	19

(*Source:* by courtesy of the Ministry of Education, Cairo.)

221

higher education. The proposed schools would have a capacity of between 864 and 1,080 pupils (24–30 groups). The two schools for conversion would need to be structurally sound and have teaching spaces suitable in design and size for the proposed groups, and adequate land for building workshops, laboratories, a library and other specialized rooms where necessary. It is suggested that the more recently built agricultural high schools might be suitable and that the proposed schools should be located in different parts of the country as models. Preliminary consideration is being given to one in the Canal area, one in the New Valley, one in the textile industry area and one in a predominantly rural area. With technical assistance it would be possible to make first-class staffing arrangements (World Bank Survey, 1975). Mimeo, Ministry of Education.

Technician training institutes

The shortage of technicians has occasioned comment in this survey. In the five-year plan (1976–80) the Ministry of Education hopes to establish ten industrial and agricultural institutes for training technicians (Grades 10–14 five-year courses) in the specializations of wool and allied textile trades, petrochemical, shipbuilding, electrical equipment of industrial enterprises, tractors and agricultural machinery, etc. They will be located in various parts of the country near existing industries and in accordance with the density of population. The project will involve constructing and equipping four to six new technician training institutes and equipping three to five secondary technical schools which will be upgraded. It is proposed that the industrial institutes would each have a capacity of 1,200–1,500 students and the two agricultural about 750. A total of 9,000–13,000 students would produce an annual output of 1,500–2,000.

In this project full use will be made of pilot studies in two new institutes at Kobba and Alexandria. Part of the proposal is to convert an existing secondary agricultural school into a technician level Food Technology Institute. The annual needs of the Ministry of Industry for the twenty-five companies of the public sector of the Egyptian General Organization for Food Industries is estimated at 120. The areas needing technicians include sugar and alcohol, beer, wine, dairy, canned food fruits, juices, dehydrated food, tobacco, edible oils, detergents, soap, margarine and animal feed, while the Ministry of Supply requires technicians for its bread-making industries. In the specialized two years following the three years' secondary course, the students will receive practical training under supervision at factories and paid work for longer periods (two-three months) each year during the latter part of the course. An Advisory Board will be available.

The other agricultural institute is planned as part of Egypt's policy of reconstruction and land reclamation. In view of the existing shortage of agricultural land in Egypt, the 1976–80 plan is giving high priority to an integrated development of reclaimed land on approximately 900,000 feddans and the reclaiming of another 300,000 feddans (acres), beginning with the area covered by Ismailia, Port Said, Suez and later the area east of the Canal, totalling approximately 450,000 feddans. The new institute will be a Land Reclamation Training Institute, designed for the training of practically orientated personnel who would be able to cope with the technological aspects connected with land reclamation and development as well as agriculture in the Canal region. Graduates from the course will also be involved in the settling of farmers in the area, and, as model settlers, will be granted twenty to twenty-five feddans each as well as all the agricultural inputs and credit required. It is hoped for a technical assistance component which would enable the Institute to begin with expert management while the Egyptian personnel receive on-the-job training and, where desirable, specialized training in a polytechnic institute abroad.

University education

As already discussed under 'Higher education', the five-year plan for the universities concentrates on the governorates; in fact, 1976 was named the 'Regional Universities Year'. It is hoped to solve two major problems at a stroke: to increase the number of students, and thereby the number of educated people in the province, and to relieve the pressure on Cairo and Alexandria which entails intractable problems of transport and residence. It is hoped that help will be available from the wealthier Arab countries for this purpose. Another concentration is in the reclaimed territories, where educational provision at all levels is being increased every year. Plans for new universities are already in hand for the Canal Zone. However, the older universities are not left out of the next five-year plan. Alexandria, for example, will, during 1976–80, acquire a number of new buildings and laboratories for some faculties as well as additions to the present buildings. Included in the projects are a new building for the Faculty of Science and another for the Faculty of Engineering as well as a postgraduate research centre. Faculties of Dentistry and Pharmacy will be extended and student hostels will be completed under the plan. Another boost for Alexandria University will be the affiliation of a new Science Research Centre, contributed to by the United Nations, which will provide facilities for specific research work which cannot be carried out at the University.

Renascence in Egyptian education?

References in the literature to the 'Arab awakening' of the nineteenth and twentieth centuries have been sufficiently frequent to provoke from Sharabi (1966), the denial that movements of reform during that period constituted a renascence, a term used by President Sadat himself in the October Working Paper of 1974. Sharabi, however, was referring to a period during which the intelligentsia of Islam were preaching that the ostensible decline of Islam could be arrested by 'resurrecting the spirit and ideals of early Islamic society and restoring moral and political strength'.

The creation of a secular state in Egypt is sufficient evidence that both Nasser and Sadat have rejected out of hand the restoration of a politically strong Islam. Indeed, a case could be made that, by doing so, they have restored the moral strength of Egypt, resurrecting the spirit and some of the ideals of early Islamic society. What is the evidence? Because of the peaceful nature of the Revolution of 1952, the continuity of institutions and the old economic system was more evident in the first years of the new government than innovation. However, according to Mabro (1974), the first years of the Revolution did, in fact, constitute a turning point in economic performance.

> A new orientation was taken, involving a large measure of state intervention both in agriculture and in industry, and later steps, e.g. planning and nationalization, followed logically from this earlier commitment. The suggestion is not that these steps were inevitable but that we can discern with hindsight, a consistent purpose throughout the period. More fundamentally, the early policies of the Revolution had a profound influence on the structure of the economy, and long-term repercussions.

This survey suggests that the same can be said of education, whether one is thinking in terms of institutions, of legislation or of the indomitable spirit of teachers and administrators in face of what appear to be insuperable obstacles. In the last few years, a pride in the achievements and contributions to Western society of the emigrants has been reinforced by success in Middle East politics. Above all, national pride and confidence have responded to the events during and following the October War of 1973. The result has been a growth of tolerance and open self-criticism. The ordinary citizen, commonly known as 'the man in the street' offers himself for voluntary service in reconstruction, while, for example, the professors of Ain Shams University find time, without payment, to organize and teach in a Higher Institute for Management for industrial workers seeking to fill educational gaps on a part-time basis. Sensitivity to foreign criticism has largely given way to co-operation, as evidenced by the existence of this survey, for the Egyptian is confident in his own future and the future of his country in an international context. Progress in education is not a finite accomplishment, but a continuing process, and, if, as Bronowski (1976), believes, the dignity of man established by the Renascence, is the most powerful step in the ascent of man, the educational progress made by Egypt since the Revolution and its promise for the future are a formidable contribution to that dignity.

Appendix 1

Faculties in The University of Cairo

The Faculty of Arts   This faculty has twelve departments: Arabic language and literature; oriental languages and literature; English language and literature; French language and literature; German language and literature; classics, history, geography, philosophy, psychology, librarianship and archives; and sociology. One of the most interesting recent expansions has been the inclusion of Japanese in the department of oriental languages. Besides the BA degree after four years of study, the MA or the PhD after at least two years, postgraduate diplomas are awarded after one year's study in English translation, French translation, cartography, industrial sociology, archives, applied psychology and comparative literature, while a general or special diploma is available in librarianship.

The Faculty of Law   This faculty consists of eleven departments: civil law; mercantile and maritime law; law of civil and commercial procedure; public law; criminal law and criminal procedure; special international law; philosophy and history of law; Islamic laws public finance and fiscal law; and social law. A BA takes four years, one year is needed for a postgraduate diploma in private law, public law, Islamic law, criminal science, tax law, administrative law and the degree of 'Docteur en Droit'. Students who obtain two diplomas may study for a minimum of two years for a doctor's degree.

The Faculty of Economics and Political Science   This faculty consists of three departments: economics; statistics; and political science. It awards degrees of BSc in each of these disciplines, taking four, two and two years respectively.

The Faculty of Commerce   This faculty also consists of three departments: accountancy; business administration; and mathematics and insurance. It awards a bachelor's degree in commerce and a master's degree in accountancy, business administration or insurance, and postgraduate diplomas in accountancy, state and national accountancy, cost accountancy, production management, public administration, manpower, planning, marketing, finance and insurance. The BSc Comm takes four years, the Master's or PhD a minimum of two years and the diploma one year.

The Faculty of Science This faculty consists of eight departments: geology; mathematics; physics; chemistry; botany; zoology; astronomy; entomology. It awards a BSc in the physical sciences and in the geological and biological sciences, as well as an MSc, a PhD and a DSc, and the postgraduate diplomas in radio-physics, nuclear physics, analytical chemistry, meteorology, applied chemistry, applied geology, applied geophysics and medical entomology. The duration of studies is the same as for commerce.

The Faculty of Medicine This faculty consists of nineteen departments: anatomy and histology; physiology; biochemistry; pathology; pharmacology; bacteriology and parasitology; surgery (experimental and plastic); anaesthetology; special surgery (orthopaedic, urology, brain and neuro-surgery, ear, nose and throat); medicine (including experimental); special medicine (nervous diseases, psychiatric, skin and venereal, endemic diseases, physical); cardiology and chest diseases and surgery; paediatrics; eye diseases and surgery; radiology (radiodiagnosis and radiotherapy); clinical and chemical pathology; hygiene (public health, preventive and social medicine, industrial medicine); forensic medicine and toxicology; obstetrics and gynaecology. The bachelor's degree in medicine and surgery takes five years, preceded by a preparatory year and followed by a year for training. Master's degrees are awarded in twenty-two clinical specializations and in eight basic medical science specializations. In each case the duration of study is divided into two one-year sections. Strict regulations must be followed throughout the period and successful students can qualify for a doctor's degree after two years' research followed by written, clinical and oral examinations.

The Faculty of Dentistry This faculty consists of seven departments: operative dentistry; oral anatomy and histology; oral pathology; oral surgery; dental prosthesis; oral medicine; and orthodontics. It awards a bachelor's degree of medicine and surgery, a specialization diploma in oral surgery, dental prosthesis, orthodontics, oral medicine and dental histopathology, a doctor's degree of dental medicine in oral anatomy, histology and pathology or predadentics or oral medicine and a master's degree of dental surgery in orthodontics or dental prosthesis or oral surgery or operative dentistry. Study takes four years preceded by a preparatory year of the bachelor's degree and one year for each of the specialization diplomas.

The Faculty of Pharmacy This faculty consists of six departments: pharmaceutics; pharmacognosy; analytical chemistry; organic chemistry; pharmaceutical chemistry; and pharmacology. Degrees awarded are a bachelor of pharmacy, a master of pharmaceutical sciences, a PhD in pharmaceutical sciences, and graduate diplomas in food analysis, analysis and biological analysis of drugs, biochemical analysis, industrial pharmacy, hospital pharmacy, micro-biological pharmacy, medicinal plants and forensic chemical analysis. The duration of study is the same as for commerce.

The Faculty of Engineering This faculty consists of twelve departments: mathematical and physical sciences; construction engineering; irrigation and hydraulics; public works; architecture; machine design; mechanical powers; electronics and electric networks; electric power; chemical engineering; aeronautics; mining, petrology and metallurgy. The bachelor's degree is awarded in the following fields: architecture, civil engineering, mechanical engineering, electrical engineering, and mining, petrology and metallurgy engineering, followed by a master's degree and a PhD, while diplomas can be obtained in the various branches of all the subjects listed above. The duration of study follows the usual pattern except that the higher diplomas take a minimum of two years.

The Faculty of Agriculture This faculty consists of seven departments: soil; agricultural economics; animal production; plant production; agricultural industries; agricultural botany; plant protection; and BSc degrees are awarded in general agricultural production, soil, animal production, plant production (field crops and gardening), agricultural economics and sociology (rural home economics for women students), nutrition (nutrition industries, dairying, agricultural biochemistry), plant production (plant diseases and insecticides). There are also MSc and PhD degrees and higher diplomas in agricultural guidance, bee-keeping and silk-worm breeding, technology of cooling and freezing and agricultural bacteriology, requiring one year's study.

The Faculty of Veterinary Medicine This faculty consists of eight depart-ments: veterinary anatomy; veterinary surgery, obstetrics and gynae-cology; veterinary pathology and parasitology; veterinary hygiene and food control; pharmacology and forensic medicine; veterinary physiology and biochemistry; veterinary internal medicine; and veterinary microbiology; offering the degrees of BSc and PhD in veterinary medicine as well as higher diplomas in veterinary hygiene and animal care, veterinary surgery, food control, artificial insemina-tion, veterinary diseases, clinical pathology and pathology, duration of study following the usual pattern.

Faculty of Dar el-Uloum (Arabic and Islamic studies) This faculty consists of seven departments: literary studies; rhetoric, literacy criticism and comparative literature; Islamic studies; Islamic history and civilization; Islamic philosophy; linguistics, Semitic and Oriental studies; and Arabic grammar and prosody. The three degrees are awarded, spread over eight years.

The Faculty of Archaeology This faculty consists of two departments Egyptian archaeology; and Islamic archaeology; awarding the three degrees and a diploma, after the normal duration of study.

The Faculty of Mass Communications This Faculty has three departments: journalism and publishing; broadcasting (radio and television); and public relations and advertising. The three degrees and diploma follow the usual pattern.

The Higher Institute of Nursing This Institute gives a course of studies in the basic social, biological and physical sciences, humanities and special studies in nursing, including basic nursing, medical and surgical nursing, maternal and child health nursing (obstetrics, gynaecology and paediatric nursing). Operating theatre nursing is also taught, as well as a basic introduction to the methods of teaching as applied to nurses and an introduction to basic nursing service administration and manage-ment. All subjects are taught in English except Arab national social

Appendix 1

studies, Arabic literature and Arabic language. Admission requirements include a secondary school certificate from the science section, a medical examination and proficiency in English. The degree of Bachelor of nursing takes four years, followed by one year nursing internship under the supervision of the faculty of medicine. Successful graduates are able to take first-level teaching and management positions in hospitals, health centres and schools of nursing.

The Cancer Institute This consists of four departments: surgery; radiology and radiological science; medical oncology; and pathology and cell research. Master's and doctor's degrees are awarded after a minimum of two years' study for each.

The Institute of African research and studies This Institute has six departments: natural resources; geography; anthropology; history; languages and dialects; political and economic methods; leading to master's and doctor's degrees after a minimum of two years' study for each.

The Institute of Statistics This Institute consists of three departments: mathematical statistics and computation; applied statistics and econometrics; and demography and bio-statistics. A diploma of statistics is awarded after two full-time academic years of study. Admission is open to employees of ministries, government departments, institutions and private companies working in statistical planning, but part-time students may be accepted. High marks in the mathematics entrance examination are required. A good diploma can be followed by an MA in Statistics after a further year, followed by a minimum two years for a PhD thesis.

The Scientific Computation Centre This grew out of the activities of the Institute of Statistical Studies and Research. The Centre is designed for the performance of a variety of computation tasks, with the help of a modern and powerful computer, thus providing for the needs of the country at large in the field of research projects. An ICL English electric computer consists of: a central processor unit, an input unit, output units, back storage units and a console typewriter.

The Khartoum Branch This consists of five departments in the Faculty of Arts, namely Arabic language and literature; geography; history, social studies; and philosophy; three in the Faculty of Law, namely special law; general law; and political economy; and four in the Faculty of Commerce, namely accounting, mathematics, insurance and statistics, economics and business administration.

The University Library This consists of the main library, the libraries of faculties, departments and the institutes affiliated to the university. In 1974 there were more than 700,500 volumes including 107,514 titles in Arabic and other Oriental languages; 348,245 titles in foreign languages and 1,512 theses. There is a general complaint from students that access to books is difficult in Egyptian universities. (Source: University of Cairo (1974) Prospectus)

Appendix 2

Some faculties in The University of Ain Shams

The Faculty of Education The Faculty of Education at Ain Shams has been built up from all the previous institutions engaged in the training of teachers at the secondary level, such as the Higher School for Teachers, later known as the Teachers' Higher Institute, the Institute of Education (which later became the Faculty of Education) and Cairo Teachers' College. As early as 1951 the Institute of Education was given the right to grant higher degrees in education, but it was not until the end of 1970 that Republican decree No. 1803/1970 was issued amalgamating in one faculty the academic studies of education and the training of secondary teachers. The Faculty of Education and the Teachers' College were both annexed to Ain Shams University and called the Faculty of Education. The Calendar of the University (1973) lists its functions as:

1. Training individuals who have obtained the general certificate of education, university graduates and people of similar standard for educational professions.
2. Training researchers in the various spheres of education and teaching.
3. Training specialists and leaders in the spheres of education and teaching.
4. Undertaking scientific researches about problems and issues of education and teaching, and publishing the results of these researches.
5. Raising the professional standard of those working in the field of education.

The faculty consists of ten departments: foundation of education; curricula; educational psychology; mental hygiene; comparative education; mathematics; physics and chemistry; natural history; social sciences; and foreign languages. It awards a Bachelor of Science and Education degree, specializing in mathematics, physics and chemistry and natural history; a Bachelor of Arts and Education degree in English language, French, history, geography, philosophy and socio-

232

logy; a General Diploma in Education; a Professional Diploma in Education in one of the specializations mentioned above; a Special Diploma in Education; an MA in Education and a PhD in Education, each in one of these specializations.

The University College for Women This college of Ain Shams has been selected for a brief description because its very existence is an indication of the rapid advances made in girls' education since the Revolution of 1952. Its actual birth took place just prior to this period, when in 1950/1 the Education Institute for Women Teachers at Zamalek, Cairo, with its two departments was affiliated to Ain Shams University as a nucleus for the University College for Women. The curricula were changed to bring them in line with those at Ain Shams, likewise the names of degrees and diplomas awarded, and in 1956 the name of the Institute itself was changed. Also, a unique Department of Home Economics was established. The higher degrees were established in 1959 by the executive decree for organization of the universities, and within ten years a ministerial decree took steps to bring the courses of study, including those in the Faculties of Science, up to the level of those provided at Ain Shams and other universities. Indeed, with its thirteen departments and wide degree coverage, the Girls' College could well be regarded as a university in its own right.

The Faculty of Arts – Sociological and Psychological Studies Department In the social sciences, whereas Alexandria University has a flourishing Department of Anthropology, Ain Shams University specializes in sociology and psychology, subjects which accord well with educational studies and research. In his speeches on education, the President of the Republic himself has affirmed the importance of developing the social sciences to balance present-day emphasis on the physical sciences and technology. Unlike the normal practice in England, in both cases applied subjects are taught at the undergraduate level and courses are concentrated in a particular year, approaching the American pattern. Lecture time is also taken up with textbooks, no doubt reflecting the shortage of Arabic texts available as well as the necessity to be guided through those involving a foreign language. There are other features which are interesting to specialists in these two disciplines. (Source: University of Ain Shams (1973) Calendar)

Bibliography

ABD-EL-RAHMAN, GABER GAD (1974), 'Socialism and Democracy in Modern Egypt', in Kotb (ed.).

ABU-LUGHAD, IBRAHIM (1967), 'The Transformation of the Egyptian Elite: Prelude to the 'Urabi Revolt',' *Middle East Journal*, Summer, pp. 325-44.

AL-ABD, SALAH (1974), 'Human Settlements in the Newly Reclaimed Areas of the A.R.E.', in Kotb (ed.).

AHMED, JAMAL MOHAMMED (1960), *The Intellectual Origins of Egyptian Nationalism*, Oxford University Press.

AL-AHRAM and AL-GOMHOUREYA: Arabic Egyptian Newspapers.

AL-SAYYID, AFAF LUTFI (1968), *Egypt and Cromer*, Praeger, New York.

AMMAR, HAMED (1954), *Growing Up in an Egyptian Village*, Routledge & Kegan Paul, London.

ATIYAH, EDWARD (1955), *The Arabs*, Penguin, Harmondsworth.

BADEAU, JOHN S. (1966), 'The Arab World in Quest of a Future', in Thompson and Reischauer (eds).

BOKTOR, AMIR (1936), *School and Society in the Valley of the Nile*, Elias' Modern Press, Cairo.

BOKTOR, AMIR (1963), *The Development and Expansion of Education in the United Arab Republic*, The American University in Cairo Press.

BRONOWSKI, J. (1976), *The Ascent of Man*, British Broadcasting Corporation, London.

BYRD, CECIL K. (1974), *The President's Review 1973-4*, The American University in Cairo Press, *The President's Review 1974-5*, The American University in Cairo Press.

CHEJNE, ANWAR G. (1965), 'Arabic: Its Significance and Place in Arab Muslim Society', *Middle East Journal*, 19, pp. 447-68.

EGYPTIAN GAZETTE 1970-6.

EL-GHANNAM, MOHAMMED A. (1970), *Education in the Arab region viewed from the 1970 Marrakesh Conference*, UNESCO.

EL-GHARIB, RAMZIA (1974), 'The Family in Egypt', in Kotb (ed.).

EL-KOUSSY, ABD EL-AZIZ (1953), 'Education in Egypt 1945-52', in *Year-book of Education*, Evans, London.

EL-MAHALLAWI, M.N. (1974), 'The Role of Higher Education in the Modernization of Egypt', in Kotb (ed.).

Bibliography

FAHMY, MOHAMMED SEIF EL-DIN (1973), *Assessment of Children's Needs in Egypt: Report of the Educational Committee*, The National Centre for Social and Criminological Research, Cairo.

FAHMY, SUMAYA (1974), 'The Role of Women in Modern Egypt', in Kotb (ed.).

GALT, RUSSELL (1936), *The Effects of Centralization on Egyptian Education in Modern Egypt*, American University of Cairo Press.

GIRGIS, SABRY (1967), *The History of Mental Health in Egypt from the Pharaohs to the Nuclear Period*, El-Kateb el-Araby, Cairo (in Arabic).

HANNA, BADR MASRI (1974), 'Some Aspects of Population Growth in Egypt', in Kotb (ed.).

HASSAN, MOHAMMED M. (1974), 'The Role of Institutions of Higher Education in National Development', in Kotb (ed.).

HOLMES, BRIAN (1965), *Problems of Education, A Comparative Approach*, Routledge & Kegan Paul, London.

HOLT, P. M. (1968), 'Political Change in Modern Egypt', in Vatikiotis (ed.).

HONIGMANN, JOHN J. (1959), *The World of Man*, Harper, New York.

HOURANI, A. H. (1947), *Minorities in the Arab World*, Oxford University Press.

HOURANI, A. H. (1960), Preface to Ahmed, J. M. (1960).

HUREWITZ, J. C. (1966), 'The Politics of Rapid Population Growth in the Middle East', in Thompson and Reischauer (eds).

HUSAYN, TAHA (1938), *Mustaqbal al-Thaqafah fi Msr* (*The Future of Culture in Egypt*), Dar el-Ma'arif, Cairo (in Arabic).

HUSAYN, TAHA (1948), *The Stream of Days: A Student at the Azhar*, trans. Hilary Wayment, Longman Green, London.

KAZEM, MOHAMMED IBRAHIM (1974), 'Towards Understanding Islam', in Kotb (ed.).

KOTB, YUSEF SALEH EL-DIN (ed.) (1974), *Education and Modernization in Egypt*, Ain Shams University Press, Egypt.

MABRO, ROBERT (1974), *The Egyptian Economy 1952-72*, Oxford University Press.

MATTHEWS, R. D. and MATTA AKRAWI (1949), *Education in Arab Countries in the Near East*, American Council on Education, Part I.

MINISTRY OF INFORMATION, STATE INFORMATION SERVICE (1962), *The Charter*, United Arab Republic.

MINISTRY OF INFORMATION, STATE INFORMATION SERVICE (April 1974), *The October Working Paper*, presented by President Mohammed Anwar el-Sadat, April, Cairo, Arab Republic of Egypt.

MINISTRY OF EDUCATION: mimeographed material, Reports (Documentary Centre for Education), Pamphlets, Notes, etc. (some undated).
Annual Reports 1970-1975.
Pamphlet on Special Education.
Pamphlet on Social Work, Department of Youth Care for Boys.

Bibliography

Eastern District of Education, Cairo: The Message and Aims of School Social Services in Abbassiya.

Drop-out in Primary Education and its Relation with Wastage in Education Resources. Cited by M. S. Fahmy, Cairo, 1971.

Failure and Drop-out, and their impact on the Economics of General Education in the United Arab Republic. (in Arabic) Cited by M. S. Fahmy.

Guide to the National Centre for Educational Research, Arab Republic of Egypt, (1975).

The Changing Role of the Teacher and its Influence on Preparation for the Profession, and on In-Service Training, (1975).

MOUSSA, TOHAMY A. (1974), 'Planning of Scientific Research in Egypt', in Kotb (ed.).

POLK, WILLIAM R. and RICHARD L. CHAMBERS (eds) (1968), *Beginnings of Modernization in the Middle East,* Part 5, University of Chicago Press.

POPPER, K. R. (1974), *The Open Society and its Enemies,* 5th Edn (revised), Routledge & Kegan Paul, London.

QUBAIN, FAHIM I. (1966), *Education and Science in the Arab World,* Johns Hopkins Press.

QUBAIN, FAHIM I. (1969), 'United Arab Republic', chs 11 and 12 in Wilbur.

RADWAN, ABU AL-FUTOUH AHMED (1951), *Old and New Forces in Egyptian Education,* Teachers' College, Columbia University, New York.

SAFRAN, NADAV (1961), Ch. 12 'The Historical Crisis of Liberal Nationalism', *Egypt in Search of a Political Community,* Part IV. Harvard University Press.

SALEH, SANEYA ABDUL WAHAB (1975), *Attitudinal and Social Structural Aspects of the Brain Drain: The Egyptian Case,* Unpub. MA Thesis, American University in Cairo.

SARHAN, EL-DEMERDASH (1974), 'Teacher Education and In-Service Training in the A.R.E.', in Kotb (ed.).

SELIM, IMAM (1974), 'Planning for Development in Egypt', in Kotb (ed.).

SHARABI, HISHAM (1966), 'Islam and Modernization in the Arab World', in Thompson and Reischauer (eds).

SMELSER, NEIL J. and SEYMOUR MARTIN LIPSET (1966), 'Social Structure, Mobility and Development', pp. 1–50 (see especially pp. 29–42) in Smelser and Lipset (eds), *Social Structure and Mobility in Economic Development,* Routledge & Kegan Paul, London.

STEIN, HERMAN D. (ed.) (1965), *Planning for the Needs of Children in Developing Countries: Report of a Round-Table Conference,* UNICEF.

SUPREME COUNCIL FOR THE UNIVERSITIES (Source: Secretary General, Professor Dr Shafik Balbaa), All the following in Arabic.

A Short Review, May 1976.

Law No. 48(1972), University Organization.

Law No. 54(1973), Adjustment for No. 49.

Bibliography

Motion of Prime Minister No. 376(1973).

Law No. 120(1974), Adjustment for Law No. 49.

Law No. 11(1974), Adjustment for Law No. 49.

Law No. 18(1974), Adjustment for Law No. 49.

Law No. 83(1974), Amendments to Law No. 49.

Law No. 70(1975), Adjustments to Law No. 49.

Motion from the Prime Minister, No. 924(1975), Adjustments to Implementation chart concerning organization of the universities.

The Implementation Chart concerned with laws for university organization (1975).

SZYLIOWICZ, JOSEPH S. (1973), *Education and Modernization in the Middle East*, Cornell University Press.

TAWADROS, SAMUEL MAKARIUS (ed.) (1973), *Assessment of Children's Needs in Egypt: Report of the Psychological Committee, the National Centre for Social and Criminological Research, Cairo.* (1974), *Mental Health and School Work*, el-Nahda el-Masriya, Cairo, 2nd edn, in Arabic.

THOMPSON, J. H. and R. D. REISCHAUER (eds) (1966), *Modernization of the Arab World*, D. Van Nostrand Company, New York.

UNESCO REPORT (1970), *Third Regional Conference of Ministers of Education for Economic Planning in the Arab States*, Minedarab 4. Marrakesh 12–20 January, 1970.

UNESCO (1972), *Arab Republic of Egypt: An Outline Strategy for the Reform and Development of Education.*

UNESCO (1975), *Unedbas Mission to the Arab Republic of Egypt Concerning the Reorganization of Secondary Education.*

UNICEF (1974), *Assessment of Children's Needs in Egypt: Final Report.*

UNIVERSITY OF CAIRO (1974), *Prospectus 1974–1975*, Cairo University Press.

UNIVERSITY OF AIN SHAMS (1973), *Calendar of the University of Ain Shams.*

UNIVERSITY OF AIN SHAMS (1974–5), *Report Psychological Clinic Department of Mental Health, College of Education.*

VATIKIOTIS, P. J. (1968), *Some Political Consequences of the 1952 Revolution in Egypt.* Oxford University Press, London.

WAHBA, MAGDI (1972), *Cultural Policy in Egypt*, UNESCO, Paris.

WILBUR, DONALD N. (1969), *Survey of World Cultures*, HRAF Press.

Index